MW01676003

Building Simulation Models with SIMSCRIPT II.5®

Edward C. Russell

CACI

12011 San Vicente Boulevard, Los Angeles, California 90049 • (213) 476-6511

Copyright ©1983
CACI, Inc.-Federal Los Angeles, California

All right reserved. No part of this publication may be reproduced by any means without written permission from CACI, Inc.-Federal.

The information in this publication is believed to be accurate in all respects; however, CACI cannot assume the responsibility for any consequences resulting from the use thereof. The information contained herein is subject to change. Revisions to this publication or new editions of it may be issued to incorporate such change.

Any questions regarding this documentation or about SIMSCRIPT II.5 should be addressed to:

CACI, Inc.-Federal
Modelling and Simulation Department
12011 San Vicente Boulevard
Los Angeles, California 90049
(213) 476-6511

September 1983

SIMSCRIPT II.5 is a registered trademark and service mark of CACI, Inc.-Federal.

ISBN 0-918417-00-7

PREFACE

SIMSCRIPT II.5 is a powerful, free-form, English-like, general-purpose simulation programming language. It is not dependent on any predefined coding forms, nor does its implementation depend on any intermediate language such as FORTRAN or assembler. It supports the application of software engineering principles, such as structured programming and modularity, which impart orderliness and manageability to simulation models.

This book stresses the use of SIMSCRIPT II.5 for conceptualizing models and implementing them in computer-readable form.

Previous books have used different approaches in presenting the language. The SIMSCRIPT II.5 Programming Language, by Kiviat et al., [8] presented it in a series of levels comparable to BASIC, FORTRAN, and PL/1. The emphasis was on programming examples rather than simulation and model building. The SIMSCRIPT II.5 Reference Handbook [3] presented explicit rules of syntax for the statements of the language and gave brief examples. The differences between the various compiler implementations, as well as system dependencies, are described in a series of User Manuals.

This book presents the use of SIMSCRIPT II.5 for discrete-event simulation through a sequence of case studies. These range from a very simple model of a single-queue-single-server to a complete, complex network model. The examples have been thoroughly tested and used in a short course regularly offered by CACI. Although the examples illustrate all the features of SIMSCRIPT II.5, the emphasis is on model building; consequently, programming concepts are introduced only as they are required. An appendix describes the syntax of the entire SIMSCRIPT II.5 language in convenient form.

The book is oriented toward real applications. Small examples are used for practical reasons, but the techniques apply to large models as well. The intent is to stress good techniques of model building, program planning, programming, and verification.

SIMSCRIPT has evolved over the last two decades. Originally, it was conceived of as an extension of FORTRAN to simplify the coding of simulation models. As such, its implementation consisted of a pre-processor or translator that read SIMSCRIPT statements and produced FORTRAN statements. This was a low-cost approach, but was rather awkward to use. Since the compiler or translator did not catch all errors, errors at execution time were, at best, keyed to the FORTRAN statements of the intermediate program.

That first version of SIMSCRIPT was developed at The Rand Corporation by Harry Markowitz [12]. The implementation required the user to fill in several coding forms for describing modelling objects, initializing data, and generating reports. The remainder of the program was coded on FORTRAN coding forms.

At CACI, Markowitz undertook a major revision of the implementation, producing a version known as SIMSCRIPT I.5. It eliminated the dependence on FORTRAN, and the translator became a compiler that produced assembly language code.

Implementations of the SIMSCRIPT I.5 compiler were done by Henry Kleine for the IBM, CDC, UNIVAC, PHILCO, and RCA computers. The NCR and IBM/360 versions were implemented by Glen Johnson, and the CDC Cyber version was implemented by Claude Delfosse. For almost a decade, SIMSCRIPT I.5 was a standard for simulation and model building.

With the experience gained from years of modelling with SIMSCRIPT I, Markowitz then designed a substantially advanced language named SIMSCRIPT II. It was described in a Rand Report [9] by Philip Kiviat. The first implementation done at Rand was improved by a company known as Simulation Associates. This version was called SIMSCRIPT II Plus. CACI acquired SIMSCRIPT Plus, and completed the full language implementation -- SIMSCRIPT II.5 -- on the major computers manufactured by IBM, CDC, Honeywell, Univac, Digital Equipment, Perkin-Elmer, NCR, and PR1ME. The language is in wide use today.

I wish to express my gratitude to Joe Annino for his most enduring patience with the extremely slow pace of development of this book, and for his encouragement and support throughout its development. I also wish to thank Bob Campbell, Claude Delfosse, and Glen Johnson for their careful reading and review of the manuscript; many useful suggestions have been incorporated as a result of their efforts. I would also like to express thanks to Celia Seelig, who has done the preparation of the manuscript and put much effort into producing a consistent form when no consistency was apparent!

Los Angeles, California

Edward C. Russell

TABLE OF CONTENTS

CHAPTER 5 - MODELLING PASSIVE OBJECTS

CHAPTER 6 - MISCELLANEOUS SIMULATION TOPICS

CHAPTER 7 - MODELLING WITH DISCRETE EVENTS

CHAPTER 8 - INPUT AND OUTPUT

CHAPTER 9 - MODEL VERIFICATION AND DEBUGGING

LIST OF EXAMPLES

LIST OF ILLUSTRATIONS

LIST OF TABLES

Chapter 1
INTRODUCTION

In this chapter, we define simulation, analyze why simulations often fail, narrow the scope of the definition to discrete-event simulation, broadly outline the steps taken in simulation and model building, and define some of the common tools needed in simulation models.

1.1 What Is Simulation?

Simulation can be defined as follows:

> A simulation of a system is the operation of a model that is a representation of the system.
>
> The model is amenable to manipulation that would be impossible, too expensive, or impractical, to perform on the system it portrays.
>
> The operation of the model can be studied and from it properties concerning the behavior of the actual system can be inferred.

Obviously, this definition is broad enough to encompass methods other than the specific approach that we wish to discuss here, but it will serve as a working definition to be refined as we proceed.

Simulation is an effective way of pretesting proposed systems, plans, or policies before developing expensive prototypes, field tests, or actual implementations. Using computer-based simulation, it is possible to trace out in detail the consequences and implications of a proposed course course of action.

Simulation is often used as an alternative to more traditional forms of analysis such as analytical solutions (e.g., closed-form solutions to steady-state queueing models), numerical solutions (e.g., to differential equations), or even to scale-model building (e.g., for harbors or waterway systems).

Over the past 20 years, simulation has proved again and again that it can be a powerful analytic tool. In small-scale applications, it has recorded countless modest successes; in large-scale applications, some of its successes have been spectacular and widely publicized. The wonder is that a tool of such power has not gained even wider adoption.

In her article "Simulation as an Alternative to Linear Programming" [17], Professor Susan L. Solomon comments wryly on the lingering distrust of simulation even as its use is becoming more widespread than ever:

> It is commonly accepted that general classes of problems are best solved using particular techniques. For example, critical path scheduling problems can often be formulated for solution by linear programming, but this approach would not recommend itself for cost reasons to the vast majority of those having access to a PERT or CPM package . . . Simulation might offer a reasonable alternative solution vehicle in many circumstances like these, yet

some operations research analysts tend to consider its use only "when all else fails." That is, simulation is the technique of last resort.

An examination of the simulation literature, including conference Proceedings, in the past decade -- by weight, by volume, by complexity and sophistication, or by breadth of applications areas -- would incline one to believe that either all else fails quite a bit of the time, or perhaps that simulation is a cost-effective alternative to the more structured deterministic methods of problem solving.

Perhaps some analysts regard simulation as too difficult or merely too strange, and feel themselves on safer ground solving familiar, purely mathematical models. More likely, they are scared off by some of simulation's spectacular -- and costly -- failures. In Section 1.2 below, we list ten reasons why simulations fail. The rest of the book tells you how to succeed.

Within the discipline of computer-based simulation, there is a rather clear-cut dichotomy between so-called "continuous simulation" and "discrete-event simulation." Continuous simulation describes systems by sets of equations to be solved numerically. These may be algebraic or differential equations, usually with time as the independent variable. Examples of problems in this area are fluid-flow or hydraulics problems, heat-flow problems such as the representation of a blast furnace in a steel mill, and orbital calculations for a communications satellite.

Discrete-event simulation describes a system in terms of logical relationships that cause changes of state at discrete points in time rather than continuously over time. Examples of problems in this area are most queueing situations: Objects (customers in a gas station, aircraft on a runway, jobs in a computer) arrive and change the state of the system instantaneously. State variables are such things as the number of objects waiting for service and the number being served. One could argue, of course, that these changes also appear to occur continuously.

For example, when exactly does an airplane join the queue at a runway? The important point is that it is satisfactory for the purposes of the study to represent certain phenomena as if they occur at discrete points in time.

Not all discrete simulations involve queueing. For example, many war gaming situations are modelled in which no queues are formed. Many communications systems are "memoryless" and hence have no queueing, yet many interesting insights into these systems can be derived from their simulation.

In the final analysis, all real systems are continuous and all digital simulation is discrete; it is merely our perception of the problems and their solutions that varies. A continuous simulation is ultimately implemented by a program that solves equations numerically in discrete (albeit very small) time increments, whereas a discrete-event simulation assumes the lack of importance of things that might occur between the modelled events or as a consequence of those events actually consuming some time.

The important question, however, is not whether a real system is discrete or continuous, but which perception of the system is most useful for the analysis.

As more complex models are built, analysts recognize that some systems are most naturally represented as a combination of discrete and continuous methodology. Considerable effort has been expended in this area [6, 14, 16].

1.2 What's Wrong With Simulation?

Before exploring good simulation procedures, let us face up to a fact of life. Simulation analysis studies too often fail to yield useful results, and the reasons for failure are frequently the same.

Why does such a powerful tool not produce useful results? There are many pitfalls, all of which can be avoided.

Before summarizing our own experiences and the principles we follow, we would like to quote from an authoritative study that supports our beliefs and experiences.

A report to the United States Congress prepared by the General Accounting Office (GAO Report LCD-75-11) said in part:

> The Government Accounting Office identified 519 federally funded models developed or used in the Pacific Northwest area of the United States. Development of these models cost about $39 million. Fifty-seven of these models were selected for detailed review, each costing over $100,000 to develop. They represent 55 percent of the $39 million of development costs in the models.
>
> Although successfully developed models can be of assistance in the management of federal programs, GAO found that many model development efforts experienced large cost overruns, prolonged delays in completion, and total user dissatisfaction with the information obtained from the model.

MOST MODELS NOW UNDER DEVELOPMENT WILL FAIL IN THE SAME WAYS THESE DID AND FOR EXACTLY THE SAME REASONS!

Ten Big Mistakes and Their Avoidance

(1) FAILURE TO DEFINE AN ACHIEVABLE GOAL

The goal of a simulation project should never be "To model the . . ." Modelling itself is not a goal; it is a means of achieving a goal. A successful simulation demands, first of all, a clearly articulated and agreed-upon set of realizable objectives. These depend on answers to questions like: What is to be learned about the system under study? What decisions will be based on the simulation results?

The objectives cannot be correctly defined without the active participation of the end user, and they must of course be realizable. Setting the goals is the first step in any simulation project and perhaps the one most commonly bypassed.

(2) INCOMPLETE MIX OF ESSENTIAL SKILLS

A successful simulation project calls for a combination of at least four areas of knowledge and experience:

Project leadership: The ability to motivate, lead, and manage the simulation team.

Modelling: The ability to design a conceptual model that imitates the system under study at the required level of detail.

Programming: The ability to transform the conceptual model into a readable, modifiable, and working computer program.

Knowledge of the modelled system: Sufficient understanding of the system to guide the modelling and to judge the validity of the simulation results.

Teams have typically lacked specialists whose expertise and professional interests lie in modelling and simulation over and above programming. In addition, people knowledgeable about the system, together with those who will use the results of the simulation study, have typically not tracked the development in sufficient detail to assure that the end product satisfies their needs.

A simulation team cannot succeed if it does not possess all of these requisite skills.

(3) INADEQUATE LEVEL OF USER PARTICIPATION

All too often, model developers simply go off by themselves for a year and then proudly drop the "completed," never-to-be-used model on the sponsor's desk.

The model-building team must work with the user organization from start to finish in order for both to have the confidence and understanding necessary to use the completed work effectively.

Provision must be made for regularly scheduled briefings, progress reports, and technical discussions with prospective users of the model.

The end user is also the only one who can inform the team about realistic considerations such as politics, bureaucracy, unions, budgets, and changes in the sponsoring organization. These will determine the success of the project as much as will the quality of the technical work.

(4) INAPPROPRIATE LEVEL OF DETAIL

A model is a simplified representation of a system, and it should incorporate only those features of the system that are important for the user's purposes.

In modelling a complex system, difficult questions must be addressed, often for the first time. There is a tendency to spend a great deal of effort modelling, in unnecessary detail, those portions of the system that are well understood while glossing over poorly defined portions that may be more important. This approach creates the illusion that great progress is being made, until it comes time to produce valid, usable results.

The goals of the project determine the appropriate level of detail, which must be consistent with the availability of data and other resources.

(5) POOR COMMUNICATION

It has been said that if you can clearly define what the problem is, you are already halfway toward its solution. To gain understanding of a problem, everyone who can contribute to its definition should be able to do so in a disciplined but natural way.

A conceptual framework and language for communication between the team members is essential. The framework, or world view, should relate closely to the language of the programmed model.

Simulation languages that are problem-oriented and readable can dramatically simplify model design and programming. They provide a vocabulary and related concepts with which system elements and their interactions can be conveniently described and discussed.

(6) USING THE WRONG COMPUTER LANGUAGE

Opinions differ regarding programming languages for simulation. Some believe that computer languages should be English-like and problem-oriented, while others feel that FORTRAN, possibly extended with simulation-related subroutines, is adequate. Our view is that the programming language should be English-like, self-documenting, and readable by the user, who is primarily interested in the system under study, not computer programming.

High-level simulation languages have been shown to substantially reduce both programming and project time. By design, they offer language, program, and data structures that make models much easier to develop and modify.

(7) OBSOLETE OR NONEXISTENT DOCUMENTATION

Over the years, we have observed numerous unsuccessful simulation projects that had no documentation except a FORTRAN listing. Many of these listings contained few explanatory comments.

Even a thoroughly commented FORTRAN listing is difficult to decipher for anyone other than the person who wrote it. Often, even the original programmer has difficulty understanding it after a short time.

We have also seen great amounts of money wasted on manuals and flowcharts intended to make it easier to develop, maintain, modify, and enhance the model.

This waste is a consequence of the realities of model development. Most models evolve over a long period of time because of new and increased understanding of the system, changing goals, and availability of new data.

Because of the evolutionary changes, flowcharts, prose documentation, detailed descriptions of routines and variables, and program comments often become obsolete, incomplete, or incorrect shortly after they are written. The longer the model is around -- and many models in use today were developed five or more years ago -- the more this type of documentation deteriorates.

For the purposes of computer program development, modification, and enhancements, the only dependable documentation in a changing environment is the source program listing. The quality and usefulness of this documentation is determined by the model design and the simulation language.

(8) USING AN UNVERIFIED MODEL

Verification involves comparing the programmed computer model with the conceptual model. Does the program implement the model as designed?

The most effective verification technique is a walkthrough, with the programmer explaining the code to someone who is familiar with the system under study. This technique frequently turns up design and coding errors that can be corrected at a fraction of the cost and time that would be required after the model is implemented on a computer.

To use the powerful walkthrough technique, the program must be readable. Hence, again we see the importance of using an English-like simulation language.

(9) FAILURE TO USE MODERN TOOLS AND TECHNIQUES TO MANAGE THE DEVELOPMENT OF A LARGE COMPLEX COMPUTER PROGRAM

Practically all large computer program developments are late. Three major reasons for this problem are:

Premature coding: The irresistable urge to begin coding before the program is designed.

Optimistic scheduling: Underestimating the time required for known tasks and neglecting to allocate time for the inevitable, unanticipated problems.

Confusing effort with progress: Forgetting that on some days a great deal of effort will be expended but progress will consist of locating and correcting a single error.

There are tools and techniques that can help in overcoming these problems. Computer-based design tools, such as JPL's Software Design and Documentation Language [10], guide the top-down development of models through statements of objectives, functional requirements, procedures, and data structures.

These tools also provide a means for capturing project management information such as progress estimates, responsibility assignments, problem areas, and design revisions.

Software engineering tools and related principles, such as structured and modular programming, make programs orderly and manageable. Lack of complete understanding of these methods and failure to use them virtually dooms any effort to develop a large, complex model.

(10) USING MYSTERIOUS RESULTS

The results from simulation studies should be presented in a way that the user can easily relate to the system under study. Otherwise the user cannot effectively judge the validity of the model and will not have confidence in it.

A model that gives unexpected or illogical results may do so because certain parameters turn out to be far more significant or insignificant than expected, or because unanticipated interactions between system elements greatly affect system performance. Insight into hidden problems of this sort are typically gained from simulation.

However, unexpected or unusual simulation results that cannot be explained are usually caused by errors, invalid assumptions, or lack of understanding of the real system. The model will be useless until these faults are found and corrected.

New simulation and programming tools and techniques can help bring order to model design, implementation, evolution, and analysis. It is now easier than ever before to define and design models, to generate correct computer programs, and to produce readable, more meaningful reports. One key to the successful use of simulation analysis lies in understanding and applying these new methodologies.

1.3 A First Look At The Simulation Task

We shall now narrow our focus somewhat to those areas where a simulation programming language such as SIMSCRIPT II.5 has been demonstrated to be of particular value.

We shall use, as a checklist, some of the points addressed in the previous section. In particular, SIMSCRIPT aids in the following:

1. Articulate simulation goals.

2. Analyze the system to determine appropriate level of detail for the model.

3. Synthesize the system (realize the model).

4. Collect and prepare input data.

5. Verify model correctness.

6. Validate model results.

7. Prepare for system experiments.

8. Analyze experimental results.

Although these points are ennumerated as if they might be accomplished sequentially, it is more realistic to envision a test after, or even during, the performance of each step that might send one back to re-perform any or all of the preceding tasks!

Articulate Simulation Goals

Defining the problem often is the problem. Setting goals does not necessarily mean determining the outputs to be produced (although it might). Rather, it means describing relationships that need to be studied and quantifying the information to be obtained.

Analyze the System to Determine the Appropriate Level of Detail for the Model

There is always more information available about a system than can (cr should) be incorporated in a simulation model. The real art of model building is the ability to capture the essence of a system without building extraneous information into the model and yet omitting nothing of importance. A modelling approach that uses good design techniques such as top-down, structured design with clearly defined modularity, will enhance the quality of the product.

Synthesize the System (Realize the Model)

An aspect of simulation languages that is often overlooked when comparison is made to modelling with a general-purpose programming language is the "world-view" of the language. With a general-purpose language, this amounts to looking at the data structures of the language; but with a simulation programming language, it involves much more.

The world-view of a simulation language, in a sense, defines the class of problems for which the language is suitable. Another way of characterizing the world-view of a language is quite literal: how one views the world with the language. For example, in SIMSCRIPT, one begins to describe the modelled system in terms of entities. These entities are characterized by their attributes. If there are logical associations or groupings of entities, they are described as sets. The actions in the modelled system are described as events or processes. The world-view of the language, together with the support of the constructs by the compiler, is one of the most important reasons for using a simulation language. Logical consistency tests are performed -- some during compilation of the model, others during execution of the model -- which are related to the correct application of the world-view, not just to programming details.

Collect and Prepare Input Data

A simulation study of any magnitude entails gathering massive amounts of data and reducing them to usable form. Tools are available to aid in this data reduction task. We shall see that SIMSCRIPT has several techniques for the representation of data; they include:

- Direct input of observed phenomena (external events).
- Reduction of data to an arbitrary distribution function (represented numerically).
- Use of any of a number of built-in random deviate generators to approximate the observed phenomena analytically.

Verify the Model

This is the traditional "debugging" phase. With a simulation model it involves assuring that the implemented code faithfully represents the model as abstracted from the real system. If it does not, there are two possibilities: Either there are latent errors in the code, or the model is not a correct abstraction.

Validate the model

A model may run "correctly" -- produce reams of results, pass all kinds of benchmarks -- and yet be worthless! Why? Because the model may not correctly represent the real system. This is a subtle problem. With a payroll program or other well-defined programming task, fairly exhaustive testing can detect programming errors and a hand calculation can, perhaps, be used to show program correctness.

With a simulation model, the best we can hope for is either a reduction to a simple case, with all randomness eliminated, or a real-world system in operation, with which we can compare our results. This is usually termed "face validity." It doesn't guarantee that the model and real system will respond in the same manner when parameters are varied, but it may be the best we can do!

Conduct Experiments

Once a model has been validated, it is ready for experimentation use. The experiments to be performed will have been articulated (optimistically) as early as the goal-setting phase, or may involve (usually) some modifications to the model at this stage.

Techniques exist for controlling the experiments, replicating runs, resetting random sequences for comparisons under identical situations, and for isolating random processes to reduce or eliminate correlation.

Analyze the Results

Again, a great deal of planning will have preceded this stage. Decisions as to which performance measures best describe the phenomena under study and the best form for their display will be incorporated in the code.

SIMSCRIPT includes facilities for automating the collection of such information and for displaying it in a natural, implementation-independent manner.

1.4 The Plan For This Book

This book is designed to teach simulation and modelling principles. It is designed to teach one simulation language. Other books are available that focus on principles and give minimal or even no attention to the simulation language. The only previous complete exposition of SIMSCRIPT II.5 did not focus on modelling and simulation, but rather approached SIMSCRIPT by comparing it with several general-purpose languages.

In a language as general as SIMSCRIPT II.5, there are some "traps" the unsuspecting user can fall into. These will be clearly pointed out. There are many common modelling situations which at first glance seem formidable or "beyond the capability of the language," but are really quite simple to handle. Many of these will be included in the examples.

Style is as much a concern as content of a model. The author has developed his own style (with many suggestions from others). This style will be used and discussed in the examples.

In Chapter 2, we shall plunge into a simple modelling task. We introduce the concepts of processes and resources, apply them to the model, and go through a step-by-step walkthrough of the execution.

In subsequent chapters, more and more complex systems are modelled and more of the richness of SIMSCRIPT II.5 is displayed.

One of the unique features of SIMSCRIPT II.5 is that it endows the user with the ability to change basic constructs of the language. In earlier examples we use the default language constructs, but in later examples we illustrate the model builder's freedom to increase the usefulness of the language for his specialized task or application.

Chapter 2

ELEMENTARY MODELLING CONCEPTS

2.1 Model Structure

Simulation models exhibit many common properties. Every model has the following three ingredients:

(1) A mechanism for representing arrivals of new objects.

(2) The representation of what happens to the objects within the modelled system.

(3) A mechanism for terminating the simulation.

The arrival of new objects into the system from the external world (i.e., outside the system being studied) is usually independent of what happens within the system. This process can be characterized by describing the number of objects that arrive simultaneously and specifying the time between arrivals. Two common methods for modelling this situation are (1) to supply as data an explicit sequence of arrivals, or (2) to arrange for sampling from a stochastic process each time an arrival "occurs" in order to determine the time delay between that arrival and the next. This latter method can use arbitrary distribution functions for the representation of time delays. These may range from constant delay to uniform intervals of delay or exponentially distributed delays with a specified mean. Representation of such phenomena will be dealt with more thoroughly in Chapter 4.

Many arrival processes may be superimposed on a model of a system. This generalization will not present any modelling difficulty to our SIMSCRIPT II.5 implementation.

The primary focus of our modelling effort is the representation of what happens to the objects within the modelled system. It is natural to focus on one object at a time and to describe its interaction with other objects. For example, objects may compete for scarce commodities, leading to queueing or preemption or balking (i.e., "giving up" without receiving whatever service was expected).

Finally, a model must be provided with a means of termination. There are two primary methods of model termination. The first is the planned-termination-time method, in which the termination is scheduled for a definite simulated time regardless of what else might be happening in the model. The second method is to allow everything in the model to come to rest. Either method can be used effectively. Models of the same system might use one method or the other, depending on the goal of the simulation.

As an example of the difference between the two methods, consider a model of a commercial system such as a bank or gas station. In the first method of termination, one would merely stop the simulation at a predetermined time and report the results. In the second method, one would stop the arrival mechanism at a predetermined time but allow the model to complete all started or pending activities. For example, in the bank, a guard closes the door to new arrivals at closing time, but people already inside are permitted to finish their transactions before the tellers close their windows.

2.2 The Process Concept

In SIMSCRIPT II.5 we shall use the notion of a process as our primary dynamic object.

A process represents an object and the sequence of actions it experiences throughout its life in the model. There may be many instances (or copies) of a process in a simulation. There may also be many different processes in a model.

A process object enters a model at an explicit simulated time, its "creation time." It becomes active either immediately or at a prescribed "activation time." From then on, the description of its activity is contained in the process routine. A process routine may be thought of as a sequence of interrelated events separated by lapses of time, either predetermined or indefinite.

Predetermined lapses of time are used to model such phenomena as the service time (deterministic or stochastic), whereas indefinite delays arise because of competition between processes for limited resources. In this latter case processes will automatically be delayed until the resource is made available to it.

At each (re)activation of the process routine, it may execute statements representing changes to the system state. The process routine may test for system conditions and take alternative courses of action.

Processes interact either implicitly (for example, through resource competition) or explicitly (through executing statements to "activate," "interrupt," or "resume" one another).

2.3 The Resource Concept

Resources are the passive elements of a model. A resource is used to model an object which is required by the process objects. If the resource is not available when required, the process object is placed in a queue or waiting line and made to wait until the resource becomes available.

A resource becomes available when the process holding it "relinquishes" it. The first process object in the queue is then given the resource and reactivated. If a resource is relinquished when no process object is waiting for it, it is merely made available to be allocated when requested.

The simplest form of a resource consists of a single "unit" of a single type. For example, a one-teller bank or a single-runway airport night be modelled in this manner. To expand to multiple resources in the model, there are two alternatives:

(1) Add more identical units of the resource. They are identical in the sense that they are indistinguishable and they serve processes from a single queue.

(2) Add more separate units of the resource. These are isolated from the other units in that they have separate queues of processes waiting for them and are reallocated only to those processes that have specifically requested them.

A third possibility is to name different resources; then both the above alternatives apply equally well to these new resources.

More capabilities of resources will be illustrated in subsequent examples. For instance, it is not necessary to request single units of a resource. Multiple units may be requested and relinquished collectively or individually. Further, the queueing for resources by default is first-come-first-served, but it can be made to be prioritized by various criteria.

2.4 Program Structure

A SIMSCRIPT II.5 program consists of three primary elements:

1. A preamble giving a static description of each modelling element is given.

2. A main program where execution begins.

3. A process routine for each process declared in the preamble.

Each element will be described in detail.

PREAMBLE

The first section of any SIMSCRIPT II.5 model is the PREAMBLE. Purely declarative, it includes no executable statements. All the modelling elements (processes and resources) must be named in the preamble.

If we draw an analogy between constructing a SIMSCRIPT model and writing a play, the preamble would be like the cast of characters, which describes their static features and lists all the props they might use, but does not describe how or why they might interact.

Many other declarations which can be made in the preamble. These include changing background conditions, specifying data structures other than processes and resources, and listing performance measurements to be made.

MAIN

Execution of a SIMSCRIPT program begins with the first statement in the MAIN program. Several necessary steps are taken in the MAIN program for a simulation.

Resources must be created and initialized before they can be used by processes. This is usually accomplished in MAIN.

SIMSCRIPT requires that something be awaiting execution before a simulation commences. This is done by activating initial processes in MAIN.

A simulation begins when control passes to a system-supplied timing routine. This is done by executing the START SIMULATION statement.

Any statements following the START SIMULATION statement will not be executed until the simulation has terminated (by running out of things to do, i.e., coming to rest). At this point final reports could be produced and a new simulation could be run.

The Timing Routine

Parenthetically at this point, it may be useful to describe a very important simulation routine that is transparent to the model builder. The timing routine is at the heart of a discrete-event simulation. From a programming perspective, this is the routine that ties the entire collection of processes together. Let us define an "event" as a pending (re)activation of a process. Then the timing routine is as shown in Figure 2.1.

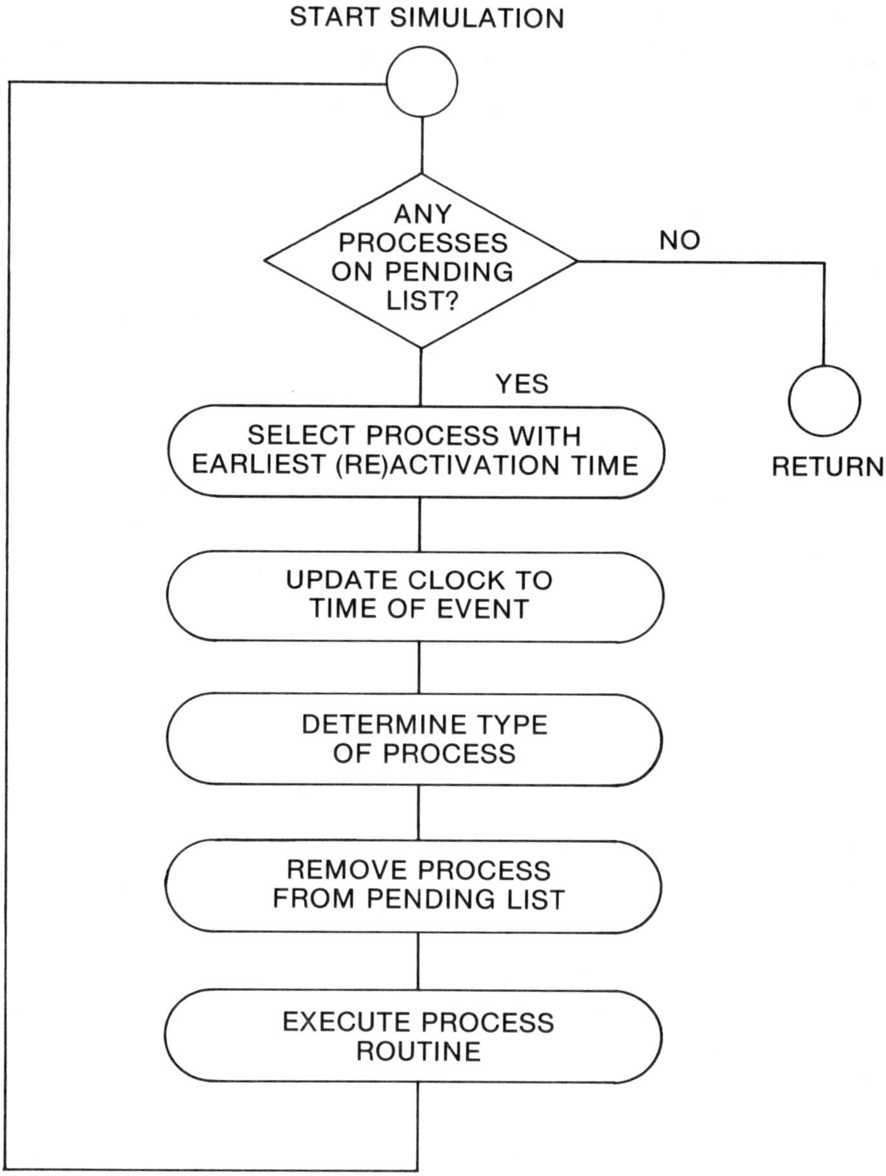

Figure 2.1 - Basic SIMSCRIPT II.5 Timing Routine

As can be seen from the figure, processes must be on the pending list prior to entry into this routine or the simulation will terminate immediately. It is natural to assume that the execution of one process will (or may) activate other processes and thus perpetuate this sequence for some time. Termination will occur either for the algorithmic reason shown in the figure or because some process executes a STOP statement.

Process Routines

Each process declared in the program preamble must be further described by a process routine. The names of the process object and process routine are identical. Continuing our analogy with playwriting, a process routine is like the script for a single character. Or, if several characters do very similar things, we might think of the process description as a prototype description into which we plug different parameters.

From a programming point of view, the process routine embodies the logic description of a process, telling what the process object does under all circumstances. Information pertinent to each process-instance is stored with the process notice telling, for example, the values of local variables in the routine, the time at which the process routine will next reactivate, the resources the process currently holds, and the reactivation point for the process-instance (a line number in the source code).

2.5 Example 1: A Simple Gas Station

To solidify these concepts, let us construct a simple model and implement it in SIMSCRIPT II.5.

Consider a small gas station where customers arrive randomly, queue up for service, receive service, and leave. Our goal might be to determine the effects of adding or deleting pumps (or attendants) from the system. For the moment, however, our real goal is merely to construct and execute a very simple SIMSCRIPT model!

To introduce randomness, assume that we have a source of uniformly distributed random numbers for which we can establish bounds. In SIMSCRIPT this is referenced as UNIFORM.F. This function has three parameters: the lower bound, the upper bound, and a random number stream. Each time the function is executed, a new sample from the interval is computed. (The details of representing random phenomena are contained in Chapter 4.)

We choose now to model the customers as processes. They arrive, request service, wait if no server is available, occupy the server for a while, and then depart. For this model, it is sufficient to model the attendant (server) as a resource.

This program will be discussed in two phases: first, a walk-through of the SIMSCRIPT code as presented in Figure 2.2; and second, a walk-through of a sample execution.

Each segment of a SIMSCRIPT program begins with a keyword and ends with an END statement.

In the PREAMBLE, we have declared two processes, a GENERATOR (of new customers) and the CUSTOMER. We have chosen to model the attendant(s) as a resource since it can be described passively.

In the MAIN program the initialization of resource ATTENDANT is accomplished by the CREATE EVERY statement, in which the number of "kinds" (or subgroups) of attendants is specified as one, and by the assignment statement "LET..." in which an automatically defined variable U.attendant is initialized to specify two "units" of attendant resources. That is, we now have two identical attendants who draw customers from a single queue. The ACTIVATE statement creates a process object called GENERATOR and places it on the pending list with an immediate time of activation (NOW). START SIMULATION passes control to the timing routine. Note that without this statement, no processes would ever be executed! Finally, in this model, when control returns from the timing routine (because all processes are complete), control immediately will pass out of the program, i.e., back to the operating system. No output is produced from this model. We shall remedy that in the sequel.

Each PROCESS is described as a separate routine which begins with a PROCESS statement naming the process. This name must correspond to one of the processes named in the preamble.

The process GENERATOR contains a sequence of two statements, which are executed repetitively under the control of a simple iteration phrase FOR I=1 TO 1000. The statements DO and LOOP delimit the scope of the FOR phase, i.e., statements between the pair will be executed 1000 times before the loop control logic is satisfied. Within the loop, the two statements create a new customer process object and place it on the pending list with an immediate time of activation. Then the WAIT statement puts the GENERATOR process object back on the pending list with a new reactivation time. The new time is determined by first drawing a sample from the population of real numbers between 2: and 8: (uniformly distributed), and then adding that value to the current "clock" time.

The process CUSTOMER describes everything that happens to a customer from the time he arrives until he departs. This is very simple in this example. The customer requests an attendant. If neither attendant is available, the customer process object is automatically placed on a list of objects waiting for the attendants. By default this list is ordered as "first-come-first-served." The process is then suspended until this "blocking" condition (no available attendant) is alleviated.

When an attendant is available, one is assigned to this customer and the customer executes the WORK statement, which operates identically to the WAIT in GENERATOR except for the difference in distribution parameters. Finally, when the customer is REACTIVATEd after a period representing his service, the attendant is RELINQUISHed, either to be made available (if no customers are waiting) or to be allocated to the first customer in the queue. (This allocation automatically reactivates the other customer, who will then execute his WORK statement). The present customer is finished, so his process object is automatically DESTROYed and no trace remains of his ever having been in the system.

In Figure 2.3, the detailed execution is traced using the following notation:

> [P_i, n, t] represents the i-th instance of process P ready to resume execution at line n at time t. Customers in queue have a time designated "*" to indicate that the time is unknown.

The progress of the program may be followed by reading the table thus:

The current process is executed at its reactivation time and line. It continues executing, line by line, until it either encounters a delay (unavailable attendant or WORK/WAIT statement) or successfully completes execution. The system status recorded on the remainder of the line is <u>after</u> the process has progressed as far as possible without a time advance.

```
''   EXAMPLE 1  A SIMPLE GAS STATION MODEL

PREAMBLE
   PROCESSES INCLUDE GENERATOR AND CUSTOMER
   RESOURCES INCLUDE ATTENDANT
END
```

```
MAIN
   CREATE EVERY ATTENDANT(1)
   LET U.ATTENDANT(1) = 2
   ACTIVATE A GENERATOR NOW
   START SIMULATION
END
```

```
PROCESS GENERATOR
   FOR I = 1 TO 1000,
   DO
      ACTIVATE A CUSTOMER NOW
      WAIT UNIFORM.F(2.0,8.0,1) MINUTES
   LOOP
END
```

```
PROCESS CUSTOMER
   REQUEST 1 ATTENDANT(1)
   WORK UNIFORM.F(5.0,15.0,2) MINUTES
   RELINQUISH 1 ATTENDANT(1)
END
```

Figure 2.2 - Example 1: A Simple Gas Station Model

TIME	CURRENT PROCESS	AFTER Current Process Executes: AVAILABLE ATTENDANTS	CUSTOMERS IN QUEUE	PENDING PROCESSES
0.0	[AT START SIMULATION]	2	NONE	[G_1,1,0.0]
0.0	[G_1,1,0.0]	2	NONE	[C_1,1,0.0] [G_1,6,7.547]
0.0	[C_1,1,0.0]	1	NONE	[C_1,4,6.847] [G_1,6,7.547]
6.847	[C_1,4,6.847]	2	NONE	[G_1,6,7.547]
7.547	[G_1,6,7.547]	2	NONE	[C_2,1,7.547] [G_1,6, 10.617]
7.547	[C_2,1,7.547]	1	NONE	[G_1,6,10.617] [C_2,4,14.400]
10.617	[G_1,6,10.617]	1	NONE	[C_3,1,10.617] [G_1,6,14.073] [C_2,4, 14.400]
10.617	[C_3,1,10.617]	0	NONE	[G_1,6,14.073] [C_2,4,14.400] [C_3,4,24.367]
14.073	[G_1,6,14.073]	0	NONE	[C_4,1,14.073] [C_2,4,14.400] [G_1,6,21.932] [C_3,4,24.367]
14.073	[C_4,1,14.073]	0	[C_4, 3, *]	[C_2,4,14.400] [G_1,6,21.932] [C_3,4,24.367]
14.400	[C_2,4,14.400]	0	NONE	[C_4,3,14.400] [G_1,6,21.932] [C_3,4,24.367]
14.400	[C_4,3,14.400]	0	NONE	[C_4,4,20.143] [G_1,6,21.932] [C_3,4,24.367]
20.143	[C_4,4,20.143]	1	NONE	[G_1,6,21.932] [C_3,4,24.367]

Figure 2.3 - Detailed Trace of Execution of Example 1

For example, the one instance of the generator process, G_1, is the first current process [G_1, 1, 0.0]. After it has executed lines 1-5 of its process source code, the available attendants and customers in queue are unchanged but two processes are now pending, the first customer to enter the system (at time zero) and the generator itself which has drawn a first interarrival time delay of 7.547 minutes. It is important to observe the sequence in which these actions occur. In particular, let us clarify the meaning of "NOW" as a time of activation. The customer process activated "now" in the generator is placed on the pending list and the generator process continues to execute until it, itself, is delayed (i.e., placed on the pending list) due to the execution of the wait statement. Thus we see that NOW means "as soon as control returns to the timing routine for next event selection."

Next let us observe what happens when a process requests a resource of which no units are available. In Figure 2.3 this occurs at time 14.073 when C_4 is the current process. The process is placed on the "CUSTOMERS IN QUEUE." At this time it is not known when the resource will become available. This is represented by an asterisk in the time position.

When the resource becomes available, in the example at [C_2,4,14.400], it is <u>immediately</u> reallocated and the waiting process (C_4) is moved from the queue to the pending process list. Notice that if C_2 were to now re-request an attendant, C_2 would be put on the CUSTOMERS IN QUEUE list, because the resource is no longer available.

2.6 Adding Performance Measurements

We have gone to great detail in explaining the execution of this example, moreso than we shall do again, in an attempt to clarify the basic execution of a SIMSCRIPT model. As noted, no output is produced by the program. We shall now remedy this situation.

Two measures that are commonly desired in such a model are statistics on the queue (average, variance, maximum, etc.) and the utilization of the resources. These can easily be obtained in SIMSCRIPT by introducing the ACCUMULATE statement. The ACCUMULATE statement provides the modeller with a simple means of specifying which measurements he desires without requiring detailed specification of the method of measurement. An ACCUMULATE statement is placed in the preamble. As the variable of interest changes during the course of the simulation, the system automatically captures the pertinent information.

For example, consider the variable plotted in Figure 2.4. This might represent queue length in our example.

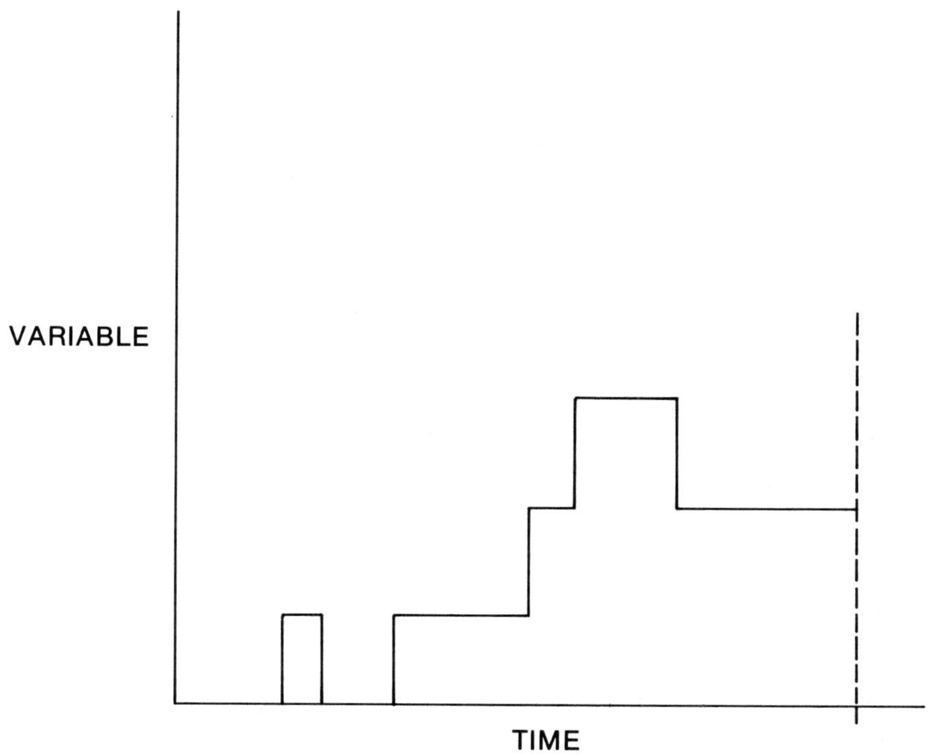

Figure 2.4 - Time-Dependent Statistics

Measurements of interest on this variable are time-dependent. The average value of the variable, for example, depends on how long the variable remains at a certain value.

Two more automatically defined variables are available for use in our measurement task. Associated with each resource are counters indicating how many requests are currently being executed and how many requests are currently enqueued. As with the number of units variable, the names of these variables are derived from the name of the resource. They are N.X.resource and N.Q.resource respectively.

To complete our example, we now lack only a means of displaying the results. For this we introduce the PRINT statement. A PRINT statement consists of three parts: the keyword PRINT and a specification of the number of lines of output to be produced from a single execution of the statement, a list of variables to be printed, and finally, a format or "picture" of the output to be produced. This picture consists of text material to be printed verbatim, together with formats for the numerical data. There must be a one-to-one correspondence between the elements in the list of variables and the formats. A numerical format is composed of a sequence of asterisks and (at most) one period. The number of asterisks after the decimal point governs the number of significant figures to be printed, with automatic rounding in the last position. The number of asterisks before the decimal point determines the maximum value that can be printed. However, automatic provision is made for blanks immediately preceding such a format to be treated as asterisks. Provision is also made for automatically detecting any overflow condition.

Figure 2.5 contains the completed program, including provision for measuring queue length and attendant utilization and for reporting these results. It should be observed that the <u>only</u> changes to the model from Figure 2.2 are the addition of two ACCUMULATE statements in the PREAMBLE and the PRINT statement in MAIN. The value printed as utilization of the attendants is the average value of N.X.ATTENDANT(1) divided by two, since the number of busy attendants ranges from zero to two and we wish to report their utilization as a percentage of possible utilization.

The placement of the PRINT statement after the START SIMULATION in MAIN causes the output to be produced only after all processes activated in the model have terminated. Another possibility is to place the PRINT statement after the LOOP statement in the generator process. This would have the effect of not including the wrap-up operation (i.e., serving customers after the door has been closed to new customers.)

The results produced by executing the program in Figure 2.5 are illustrated in Figure 2.6.

2.7 A Slightly More Complicated Example

One of our goals in modelling is to quickly explore alternatives in design. This may entail including more (or less) detail than originally anticipated, changing numerical data in the model, or including more measurement requirements.

```
''    EXAMPLE 1 A   EXAMPLE 1 WITH PERFORMANCE MEASUREMENTS ADDED

PREAMBLE
   PROCESSES INCLUDE GENERATOR AND CUSTOMER
   RESOURCES INCLUDE ATTENDANT
   ACCUMULATE AVG.QUEUE.LENGTH AS THE AVERAGE
      AND MAX.QUEUE.LENGTH AS THE MAXIMUM
      OF N.Q.ATTENDANT
   ACCUMULATE UTILIZATION AS THE AVERAGE OF N.X.ATTENDANT
END
```

```
MAIN
   CREATE EVERY ATTENDANT(1)
   LET U.ATTENDANT(1) = 2
   ACTIVATE A GENERATOR NOW
   START SIMULATION
   PRINT 4 LINES WITH AVG.QUEUE.LENGTH(1), MAX.QUEUE.LENGTH(1),
      AND UTILIZATION(1) * 100. / 2   THUS
SIMPLE GAS STATION MODEL WITH 2 ATTENDANTS
   AVERAGE CUSTOMER QUEUE LENGTH IS      *.***
   MAXIMUM CUSTOMER QUEUE LENGTH IS      *
   THE ATTENDANTS WERE BUSY   **.** PER CENT OF THE TIME.
END
```

```
PROCESS GENERATOR
   FOR I = 1 TO 1000,
   DO
      ACTIVATE A CUSTOMER NOW
      WAIT UNIFORM.F(2.0,8.0,1) MINUTES
   LOOP
END
```

```
PROCESS CUSTOMER
   REQUEST 1 ATTENDANT(1)
   WORK UNIFORM.F(5.0,15.0,2) MINUTES
   RELINQUISH 1 ATTENDANT(1)
END
```

Figure 2.5 - Example 1A: Example 1 With Performance Measurements Added

```
SIMPLE GAS STATION MODEL WITH 2 ATTENDANTS
   AVERAGE CUSTOMER QUEUE LENGTH IS      7.809
   MAXIMUM CUSTOMER QUEUE LENGTH IS    21
   THE ATTENDANTS WERE BUSY  98.64 PER CENT OF THE TIME.
```

Figure 2.6 - Output from Example 1A

To illustrate the ease of doing this in SIMSCRIPT, let us modify our example as follows:

a. Customers choose the type of gas they require (premium or regular) and must wait for the proper pump to become available. Let us arbitrarily assume that 70% require premium and 30% require regular. Initially, we shall arbitrarily have one regular pump and three premium pumps.

b. An attendant is not required until the pump is available. The attendant starts the pump and then is free until the pump stops. He is then required in order to complete the service.

c. We wish to measure the queues and utilization for the attendants and two types of pumps.

Figure 2.7 shows the program modified to incorporate these features.

The program uses three features of SIMSCRIPT not used previously:

DEFINE TO MEAN
Local Variables
Simple Decision Logic

DEFINE TO MEAN

In the interest of improved readability of programs, SIMSCRIPT allows the modeller to substitute a character string for a single word, and thus to develop his own vocabulary or shorthand notation. The general form of the statement is:

DEFINE word TO MEAN string

A constraint is that string must be confined to a single input record.

In our example we use this feature to allow mnemonic values for our pump resource subscripts (.REGULAR or .PREMIUM). It is purely a style convention we have adopted to have every "DEFINE TO MEAN" symbol begin with a period.

Local Variables

The variables we have used so far have been global in scope. That is, the same variable can be referenced from anywhere in the program. For example, the variable U.ATTENDANT was initialized in MAIN and modifed in the execution of the REQUEST and RELINQUISH statements in the process customer.

It is sometimes necessary to define variables which are private to a particular process, or even more specifically, to an individual instance of a process. This is accomplished by defining local variables in the body of a process. For example, in our model, it is necessary that each customer "remember" which grade of gasoline he wants, so that when he has been served he can relinquish the proper pump. We accomplish this by defining the variable GRADE within the process customer.

Simple Decision Logic

The final new concept introduced in this model is the ability to alter the flow of control explicitly in the program logic. The IF statement is used to describe two alternative courses of action. The form of the statement is:

```
IF   logical test
          group of statements1
ELSE
          group of statements2
ALWAYS
```

and it is executed in this manner:

The logical test is evaluated. It will be either true or false. If it is true, group of statements_1 will be executed and group of statements_2 will not. If the logical test is false, only group of statements_2 will be executed. In either case the statements which follow the word ALWAYS are executed.

In our example, this construct is used to randomly select the grade of gasoline for each customer. RANDOM.F(i) is a function that uses the i-th random number stream to return a value sampled from the population uniformly distributed between 0 and 1. This value should be less than 0.70 seventy percent of the time, corresponding to our estimate of the number of customers who use premium grade.

The results from executing this model are displayed in Figure 2.8. This more realistic model shows the breakdown of congestion between pump demands and attendant demands. However, the data are purely fictitious and no significant conclusions should be drawn without more analysis of the situation.

2.8 Some Concluding Remarks

This chapter has introduced many of the modelling concepts supported by the SIMSCRIPT II.5 language. Many problem areas can be addressed by analogy to the models presented. About 25% of the statements of the language have been illustrated. But, almost without exception, each of the statements has more complex forms or alternative applications. Succeeding chapters will go into much more detail, showing how these basic constructs may be elaborated upon in some instances and dissected in others, for purposes of greater understanding or nonstandard applications.

Quite a few readers may already have some acquaintance with SIMSCRIPT; but for those who desire a more formal expose of the language than this tutorial form permits, Appendix A contains a formal syntax of all the statements of the SIMSCRIPT II.5 language. Appendix B summarizes the coding and style conventions used in the examples. Appendices C and D give all the particulars about system-defined variables, functions, and routines.

```
''    EXAMPLE 2  A MORE ELABORATE GAS STATION MODEL

PREAMBLE
    PROCESSES INCLUDE GENERATOR AND CUSTOMER
    RESOURCES INCLUDE ATTENDANT AND PUMP
    ACCUMULATE AVG.ATTENDANT.QUEUE.LENGTH AS THE AVERAGE
       AND MAX.ATTENDANT.QUEUE.LENGTH AS THE MAXIMUM
       OF N.Q.ATTENDANT
    ACCUMULATE UTILIZATION AS THE AVERAGE OF N.X.ATTENDANT
    ACCUMULATE AVG.PUMP.QUEUE.LENGTH AS THE AVERAGE
       AND MAX.PUMP.QUEUE.LENGTH AS THE MAXIMUM
       OF N.Q.PUMP
    ACCUMULATE PUMP.UTILIZATION AS THE AVERAGE OF N.X.PUMP
    DEFINE .REGULAR TO MEAN 1
    DEFINE .PREMIUM TO MEAN 2
END

MAIN
    CREATE EVERY ATTENDANT(1)
    LET U.ATTENDANT(1) = 2
    CREATE EVERY PUMP(2)
    LET U.PUMP(.REGULAR) = 1
    LET U.PUMP(.PREMIUM) = 3
    ACTIVATE A GENERATOR NOW
    START SIMULATION
    PRINT 10 LINES WITH AVG.ATTENDANT.QUEUE.LENGTH(1),
       MAX.ATTENDANT.QUEUE.LENGTH(1),
       UTILIZATION(1) * 100. / U.ATTENDANT(1),
       AVG.PUMP.QUEUE.LENGTH(.REGULAR), MAX.PUMP.QUEUE.LENGTH(.REGULAR),
       PUMP.UTILIZATION(.REGULAR) * 100. / U.PUMP(.REGULAR),
       AVG.PUMP.QUEUE.LENGTH(.PREMIUM), MAX.PUMP.QUEUE.LENGTH(.PREMIUM),
       PUMP.UTILIZATION(.PREMIUM) * 100. / U.PUMP(.PREMIUM) THUS
SIMPLE GAS STATION WITH TWO ATTENDANTS
   AND TWO GRADES OF GASOLINE
AVERAGE QUEUE WAITING FOR ATTENDANTS IS    *.*** CUSTOMERS
MAXIMUM    "     "     "     "     "       *
THE ATTENDANTS WERE BUSY   *.**  PER CENT OF THE TIME.

THE QUEUES FOR THE PUMPS WERE AS FOLLOWS:
GRADE        AVERAGE       MAXIMUM       UTILIZATION
REGULAR:      *.***           *              *.**  PERCENT
PREMIUM:      *.***           *              *.**  PERCENT
END
```

Figure 2.7 - Example 2: A More Elaborate Gas Station Model (Continued)

```
PROCESS GENERATOR
   FOR I = 1 TO 1000,
   DO
      ACTIVATE A CUSTOMER NOW
      WAIT UNIFORM.F(2.0,8.0,1) MINUTES
   LOOP
END
```

```
PROCESS CUSTOMER
   DEFINE GRADE AS AN INTEGER VARIABLE
   IF RANDOM.F(3) > 0.70,
      LET GRADE = .REGULAR
   ELSE
      LET GRADE = .PREMIUM
   ALWAYS
   REQUEST 1 PUMP(GRADE)
   REQUEST 1 ATTENDANT(1)
   WORK UNIFORM.F(2.0,4.0,2) MINUTES
   RELINQUISH 1 ATTENDANT(1)
   WORK UNIFORM.F(5.0,9.0,2) MINUTES
   REQUEST 1 ATTENDANT(1)
   WORK UNIFORM.F(3.0,5.0,2) MINUTES
   RELINQUISH 1 ATTENDANT(1)
   RELINQUISH 1 PUMP(GRADE)
END
```

Figure 2.7 - Example 2: A More Elaborate Gas Station Model

```
SIMPLE GAS STATION WITH TWO ATTENDANTS
   AND TWO GRADES OF GASOLINE
AVERAGE QUEUE WAITING FOR ATTENDANTS IS     .138 CUSTOMERS
MAXIMUM    "       "        "        "       "       2
THE ATTENDANTS WERE BUSY  69.93 PER CENT OF THE TIME.

THE QUEUES FOR THE PUMPS WERE AS FOLLOWS:
 GRADE        AVERAGE        MAXIMUM        UTILIZATION
REGULAR:       1.237            8            79.94 PERCENT
PREMIUM:        .084            3            70.74 PERCENT
```

Figure 2.8 - Output from Example 2

Chapter 3

MODELLING INDIVIDUAL OBJECTS

3.1 The Attribute Concept

In Chapter 2, the system was modelled without a need to identify individual copies of objects explicitly.

Objects often have to be described in more detail. Processes and resources can be given attributes. In fact, we have actually used some attributes of resources in Chapter 2. These attributes were, however, automatically defined by the system. The number of units of a resource, the number of outstanding requests, and the number of currently satisfied requests are all contained in attributes of a resource. The modeller may add as many attributes as he or she chooses to characterize the resources adequately.

For example, instead of remembering that the first pump subgroup is for regular gas and the second is for premium, we may choose to have a type or grade attribute. In addition, let us suppose we wish to keep track of the remaining reserve of each grade. To do so, we write:

```
RESOURCES
    EVERY PUMP HAS A GRADE
```

When space is allocated for this resource, the data structure can be represented as shown in Figure 3.1.

```
CREATE EVERY PUMP (3)
```

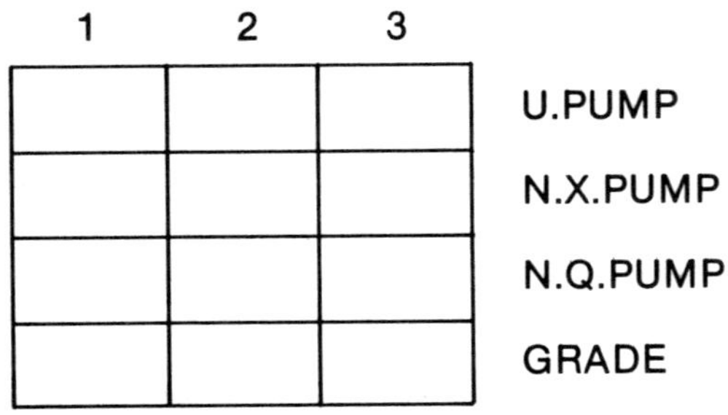

Figure 3.1 - PUMP Resource Data Structure

Each column in the figure represents the storage for the attributes of a different pump group.

Two more variables are automatically associated with each resource. One is a variable with the same name as the resource; the other is a variable whose name is derived from the resource name by prefixing "N.". N.resource contains the number of resource objects in existence whereas <u>resource</u> is used as a reference to a particular object (or column in Figure 3.1). Thus in our example, N.PUMP has a value of 3, taken from the CREATE statement. The initial value of all SIMSCRIPT variables is zero. Therefore, before using the variable PUMP we must initialize it to a valid value -- in this case 1, 2, or 3. We use the entity name like a subscript and refer to specific attributes as GRADE(PUMP) or "grade of pump."

3.2 Variables

Several SIMSCRIPT variables have been used in previous examples without a precise definition of their characteristics. This will now be remedied.

SIMSCRIPT variables are of numerous types. Attributes, reference variables, and simple variables are only a few of the types available, but they will suffice to introduce the concepts.

Variables are either global or local in scope. A global variable must be defined in the program preamble. If a variable is not explicitly defined anywhere, it becomes a local variable by default, provided that it is used in a proper context.

All variables have a mode. This may be integer, real, alpha, or text. Real is the background or default mode, i.e., if a variable is defined implicitly or even explicitly without specifying the mode, it assumes the background mode.

The background mode may be changed by use of the statement,

```
NORMALLY, MODE IS mode
```

If this statement appears in the preamble, it has the effect of changing the background for the remainder of the preamble AND all programs compiled with the preamble. It may, of course, be superseded by subsequent NORMALLY statements. If a NORMALLY statement appears in an individual routine, it applies only to variables in that routine. It is better programming practice to define every variable explicitly and not to rely on the system defaults.

Global/Local Conflicts

A variable which is defined in the preamble (and is thus global) may also be defined explicitly in an individual routine. When this is done, the global variable is effectively excluded from use in that routine. This is particularly useful in isolating or eliminating "side effects" of the execution of routines. This will be illustrated in a subsequent example (Figure 3.4).

A variable is initialized to zero automatically when the storage for the variable is allocated. For a global variable, this occurs at the beginning of the execution of the program. For a local variable in a routine or process, the local variables are allocated upon entry into the routine. The local variable storage remains allocated until the routine "ends." For a routine this means at the execution of a RETURN statement. The execution of process delaying statements does not cause local storage to be deallocated. The local storage for a process remains allocated until the process finally is completed. Note that this method of storage allocation provides each copy of a process with its <u>own</u> local storage and also permits recursive calls of routines.

Naming of Variables

The modeller has great freedom in naming variables. The only restriction on name-length is that it must be contained within a single record of input to the compiler (typically 80 characters). The keywords of SIMSCRIPT are not reserved words and thus may be used as variable names, if desired. A variable name is any sequence of letters, digits, and periods that does not form a number. So, for example, ABC, NO.OF.CUSTOMERS, 4F, 5.12.38, 1E6 and ABC... are all valid names, whereas 1., 567, 2+2 and

5.12 are not valid names but instead numbers or expressions. A final comment: The compiler drops terminal periods in names. Thus ABC and ABC... are representations of the same variable name.

SIMSCRIPT contains many predefined variables and constants, as well as automatically generated variables, all named according to the following conventions:

Category	Form	Examples	Meaning
Constants	name.C	PI.C	π
		INF.C	infinity
Variables	name.V	TIME.V	simulation clock
		HOURS.V	number of hours/day
Functions	name.F	SQRT.F	square root
		UNIFORM.F	uniform random deviate generator
Generated Attributes	letter. name	U.PUMP	units attribute of a resource
		N.Q.PUMP	number in queue for a resource

By SIMSCRIPT language rules, system names (of the form name.letter) and generated names (of the form letter.name) are used only for purposes defined by the language implementation. Appendix D describes in full all such system names.

3.3 Arithmetic

The usual arithmetic operators and precedence rules are used in SIMSCRIPT. Parentheses are used to change the order of evaluation, forcing evaluation of expressions within parentheses before using the result in outer expressions. There is no limit to the length of an expression or the depth of nesting of parentheses.

For example, the statement

```
LET A = B+D/(C-E*F)**2
```

is evaluated as follows:

1) multiply E by F
2) subtract the product from C
3) square the difference
4) divide D by the result of (3)
5) add B
6) store the result in A

3.4 Data Input

Models are usually constructed in order to perform parametric studies. Quite often a wide range of values need to be tested and the specific values or sequence of values are not known a priori. Rather than build constant values into a model and then require recompilation each time one value needs to be changed, it is much more common practice (at least in real applications) to provide for parameters to be changed at time of execution of the model, without change to the source code. For this purpose we introduce our first input statement, the free-form READ statement. An example of the statement is:

```
READ  X, N.TELLER, U.PUMP (1)
```

i.e., the READ statement consists of the keyword READ followed by a list of variables separated by commas. The format of the data is not specified in the statement but rather is implied by the language. The implied format is that a sequence of data fields will be read corresponding to the variables in the READ statement.

A data field is a sequence of non-blank characters. It is terminated by either a blank or the end of a record (card or line of type from a terminal, etc.). Thus, a single READ statement may use several records to satisfy its input data requirements. A READ statement does not automatically start a new record. Thus, if successive READ statements are executed, the first one might read several entire records and part of one more. The second READ will read any data fields on the current record before starting a new record.

If there is disagreement between the mode of the data field and the mode of the variable, conversion will be made automatically where the conversion is permitted. The allowable conversions are shown in Figure 3.2.

		VARIABLE MODE			
		INTEGER	REAL	ALPHA	TEXT
FORM OF DATA	INTEGER	INTEGER	REAL	ALPHA	TEXT
	REAL	X	REAL	ALPHA	TEXT
	CHARACTERS	X	X	ALPHA	TEXT

where X denotes an error condition.

Figure 3.2 - Input Data Mode Conversions

The mode of an input data field is determined in the following manner:

(1) A sequence of digits, possibly including a preceding sign, is regarded as INTEGER.

(2) A sequence of digits (with optional sign) with a decimal point is regarded as REAL. In addition, a scientific notation is recognized as REAL. It consists of a real representation plus an exponent in the form

SXX.XXESXX

where S represents an optional sign,
X represents a digit, and
E is an optional separator between fraction and exponent (either E or the sign of the exponent is required).

(3) Anything else is regarded as an ALPHA or TEXT mode string.

3.5 Program Control Structures

There are several statements in SIMSCRIPT for altering the flow of program control. The IF statement in its most general form was used in Example 2.7, and a simple loop structure was used to control the generation of new customers. We shall now elaborate on these structures.

The IF Statement

Sometimes the full structural power of the IF statement is not needed to describe a branching condition. For example, when a block of statements is executed conditionally, but no alternative is needed (other than _not_ to execute those statements), the ELSE can be omitted.

For example,

```
IF  STATUS = BUSY
     ADD 1 TO BACK.LOG
ALWAYS
```

On the other hand, the first path may end with an unconditional transfer of control such as STOP or RETURN. In this case, the alternative _is_ the remainder of the routine and no ALWAYS is needed. The ALWAYS should not be included in this case as it may cause another IF structure to be terminated. (IF structures can be nested to any depth.)

```
IF  BACK.LOG= 0
     LET STATUS= IDLE
     RETURN
OTHERWISE
```

LOOPING

The indexed FOR phrase used previously for simple counter control can also be applied to a resource entity in the following manner:

FOR EACH resource

is equivalent to

FOR resource = 1 TO N.resource

(resource in this example is a defined resource entity.) This illustrates that the variable associated with each resource is incremented over its range of valid values from one to the number of subgroups of the resource (N.resource). An alternate form of this phrase is:

FOR EACH resource CALLED name

which is equivalent to

FOR name = 1 TO N.resource

It is often desirable to be selective in this searching operation. For this purpose it is possible to build into the control structures phrases for specifying conditions which must be met either to include or exclude a certain case, or conditions for continuing or terminating the search.

The logical comparisons that may be used in these phrases are the same as those used in the IF statement; they include:

EQUALITY	=	EQ
INEQUALITY	¬ =	NE
LESS THAN	<	LT
GREATER THAN	>	GT

and combinations of these. For program readability, a large collection of synonyms is available. See Appendix A.

Each logical expression will be evaluated to a true or false value. In addition to these simple expressions, compound expressions may be composed by using the logical connectives AND, OR, and parentheses. For example, we might need a certain combination of attribute values on a resource to exist before the resource is of use.

For example,

```
FOR EACH PUMP,
     WITH GRADE (PUMP) = DESIRED.GRADE
     AND RESERVE (PUMP) >= 10.0,
FIND THE FIRST CASE
```

specifies a search over all the pump resource subgroups, looking for the first one that has a grade attribute whose value matches a desired grade, and simultaneously has a value greater than or equal to 10 in its reserve attribute. The FIND statement causes the search to terminate on the first success. It may be followed, optionally, by an IF statement to determine the outcome. The format of this statement is IF FOUND, or alternatively, IF NONE.

Sometimes the search is for the maximum (or minimum) over all the subgroups. In this case the COMPUTE statement is used in place of the FIND statement, since we must necessarily look at all the cases before ascertaining that the maximum (or minimum) has indeed been found. As an example:

```
FOR EACH TELLER,
     COMPUTE SHORTEST.QUEUE.LENGTH
       AS THE MINIMUM OF N.Q.TELLER(TELLER)
```

will examine the N.Q.TELLER attribute of each subgroup of tellers and record, as the value of the variable SHORTEST.QUEUE.LENGTH, the minimum value of this attribute among all the teller subgroups.

Often it is not the value of the variable that is important, but rather the index corresponding to the value that maximizes or minimizes the variable. To record the index, a slightly different form of the statement is used:

```
FOR EACH TELLER,
     COMPUTE SHORTEST.QUEUE
       AS THE MINIMUM (TELLER)
       OF N.Q.TELLER(TELLER)
```

This is interpreted as "Examine the value of the length attribute of each teller queue and record in SHORTEST.QUEUE the value of the index TELLER for which this variable is a minimum."

3.6 The Representation of Time

We have used time expressions in our simulation models without precisely describing the representation of time internally to the system. The SIMSCRIPT simulation "clock" is a system-defined, real variable called TIME.V.

Initially TIME.V has a value of zero, although it may be initialized to any starting value. The default units for time are days. If time expressions are given in hours or minutes, appropriate adjustments are made using two system-defined variables, HOURS.V and MINUTES.V. The default values for these variables are 24 and 60, respectively, indicating the expected conversions of 24 hours per day and 60 minutes per hour. The modeller may change these values, for example, to represent an eight-hour day.

In combination with the DEFINE TO MEAN feature, the entire time domain may be easily changed, For example, in modelling computer systems it is often convenient to represent times in units of seconds, milliseconds, and microseconds. While these words are not a part of the SIMSCRIPT vocabulary, they may easily be added as shown here:

```
PREAMBLE
   DEFINE .SECONDS TO MEAN DAYS
   DEFINE .MILLISECONDS TO MEAN HOURS
   DEFINE .MICROSECONDS TO MEAN MINUTES
END
MAIN
   LET HOURS.V = 1000
   LET MINUTES.V = 1000
END
```

Now the modeller can write statements such as WAIT 32 .MILLISECONDS.

Note, however, that the conventional meanings of days, hours, and minutes have been substantially altered!

The timing routine, as noted in Chapter 2, updates TIME.V as it causes the simulation to progress. It should be noted that any attempt to retrogress in simulated time causes a terminal error in the execution of the model.

3.7 Time Measurements

In the ACCUMULATE performance measurements (Section 2.6), we saw that it is often necessary to measure phenomena as they change over simulated time. There are also many measures which are not time-dependent, but rather depend on the number of samples taken. (Actually, all of our measures could be performed in this manner; the accumulated technique is simply much more convenient.)

For the sample-based measurements, we introduce the TALLY statement. Like the ACCUMULATE statement, it is a declarative statement appearing in the preamble. There are many applications of the TALLY statement. Many involve sampling time measurements such as delays, actual service times, total cycle time, etc.

Figure 3.3 illustrates an example of measuring the waiting time of the first several customers in a system.

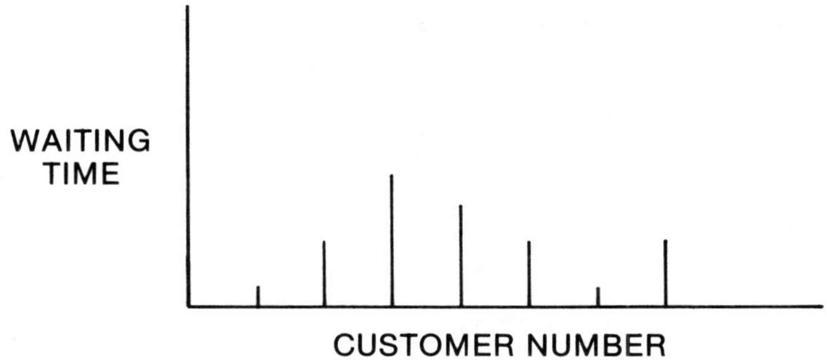

Figure 3.3 - Time-Independent Statistics

Notice that zero waiting times are explicitly recorded as sample values in order to be included in the statistics.

If the default time values are used, these measurements will be recorded in units of days. The results may be converted to hours or minutes by using the system variables HOURS.V and MINUTES.V.

3.8 Example 3: A Bank With a Separate Queue for Each Teller

Let us now illustrate all of the features discussed so far in this chapter by modelling a bank in which customers arrive, go immediately to any available teller, receive service, and leave. If all tellers are busy, let us assume the arriving customer will select the shortest line, join it, and wait there until served. While this is an unreasonable assumption (customers remaining in one line when another teller becomes free), it will give us an extreme value for comparing this system with the new-style bank in which all customers form a single line to be served by the next available teller. (It might be interesting to show that when jockeying is permitted, the single line is the optimum equivalent.)

The measurements required are the average and maximum queues, the utilization of each separate teller, and the mean waiting time for all customers.

Model Formulation

This system will be modelled using two processes and one resource. The generator process will inject customers into the system with an exponential distribution of interarrival times until a prespecified closing time. The model will terminate after all customers who arrived before closing time finish being served. (See Chapter 4 for details of the exponential distribution.)

The customer process will contain the complete description of the actions of one customer from arrival at the bank until departure.

The single resource, teller, is used with the subgroup concept -- one subgroup per individual teller -- so as to easily accomplish the separate queueing and measurements.

Certain model parameters are explicitly defined as global variables to permit initializing them in one program (MAIN) and using them in another (processes generator and customer).

The program listing for this example is shown in Figure 3.4.

```
''    EXAMPLE 3  A BANK WITH SEPARATE QUEUES FOR EACH TELLER

PREAMBLE
    PROCESSES INCLUDE GENERATOR AND CUSTOMER
    RESOURCES INCLUDE TELLER
    DEFINE MEAN.INTERARRIVAL.TIME, MEAN.SERVICE.TIME,
        DAY.LENGTH AND WAITING.TIME AS REAL VARIABLES

    ACCUMULATE UTILIZATION AS THE AVERAGE OF N.X.TELLER
    ACCUMULATE AVG.QUEUE.LENGTH AS THE AVERAGE,
        MAX.QUEUE.LENGTH AS THE MAXIMUM OF N.Q.TELLER
    TALLY MEAN.WAITING.TIME AS THE MEAN OF WAITING.TIME
END

MAIN
    READ N.TELLER, MEAN.INTERARRIVAL.TIME,MEAN.SERVICE.TIME
        AND DAY.LENGTH
    CREATE EVERY TELLER
    FOR EACH TELLER,
        LET U.TELLER(TELLER) = 1
    PRINT 8 LINES WITH N.TELLER, MEAN.INTERARRIVAL.TIME,
        MEAN.SERVICE.TIME AND DAY.LENGTH THUS
SIMULATION OF A BANK WITH   *  TELLERS
  (EACH WITH A SEPARATE QUEUE)
CUSTOMERS ARRIVE ACCORDING TO AN EXPONENTIAL DISTRIBUTION
   OF INTER ARRIVAL TIMES WITH A MEAN OF   *.**  MINUTES.
SERVICE TIME IS ALSO EXPONENTIALLY DISTRIBUTED
   WITH A MEAN OF   *.**  MINUTES.
THE BANK DOORS ARE CLOSED AFTER   *.**  HOURS.
   (BUT ALL CUSTOMERS INSIDE ARE SERVED.)

    ACTIVATE A GENERATOR NOW
    START SIMULATION

    PRINT 6 LINES WITH TIME.V * HOURS.V,
        AND MEAN.WAITING.TIME * HOURS.V * MINUTES.V THUS
THE LAST CUSTOMER LEFT THE BANK AT   *.** HOURS.
THE AVERAGE CUSTOMER DELAY WAS   *.** MINUTES.

TELLER         UTILIZATION                   QUEUE  LENGTH
                                          AVERAGE         MAXIMUM

    FOR EACH TELLER,
        PRINT 1 LINE WITH TELLER, UTILIZATION(TELLER),
            AVG.QUEUE.LENGTH(TELLER), MAX.QUEUE.LENGTH(TELLER) THUS
  *                 *.**               *.**                *
END
```

Figure 3.4 - Example 3: A Bank With a Separate Queue for Each Teller

```
PROCESS GENERATOR
   DEFINE TIME.TO.CLOSE AS A REAL VARIABLE
   LET TIME.TO.CLOSE = DAY.LENGTH / HOURS.V
   UNTIL TIME.V >= TIME.TO.CLOSE,
   DO
      ACTIVATE A CUSTOMER NOW
      WAIT EXPONENTIAL.F(MEAN.INTERARRIVAL.TIME,1) MINUTES
   LOOP
END
```

```
PROCESS CUSTOMER
   DEFINE ARRIVAL.TIME AS A REAL VARIABLE
   DEFINE MY.CHOICE AS AN INTEGER VARIABLE
   LET ARRIVAL.TIME = TIME.V
   FOR EACH TELLER, WITH N.X.TELLER(TELLER) = 0,
      FIND THE FIRST CASE
   IF FOUND,
      LET MY.CHOICE = TELLER
   ELSE
      FOR EACH TELLER,
         COMPUTE MY.CHOICE AS THE MINIMUM(TELLER)
            OF N.Q.TELLER(TELLER)
   ALWAYS
   REQUEST 1 TELLER(MY.CHOICE)
   LET WAITING.TIME = TIME.V - ARRIVAL.TIME
   WORK EXPONENTIAL.F(MEAN.SERVICE.TIME,2) MINUTES
   RELINQUISH 1 TELLER(MY.CHOICE)
END
```

Figure 3.4 - Example 3 (Continued)

```
SIMULATION OF A BANK WITH   2  TELLERS
  (EACH WITH A SEPARATE QUEUE)
CUSTOMERS ARRIVE ACCORDING TO AN EXPONENTIAL DISTRIBUTION
   OF INTER ARRIVAL TIMES WITH A MEAN OF    5.00  MINUTES.
SERVICE TIME IS ALSO EXPONENTIALLY DISTRIBUTED
   WITH A MEAN OF  10.00  MINUTES.
THE BANK DOORS ARE CLOSED AFTER   8.00  HOURS.
   (BUT ALL CUSTOMERS INSIDE ARE SERVED.)
THE LAST CUSTOMER LEFT THE BANK AT   9.49 HOURS.
THE AVERAGE CUSTOMER DELAY WAS  19.84 MINUTES.

TELLER        UTILIZATION              QUEUE  LENGTH
                                   AVERAGE        MAXIMUM

  1                .97               1.73            6
  2                .91               2.06            7
```

Figure 3.5 - Output from Example 3

Program Discussion

For the sample execution output shown (Figure 3.5) , the input data could have been prepared as:

```
2     5.0     10.     8
```

A more elaborate model might request this information in an interactive dialog.

A good programming practice is to print all the input data so as to verify that no miscommunication has occurred. This is shown in MAIN.

This model is designed to terminate by running out of active processes and returning control to MAIN for final analysis output.

The process customer has the following salient features:

1) Lines 2, 4 and 15 compute a sample of waiting time for each customer.

2) Lines 2 and 3 define local variables in order to preserve a record for each customer of the time of arrival and the selected teller. This latter is imperative so that after a time delay either for queueing, service, or both, the proper teller resource will be relinquished.

3) The customer decision-making function is broken into two steps:

   a) Look for an idle teller (lines 5-8);

   b) If no idle teller is found, look for the shortest line (lines 10-12).

This operation could have been combined into a single search of the form:

```
FOR EACH TELLER
     COMPUTE MY.CHOICE AS THE
     MINIMUM(TELLER)
     OF N.X.TELLER(TELLER)+N.Q.TELLER(TELLER)
```

The process generator is slightly different from previous examples in that the number of customers to be generated is not specified, but rather a time at which to stop generating them. The UNTIL phrase is another loop variant. This time there is no need for the FOR phrase.

There is a slight imprecision in this model-closing procedure in that, if there were no customers in the bank at closing time, the model would not actually stop and summarize statistics immediately, but would only do so at the time of next customer arrival since that is the time at which the process generator would be terminated. This can be remedied with additional commands to be discussed in the next section.

3.9 Process Attributes

Attributes may be associated with processes as well as with resources. For example, it might be necessary to carry along as attributes of the process CAR such information as the time of arrival, the grade of gasoline required, and the amount of gasoline required. These can all be defined in a statement such as:

```
PROCESSES
     EVERY CAR
          HAS A TIME.OF.ARRIVAL
          AND A GAS.GRADE
          AND A TANK.CAPACITY
```

When such a process is activated, these attributes will automatically be initialized to zero. In order to assign values to the attributes of a process or to reference the values later, the attribute is associated with the particular process through the use of a reference variable (sometimes called a pointer variable).

For example,

```
LET TANK.CAPACITY(CAR) = 15
```

This statement is read as "let tank.capacity of car be set equal to fifteen." The variable CAR is a reference variable. Its value is established by the ACTIVATE statement.

```
ACTIVATE A CAR IN 10 MINUTES
```

which is now seen to mean:

1) Create a process notice to describe a new CAR.

2) Place the reference value for this notice in the variable CAR.

3) Compute the time at which this activation will take place (current time + ten minutes) and store this value as an attribute of the process.

4) Place the process notice in the pending list.

Only one CAR process notice is accessible by this mechanism at any particular time. It is possible to refer to more than one copy of processes of the same class in the following manner:

```
ACTIVATE A CAR CALLED X IN 5 MINUTES
ACTIVATE A CAR CALLED Y IN 10 MINUTES


LET TANK.CAPACITY(X)= 17
LET TANK.CAPACITY(Y)= 20
```

This concept is summarized in Figure 3.6.

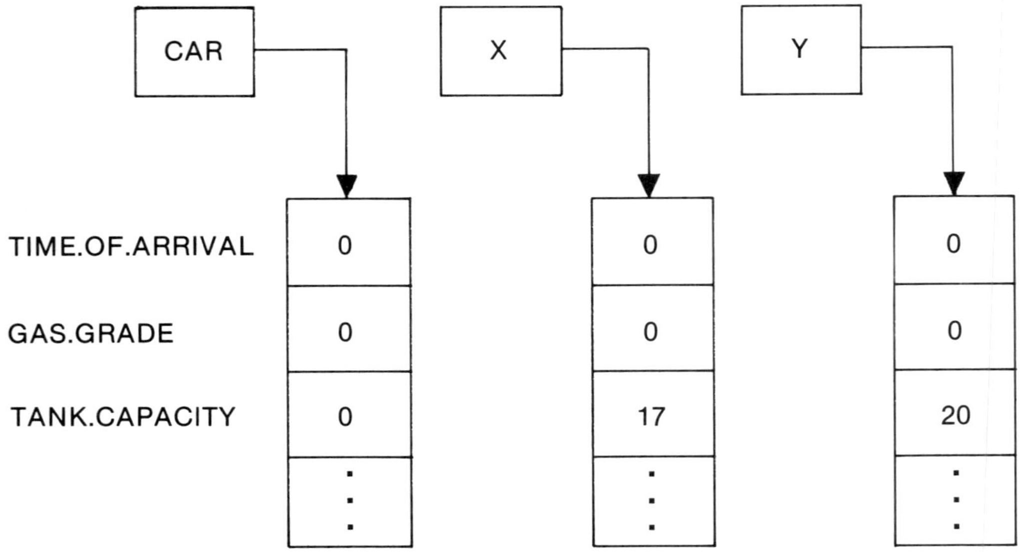

Figure 3.6 - Multiple Process Data Structures

Each process notice has space for the defined attributes plus some additional system-defined information to be discussed later. These process notices are dynamically allocated blocks of storage. The modeller need not be concerned with where they are stored, how many are allocated at any particular time, or the order of assignment of the attributes to the words within the process notice.

The variable with the generic name of the process becomes, by default, a global variable -- accessible from any part of the model -- whereas other variables default to a local context.

The attributes of a process can be initialized as part of the execution of the ACTIVATE statement. Assume, for example, that we have a process representing a message in a communications network defined as follows:

```
PROCESSES
     EVERY MESSAGE HAS AN ORIGIN
          AND A DESTINATION
```

We might represent a message to be sent from Los Angeles to Washington, D.C. as:

```
ACTIVATE A MESSAGE GIVING LA AND DC NOW
```

This is equivalent to the following sequence of statements:

```
CREATE A MESSAGE
LET ORIGIN(MESSAGE) = LA
LET DESTINATION(MESSAGE) = DC
ACTIVATE THIS MESSAGE NOW
```

This latter breakdown illustrates two further concepts: the ability to create a process notice without placing it in the pending list; and then, later on, activating the process without automatically creating a new process notice. The distinction in the form of the ACTIVATE statement is very subtle. The indefinite article (A or AN) is replaced by a definite article (THE or THIS). The values in the GIVING phrase are assigned to attributes in the order in which the attributes were defined in the preamble.

3.10 Argument Passing for Subroutines

When a subroutine is invoked, it is often necessary to pass information to that routine. Upon completion, the subroutine communicates its results to the calling routine via arguments. In SIMSCRIPT, the given information and the results are passed as separately specified arguments.

A subroutine is invoked via the CALL statement. For example,

```
CALL HARBOR.MASTER GIVING SHIP AND "ARRIVING" YIELDING STATUS
```

specifies invocation of the routine named HARBOR.MASTER, passing to it as arguments the value of the variable SHIP and the literal "ARRIVING." The result of this execution of the routine will be placed in the variable STATUS.

The corresponding procedure declaration heading might appear as:

```
ROUTINE HARBOR.MASTER GIVING NEW.SHIP AND ACTION YIELDING STATUS
   DEFINE NEW.SHIP AND STATUS AS INTEGER VARIABLES
   DEFINE ACTION AS A TEXT VARIABLE
```

Note that the arguments must agree in mode and in number between the CALL statement and the routine declaration.

3.11 Subprogram Variables

As a generalization of the subroutine calling mechanism, the subprogram variable is introduced into SIMSCRIPT. A subprogram variable is declared as, for example,

```
DEFINE DEBUG AS A SUBPROGRAM VARIABLE
```

or,

```
DEFINE TRIG AS A REAL SUBPROGRAM VARIABLE
```

When a mode is specified, it refers to the mode of the result of the subprogram when called as a function. This will be illustrated below.

To initialize a subprogram variable, a LET statement must be used to assign a subprogram literal as the value of the variable. For example,

```
LET TRIG = 'SIN.F'
```

The subprogram literal may be any SIMSCRIPT library routine or a routine to be written by the user.

A statement such as,

```
LET B = TRIG
```

would copy the address of the SIN.F function to another subprogram variable, B, whereas,

```
LET X = $TRIG(.5)
```

would compute the value of SIN.F(.5) and store the result in X.

This raises a syntactic problem. Since a subprogram variable can be subscripted, i.e., an array or an attribute, what does the quantity in parentheses represent? The answer is the argument to the routine. If it is necessary to execute a subprogram stored in an array or attribute, it must first be moved to an unsubscripted subprogram variable.

For example,

```
PROCESSES
   EVERY PORT
      HAS A PT.ROUTINE
DEFINE PT.ROUTINE AS A SUBPROGRAM VARIABLE

.

.

.
PROCESS PORT
   DEFINE LOCAL AS A SUBPROGRAM VARIABLE
   STORE PT.ROUTINE IN LOCAL
   CALL LOCAL GIVING PORT
.

.

.
```

This program illustrates that a different routine can be associated with each different process instance, i.e., each port, to be called from the process when needed.

3.12 Argument Passing for Processes

It is not necessary to explicitly pass arguments to processes, since the values of the arguments are taken from the attributes of the process notice. They may be referenced directly; however, it is occasionally convenient or more natural to specify parameters for a process. Only given parameters may be specified for processes. The arguments (or formal parameters) take their values from the user-defined attributes specified in the process notice definition in the preamble. It is not necessary to provide arguments for all of the attributes; however, the attributes will be assigned to the arguments in the order of preamble definition. The mode-mismatch problem of subroutines does not arise for processes; however, process attributes are copied to the arguments only upon initial entry to the process routine. If, for some reason, the attribute values are changed while the process is either active or passive (i.e., from within or without the process), this will have no effect on the argument values.

For example, consider the previous MESSAGE process example. With the same preamble definition and activate statement,

```
PROCESSES
   EVERY MESSAGE HAS AN MG.ORIGIN
      AND AN MG.DESTINATION
ACTIVATE A MESSAGE GIVING LA AND DC NOW
```

The process routine might start with,

```
PROCESS MESSAGE GIVEN ORIGIN AND DESTINATION
   DEFINE ORIGIN AND DESTINATION AS INTEGER VARIABLES
```

Note that it is not permissible to use the same variable names as process attributes and process routine arguments. The common solution is to give the desired name to the argument and prefix the attribute with a reminder of the process name (e.g., ORIGIN vs MG. ORIGIN). The process attribute names may not even appear in the program because of the GIVING phrase in the ACTIVATE statement.

3.13 Process Interaction Commands

We have seen two types of process interactions thus far:

(1) A process activates another process (via the ACTIVATE statement);

(2) A process restarts another process by relinquishing a resource that the latter process has requested.

Several more process interaction commands may be used to describe direct communication between processes. They allow for:

(1) Interrupting a process that is currently awaiting time passage, as in a WORK or WAIT statement;

(2) Resuming a process previously interrupted;

(3) Suspending a process (this statement applies only to the currently executing process -- a sort of "do-it-yourself" command);

(4) Destroying a process.

All of these interactions are summarized in the state transition diagram of Figures 3.7 and 3.8.

INTERRUPT

The form of the statement is

INTERRUPT [THE] process [CALLED variable]

The process must be known to be currently in the pending process list -- that is, to be in a WORK or WAIT statement (see Figure 3.7). The amount of time remaining until the process would have completed working or waiting is captured and recorded as a process attribute (TIME.A). If this process is later RESUMEd, this value is used to determine the new period of work. TIME.A may be modified by the user while the process is interrupted.

RESUME

The form of the statement is

RESUME [THE] process [CALLED variable]

The process must currently not be in the pending process list. The process is placed in the pending process list to "awaken" after a prescribed amount of time (found in TIME.A(process)).

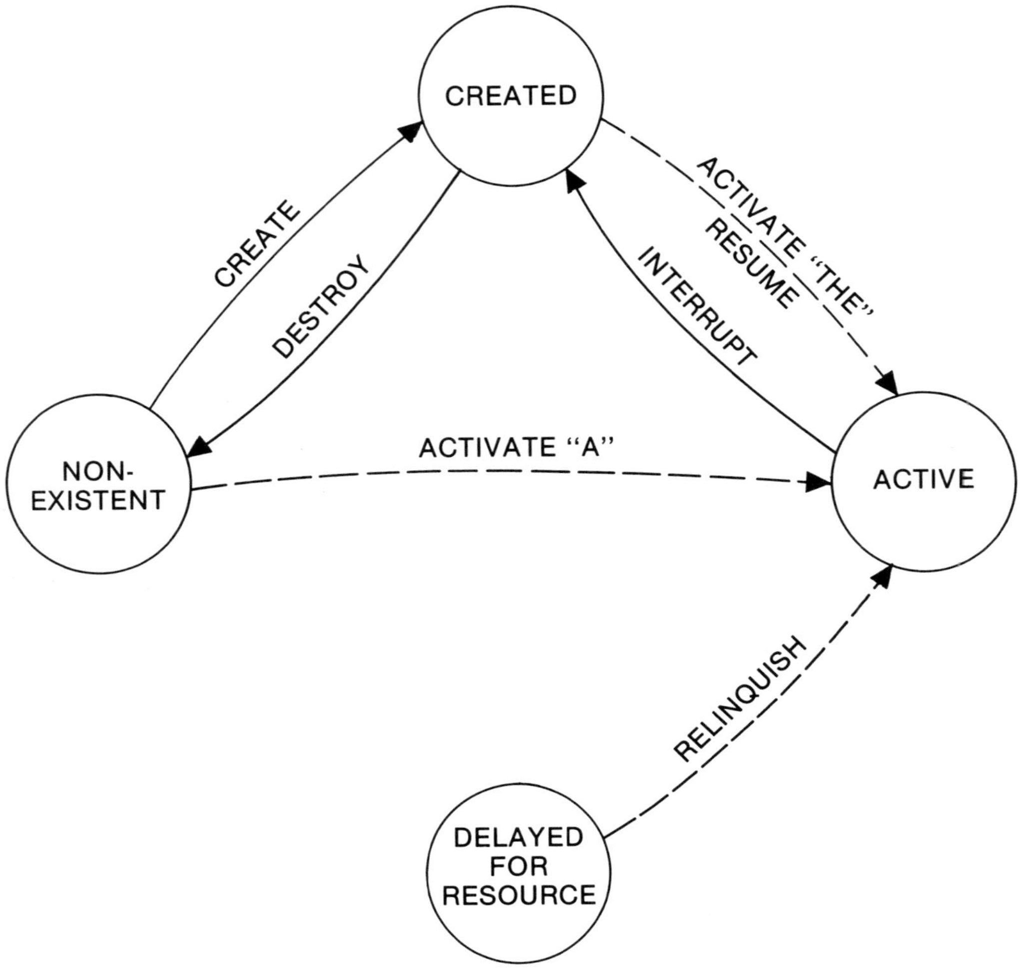

Legend:

Solid lines represent immediate actions

Dotted lines represent simulation time-delayed actions

Figure 3.7 - Actions Performed for a Process
(Externally to the Process Itself)

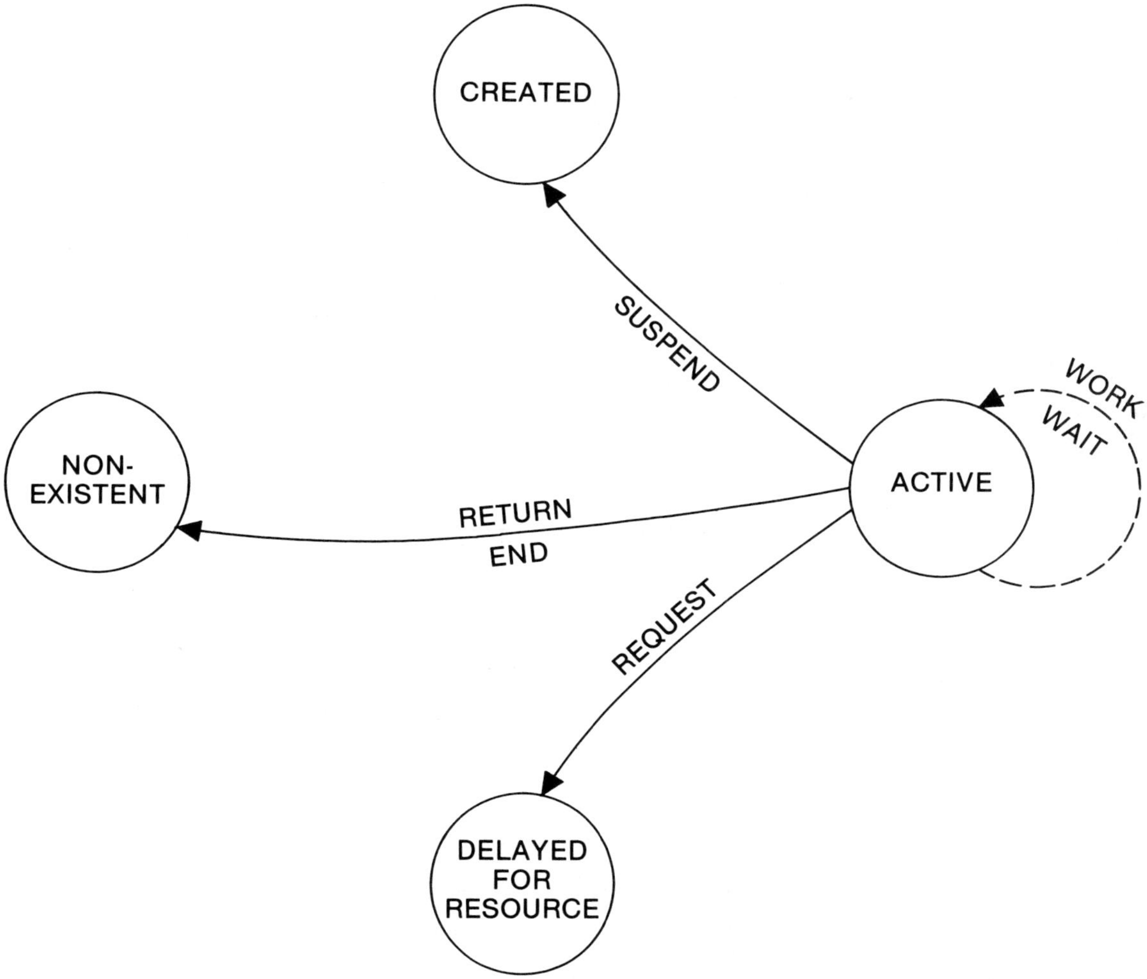

Legend:

Solid lines represent immediate actions

Dotted lines represent simulation time-delayed actions

Figure 3.8 - Actions a Process Performs for Itself

SUSPEND

This operation applies only to the process in which it appears. The process returns to the "created" state and will not progress further until stimulated from outside the process (via a RESUME or (RE)ACTIVATE "THE" statement in another process).

DESTROY

The form of the statement is

DESTROY [THE] process [CALLED variable]

The process must not be in the pending list (or any other set). A process routine must not contain a DESTROY statement to destroy itself (i.e., the "current activation") since the destroy operation occurs automatically at the end of a process routine.

These operations point out the need for taking great care in manipulating processes. When a process has been interrupted or suspended, there is a danger of "losing" it. That is, the user must preserve the reference to the process since no system-maintained mechanism has record of it (pending list or resource queue).

This is often accomplished through direct reference, either by global variable or attribute (or local variable) of another process, but most often by introducing a very powerful data structure, the user-defined set.

3.14 The Set Concept

A set is a logically ordered collection of entities (processes or resources) organized through a system of set pointers. The implementation of resources involves two sets that are automatically maintained by the system: one for the resource requests currently satisfied, and the other for the queue of pending resource requests.

A user-defined set must have a declared owner and a declared member. If there is to be only one copy of the set in the model, the owner can be defined to be "THE SYSTEM". In general, however, any process, resource, or other type of entity can either own or belong to a set. For example, we might wish to define a queue of airplanes waiting for a single runway at an airport. (Assume for some reason that it is not satisfactory to model the runway as a resource.) The structure might be:

```
PROCESSES
   EVERY AIRPLANE
      MAY BELONG TO A RUNWAY
   THE SYSTEM OWNS THE RUNWAY
```

It is represented pictorially in Figure 3.9.

The figure illustrates several aspects of set structures. First, the information describing a set is completely contained within the attributes of the owner and the member(s). The figure shows an instantaneous

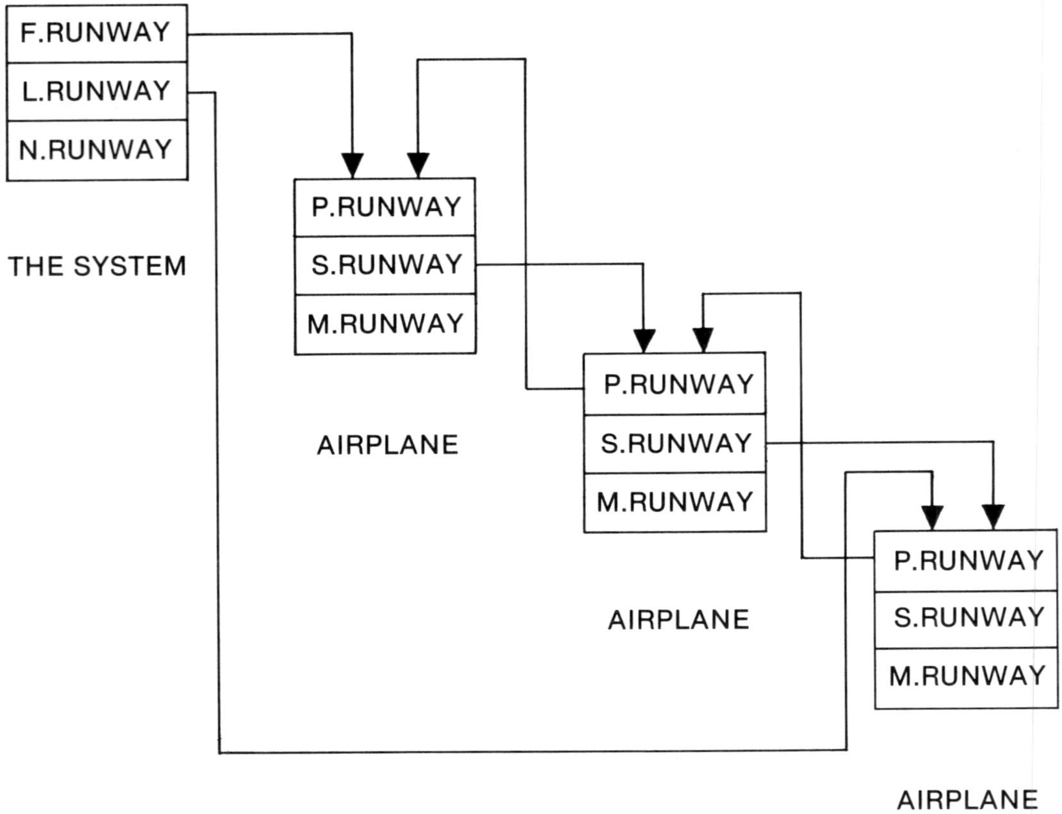

Figure 3.9 - Set Structure Linkage

snapshot of a set which has an owner (the System) and three members (airplanes). The attributes shown are automatically generated and maintained by the system. They are:

Owner Attributes:

F.RUNWAY -- A pointer to the First member of the set.

L.RUNWAY -- A pointer to the Last member of the set.

N.RUNWAY -- The Number of members currently in the set.

Member Attributes:

P.RUNWAY -- A pointer to the Predecessor member of the set.

S.RUNWAY -- A pointer to the Successor member of the set.

M.RUNWAY -- An error checking flag to record Membership in a set (and disallow multiple membership).

All of these attributes are initially zero. The set comes into existence with the creation of the owner. Note that an owner with all three attributes of zero value has an empty set. We say that set ownership is unconditional. If the owner exists, it owns the set (even though it may be an empty set). However, set membership is said to be potential.

A potential member does not become an actual member until explicitly placed in the set. The command for this purpose is the FILE statement. For example,

```
FILE AIRPLANE IN RUNWAY
```

The default set-discipline is first-in-first-out or FIFO. A new member is automatically placed at the end of the list.

Once an entity is placed into a set, we no longer need concern ourselves about preserving an explicit reference to it, since it may be recovered at will from the set. A set may be examined, in total or in part, by use of a FOR loop. For example,

```
FOR EACH AIRPLANE ON RUNWAY
DO
.
.
.
LOOP
```

This structure processes the members of the set, RUNWAY, starting from the first (or oldest member in a FIFO set), and successively setting the index variable AIRPLANE to "point" to each member in turn. If there are no members, no processing takes place and it is not an error; control merely proceeds to the next statement after the loop.

Eventually, it may become desirable to remove a member from a set. One form of the command for this purpose is:

REMOVE FIRST <u>variable</u> FROM <u>set</u>

This statement causes two things to happen: The first member of the set is logically disconnected from the set, and the variable becomes a reference to this newly removed entity.

There are several pitfalls to avoid in performing set operations. Once an entity has been removed from a set, it is once again vulnerable to becoming lost should the reference variable be modified. Secondly, a remove operation on an empty set causes a terminal error in program execution. Thirdly, an entity cannot be destroyed if it is still a member of any set, since destroying a member would essentially break the linking mechanism of a set. (So far, this would apply only to processes.) This again causes a terminal error in program execution.

There are two logical tests for avoiding these situations. They are illustrated as follows:

```
IF RUNWAY IS EMPTY
```

and,

```
IF AIRPLANE IS ON RUNWAY
```

(NOTE: This is a test for membership in any "RUNWAY" set. It is not possible to test for membership in a particular copy of a set (i.e., specific subscript).

These logical expressions may be used in IF statements or any of the selection or termination phrases associated with loops.

3.15 Example 4: A Harbor Model

A comprehensive example will illustrate the concepts of process interactions and sets.

Suppose we wish to model the unloading of ships in a harbor using two cranes mounted on a track. There is room at dockside for two ships. When two ships are there, each crane unloads one of them. If only one ship is there, both cranes work on it, reducing its unloading time by a factor of two. If another ship arrives while both cranes are serving one ship, one crane will immediately begin to serve the new ship. Waiting ships are unloaded first-come-first-served.

Assume that ships arrive on the average of three in every four days, but interarrival times are exponentially distributed (the mean is thus 4/3 days). The unloading time is uniformly distributed between 0.5 and 1.5 days.

The desired results are the maximum and average queue length and the cycle times of ships (queueing plus unloading) -- minimum, maximum and average. These results should be reported after 80 days of continuous operation.

MODEL FORMULATION

The ship will be modelled as a process. A separate process will model the arrival of ships. At first glance, it might seem natural to model the cranes as a single resource with one subgroup and two units. However, the rules for operating cranes do not readily translate into the simple operations we have learned to perform on resources (REQUEST/RELINQUISH).

There is no preemption command in SIMSCRIPT (yet!). Thus we resort to the following:

(1) A set called DOCK to contain ships being unloaded (maximum of 2);

(2) A set called QUEUE to contain ships waiting for the DOCK;

(3) A routine called HARBOR.MASTER to model the interactions between ships by allocating the cranes and adjusting unloading times of ships. This is a routine rather than a process since no time delays are represented. The harbor master responds immediately to any request for service.

This modelling approach illustrates the important concept of modularizing the system in a manner that parallels the real system. In this instance, the ship process contains only those actions that are under the control of the ship in the real world, and the harbor master routine describes those ship interactions that a real harbor master would normally control.

The level of detail is chosen to ignore the very detailed operations. For example, cranes would really require some travel time to move from one ship to the other; they would not move to a ship that was almost unloaded; etc.

The complete program and sample output are shown in Figure 3.10.

```
''      EXAMPLE 4  --  A HARBOR MODEL

PREAMBLE
   PROCESSES INCLUDE SCHEDULER AND STOP.SIM
      EVERY SHIP HAS AN UNLOADING.TIME
         AND MAY BELONG TO THE QUEUE
         AND MAY BELONG TO THE DOCK
      DEFINE UNLOADING.TIME AS A REAL VARIABLE
   THE SYSTEM OWNS THE QUEUE AND THE DOCK
   ACCUMULATE MAXQ AS THE MAXIMUM,
      MEANQ AS THE MEAN OF N.QUEUE
   TALLY NUMBER.OF.SHIPS AS THE NUMBER,
      MINCT AS THE MINIMUM,
      MAXCT AS THE MAXIMUM
      AND MEANCT AS THE MEAN OF CYCLE.TIME
   DEFINE CYCLE.TIME AS A REAL VARIABLE

   DEFINE .DOCK.IS.NOT.FULL TO MEAN N.DOCK < 2
   DEFINE .ARRIVING TO MEAN 1
   DEFINE .LEAVING TO MEAN 2
   DEFINE .OK TO MEAN 1
   DEFINE .NOT.OK TO MEAN 0
END
```

```
MAIN
   ACTIVATE A SCHEDULER NOW
   ACTIVATE A STOP.SIM IN 80 DAYS
   START SIMULATION
END
```

Figure 3.10 - Example 4: A Harbor Model

```
PROCESS SCHEDULER
   UNTIL TIME.V > 80,
      DO
      ACTIVATE A SHIP NOW
      WAIT EXPONENTIAL.F(4/3,1) DAYS
      LOOP
END
```

```
PROCESS SHIP
   DEFINE STATUS AS AN INTEGER VARIABLE
   DEFINE ARRIVE.TIME AS A REAL VARIABLE
   LET ARRIVE.TIME = TIME.V
   LET UNLOADING.TIME(SHIP) = UNIFORM.F(0.5,1.5,2)
   CALL HARBOR.MASTER GIVING SHIP AND .ARRIVING YIELDING STATUS
   IF STATUS NE .OK
      FILE SHIP IN QUEUE
      SUSPEND
   ALWAYS
   WORK UNLOADING.TIME(SHIP) DAYS
   REMOVE THIS SHIP FROM THE DOCK
   LET CYCLE.TIME = TIME.V - ARRIVE.TIME
   CALL HARBOR.MASTER GIVING SHIP AND .LEAVING YIELDING STATUS
END
```

Figure 3.10 - Example 4: A Harbor Model (Continued)

```
ROUTINE HARBOR.MASTER GIVEN NEW.SHIP AND ACTION YIELDING STATUS
    DEFINE ACTION, STATUS, NEW.SHIP, OTHER.SHIP
        AND SHIP AS INTEGER VARIABLES
    IF ACTION = .ARRIVING
        IF .DOCK.IS.NOT.FULL,
            IF DOCK IS NOT EMPTY,
                LET OTHER.SHIP = F.DOCK
                INTERRUPT SHIP CALLED OTHER.SHIP
                LET TIME.A(OTHER.SHIP) = TIME.A(OTHER.SHIP) * 2.0
                RESUME SHIP CALLED OTHER.SHIP
            ELSE
                LET UNLOADING.TIME(NEW.SHIP) = UNLOADING.TIME(NEW.SHIP) / 2.0
            ALWAYS
            FILE THIS NEW.SHIP IN DOCK
            LET STATUS = .OK
        ELSE
            LET STATUS = .NOT.OK
        ALWAYS
    ELSE  ''ACTION IS .LEAVING
        IF QUEUE IS NOT EMPTY,
            REMOVE THE FIRST SHIP FROM QUEUE
            FILE THIS SHIP IN DOCK
            REACTIVATE THIS SHIP NOW
        ELSE
            IF DOCK IS NOT EMPTY,
                    LET OTHER.SHIP = F.DOCK
                    INTERRUPT SHIP CALLED OTHER.SHIP
                    LET TIME.A(OTHER.SHIP) = TIME.A(OTHER.SHIP) / 2.0
                    RESUME SHIP CALLED OTHER.SHIP
            ALWAYS
        ALWAYS
    ALWAYS
    RETURN
END
```

Figure 3.10 - Example 4: A Harbor Model (Continued)

```
1  PROCESS STOP.SIM
2      PRINT 5 LINES WITH NUMBER.OF.SHIPS,TIME.V,MINCT,MAXCT AND MEANCT
3          AS FOLLOWS
                SHIP AND CRANE MODEL
     * SHIPS WERE UNLOADED IN  *.** DAYS
  THE MINIMUM TIME TO UNLOAD A SHIP WAS    *.***
   "  MAXIMUM   "  "    "    "  "   "      *.***
   "  MEAN      "  "    "    "  "   "      *.***
4      SKIP 3 LINES
5      PRINT 2 LINES WITH MEANQ AND MAXQ THUS
  THE AVERAGE QUEUE OF SHIPS WAITING TO BE UNLOADED WAS    *.***
  THE MAXIMUM QUEUE WAS    *
6      STOP
7  END
```

Figure 3.10 - Example 4: A Harbor Model (Continued)

```
             SHIP AND CRANE MODEL
   73 SHIPS WERE UNLOADED IN 80.00 DAYS
 THE MINIMUM TIME TO UNLOAD A SHIP WAS     .270
  "  MAXIMUM   "  "    "    "  "   "     2.230
  "  MEAN      "  "    "    "  "   "      .862



 THE AVERAGE QUEUE OF SHIPS WAITING TO BE UNLOADED WAS     .093
 THE MAXIMUM QUEUE WAS   2
```

Figure 3.11 - Output from Example 4

Program Discussion

The PREAMBLE contains definitions of the processes of this model, SCHEDULER, STOP.SIM, and SHIP. We make UNLOADING.TIME an attribute in order to permit external access to this ship's unloading time (from the HARBOR.MASTER routine).

Other communication takes place by means of the two sets, QUEUE and DOCK.

In order to improve the English-like readability of the model, lines 16-19 define several symbolic substitutions. SIMSCRIPT does not have the concept of a "full" set. We define this concept for our dock by recognizing that, at most, two ships are allowed at dockside.

The MAIN, process SCHEDULER, and STOP.SIM operate the same as previous models and should thus be self-explanatory.

When a ship arrives, it calls the HARBOR.MASTER routine, which checks the current situation at the dock and moves the new ship into the dock immediately if the dock is not full (lines 6-18). In doing so, it may be necessary to take a crane from another ship (lines 7-10). If no other ship is at the dock, this new ship gets both cranes and will take less time to unload (line 12).

When a ship signals that it is leaving, the harbor master reallocates the crane(s) to either the next ship in queue (lines 21-23) or the only ship remaining at the dock (lines 26-29). If neither of these actions is taken (because no ships remain), the cranes are effectively made idle. The ship process communicates its requests to the harbor master by passing the arguments ship and action to the harbor master, indicating which ship is requesting attention and what action is desired. If the action can be performed, the harbor master returns a status of "ok."

3.16 Summary

We have now illustrated most of the concepts of process/resource modelling in SIMSCRIPT II.5. We have not yet illustrated certain interesting and fairly general process modelling structures, but before we do so, the next chapter will concentrate on the statistical aspects of the language.

Chapter 4

MODELLING AND MEASURING RANDOM PHENOMENA

4.0 Introduction

In all of the examples so far, we have used random processes to drive the models without discussing the mechanisms for representing random phenomena in our models. The purpose of this chapter is to display all of the tools available in SIMSCRIPT II.5 for the representation and use of random processes. Further, once we have incorporated random processes into a model, the output results also become random phenomena, so it is important to have tools for measuring such phenomena and displaying these results in a convenient form. We shall expand upon previously introduced commands (ACCUMULATE and TALLY) for this purpose.

It is not the purpose of this chapter (or even of this book!) to give a complete exposé on the role of random processes in simulation or the analysis of output from models that incorporate random processes. Several excellent references on the subject are available. For an introduction to the selection of which distribution to use, see Breiman [1]. For output analysis see Law [11] or Fishman [4, 5].

4.1 Random Number Generation

The heart of any representation of random phenomena on a computer is a source of random numbers. In SIMSCRIPT II.5 a function called RANDOM.F serves this purpose. It is a generator of numbers which are uniformly distributed on the open interval (0, 1). We more properly should refer to RANDOM.F as a source of pseudo-random numbers, since any sequence of numbers can be reproduced at will merely by initializing the generator function to the same starting seed. The technique upon which RANDOM.F is based is the Lehmer technique as described in [13]. In this method, based on the multiplicative congruence technique, a starting <u>seed</u> is multiplied by a constant to produce a new seed and a sample. The constant is chosen as a function of the size of the computer word and thus is different for different architectures. Therefore, the same model using random numbers may yield slightly different results on different computers. The starting seed is actually a variable which has a default non-zero value.

In SIMSCRIPT, SEED.V (n) contains the current seed of the n-th random number stream. By default, ten starting seeds are provided. They were generated by using RANDOM.F and recording the seed after each 100,000 samples. Even after the required 1,000,000 samples, the period of the generator has not been approached. (For the 32-bit IBM implementation it is on the order of 2^{31}). The seeds are stored as integers and may be printed or altered as desired (more on this later).

To generate a random number in a program, one merely references the function; for example,

```
LET X = RANDOM.F (1)
```

will generate a sample using SEED.V(1) and replace SEED.V(1) for the next sample.

The reason for providing more than one random number stream is to allow greater flexibility in the design of experiments and to reduce the cost of simulation runs without reducing the usefulness of the results.

```
LET X = UNIFORM.F (a,b,i)

1.  draw a sample from RANDOM.F(i) (call it r)

2.  compute X as a + r (b-a)
```

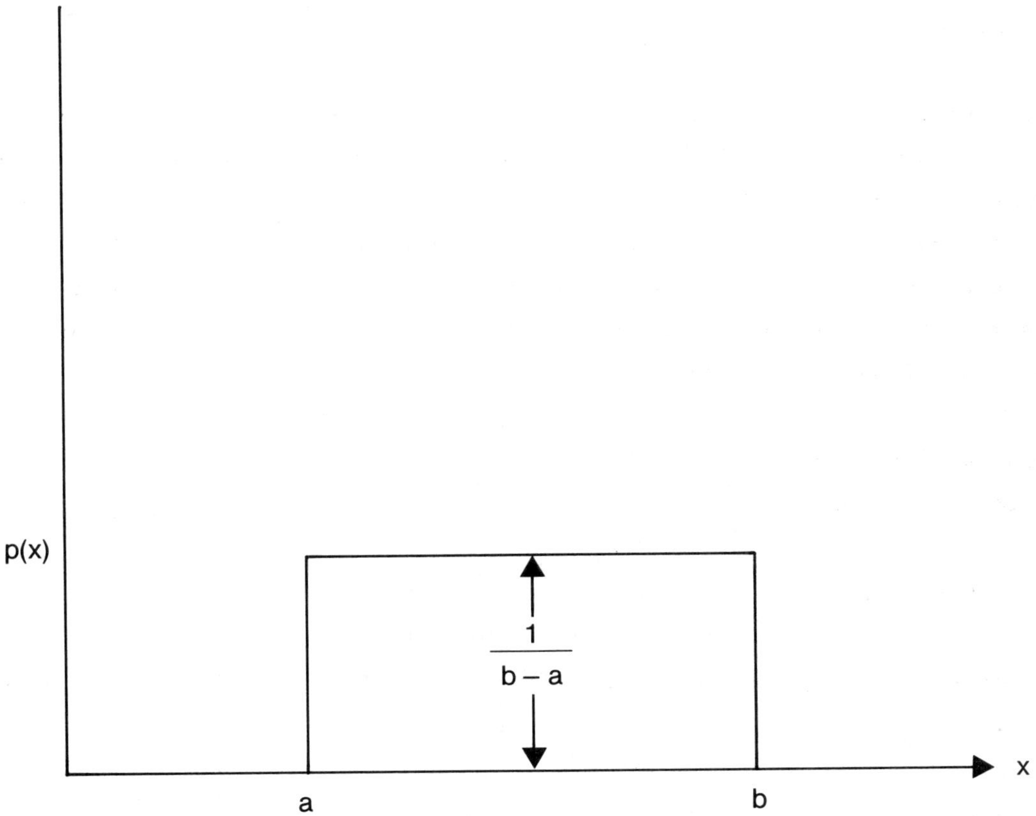

Figure 4.1 - UNIFORM Distribution

In order to restart a simulation with the same starting seeds, there are two possibilities:

(1) Make a separate run (i.e., reload the program).

(2) Save the initial values of any streams to be sampled from and restore them before the second simulation. This method will be illustrated in Example 5.

4.2 Random Deviates

Once we have a reliable source for introducing randomness into models, it is relatively easy to provide functions for the common random deviates. SIMSCRIPT provides most of the commonly used distributions. They are described briefly as follows:

UNIFORM

The uniform function (see Figure 4.1) effectively extends the range of RANDOM.F. The required parameters are the minimum and maximum values of the range of the function. As in all of these functions, the last parameter specifies which random number stream is to be used. The sampling is accomplished as follows:

In representing random processes in a model, it is important to be able to isolate various processes. For example, in a simple queueing system, one expects that the arrival distribution should be independent of the service mechanism. If we were limited to one sequence of random numbers, it would be difficult to represent this independence. (It could be done, to a degree, with very long runs.) However, by assigning different random number streams to the two processes and thereby starting from different values, we can have the desired independence. Further, from an experimental design point of view, we can more quickly perform sensitivity analysis experiments. For example, if we change the number of servers in our simple queueing system and repeat the experiment with the same starting seeds for each stream, then, through careful implementation of the model, we can show that any changes in the results from the simulations are directly due to the changes in the controlled variable (number of servers) and not due to random variations.

Another technique which can be easily used in SIMSCRIPT is the so-called method of antithetic variates. For each use of the random number generator, if r is the prescribed sample, 1-r is the antithetic sample. Two runs that are identical except for this change can be very useful for establishing bounds on random variables in the output from a simulation. See Fishman [4, 5].

To use an antithetic variate in any random deviate generator in SIMSCRIPT, it is merely necessary to negate the random number stream parameter to the function RANDOM.F. For example,

```
LET X = RANDOM.F (-1)
```

or,

```
LET SAMPLE = NORMAL.F (MU, SIGMA, -3)
```

Appendix D summarizes the parameters of all of the following SIM-SCRIPT-provided random deviate generators. It is particularly important that the user pay careful attention to the modes of the parameters to these functions when preparing programs using them. The coding for all the random deviate generators is contained in Appendix C. For an excellent treatment of the analytical formulation of these generators, including formulation of the density and distribution functions, see Law [11].

NORMAL

The normal function provides the familiar "bell-shaped curve." Two parameters are required: the mean and the standard deviation (plus the random number stream)

```
LET X = NORMAL.F (MU, SIGMA, I)
```

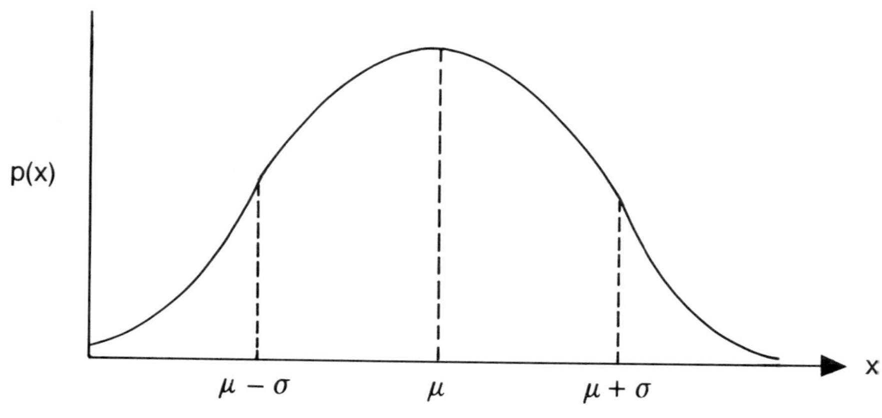

Figure 4.2 - NORMAL Distribution

One word of caution in using this distribution for sampling time intervals (for example, service times or mean time between failures): With inappropriate relative values of mean and standard deviation, the tail can extend into the negative region and occasional samples will be negative. If used directly in activating processes or in WORK or WAIT statements, this will produce an execution error, since it is not permitted to schedule actions at times which have already passed.

EXPONENTIAL

The exponential function is widely used in analytical queueing models. It is related to the Poisson function in that, if the number of arrivals in a given unit of time are Poisson distributed, the interarrival times are exponentially distributed. The only parameter required to describe the distribution is the mean. The variance is equal to the square of the mean.

```
LET Y = EXPONENTIAL.F (MU, I)
```

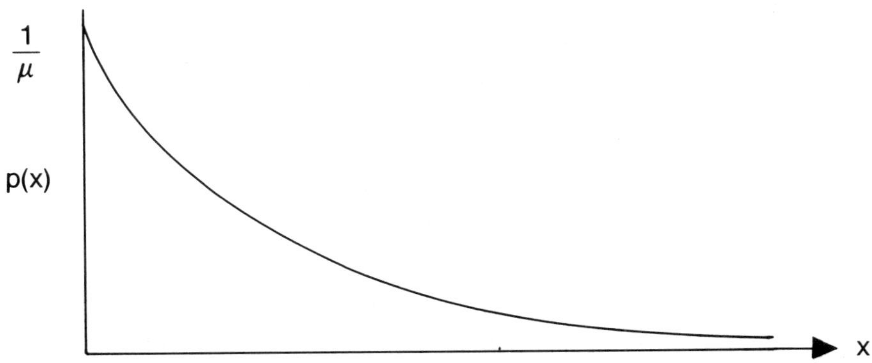

Figure 4.3 - EXPONENTIAL Distribution

GAMMA

The gamma function is often used to represent service time in preference to the exponential function. The reason is that it has smaller variance and more control in parameter selection, and therefore more realistically represents observable data. It is also closely related to the beta and Erlang distributions, which follow.

The classical representation of this distribution is given by the density function

$$f(X) = \frac{1}{(\alpha-1)!\,\beta^{\alpha}} X^{\alpha-1} e^{-X/\beta}$$

where $\alpha > 0$, $\beta > 0$, and $X \geq 0$

The mean of this distribution, $\mu = \alpha\beta$
and the variance, $\sigma^2 = \alpha\beta^2$

The parameters for the SIMSCRIPT function GAMMA.F are <u>not</u> α and β, but rather μ and α (where $\mu = \alpha\beta$).

```
LET X = GAMMA.F (MU, ALPHA, I)
```

If ALPHA is integer, this function is the same as the Erlang distribution. If ALPHA is one, this function is the same as the exponential distribution, and if ALPHA = 0.5, this function is the chi-square distribution.

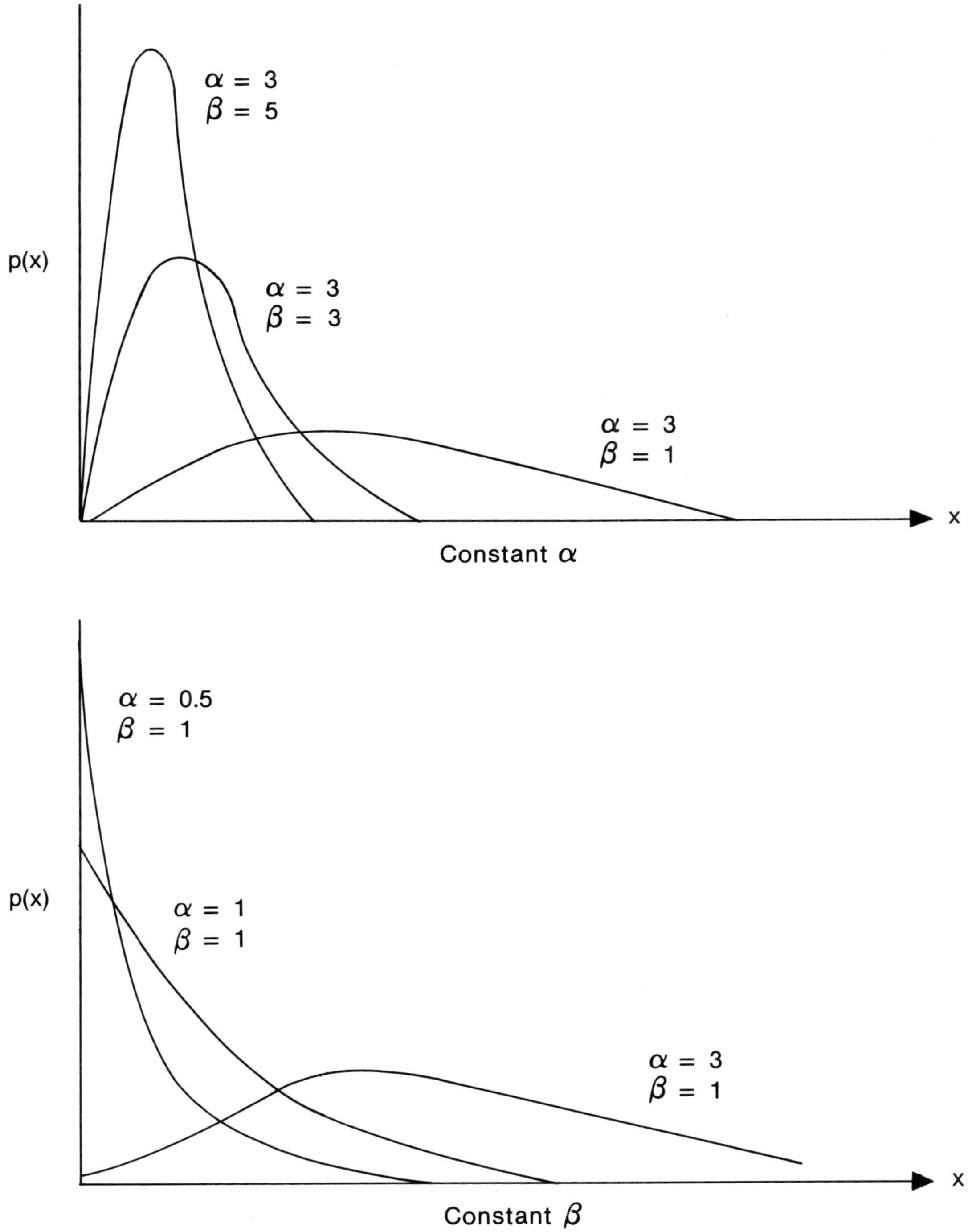

Figure 4.4 - GAMMA Distribution

BETA

The beta function generates a useful family of distributions, related to the gamma function, where the result is restricted to the unit interval. The mean of this distribution,

$$\mu = \frac{\alpha_1}{\alpha_1 + \alpha_2}$$

and the variance, $\sigma^2 = \dfrac{\alpha_1 \alpha_2}{(\alpha_1 + \alpha_2)^2(\alpha_1 + \alpha_2 + 1)}$

The parameters for the SIMSCRIPT function BETA.F are α_1 and α_2 (and the random number stream).

```
LET X = BETA.F (ALPHA1, ALPHA2, I)
```

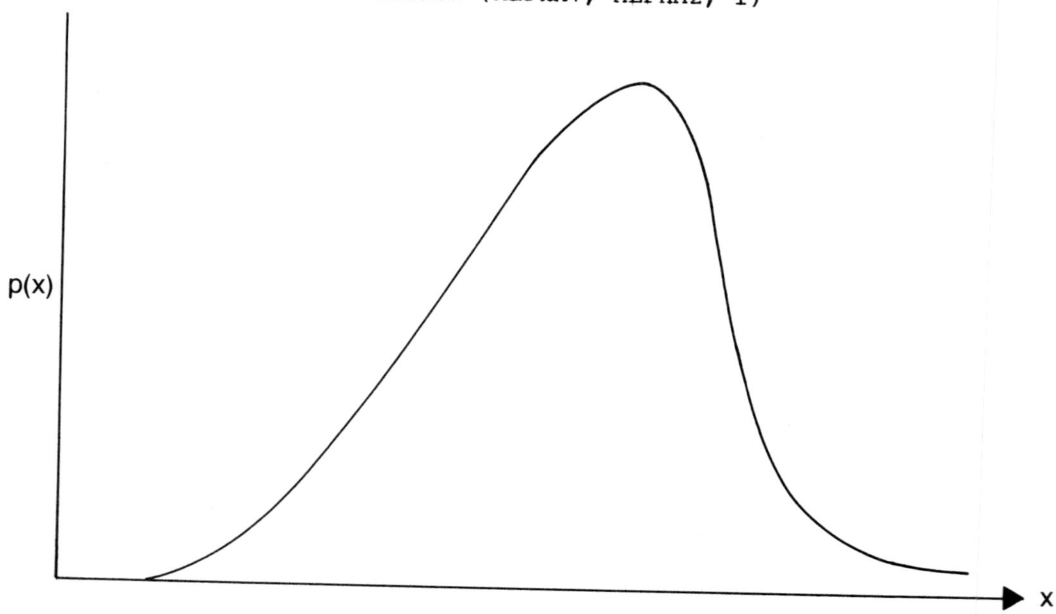

Figure 4.5 - BETA Distribution

ERLANG

The Erlang distribution is a special case of the gamma which results when α is an integer. If α = 1, this function is the same as the exponential distribution.

```
LET X = ERLANG.F (MEAN, ALPHA, I)
```

where ALPHA is integral

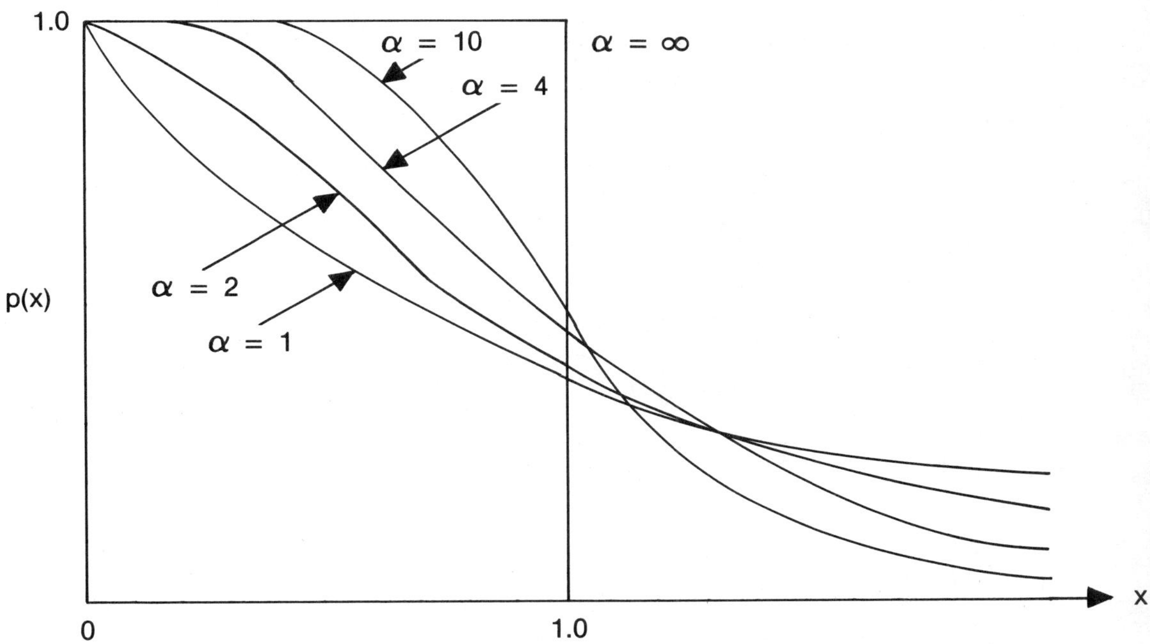

Figure 4.6 - ERLANG Distribution

LOG NORMAL

The log normal distribution is often used to characterize skewed data. The mean of this distribution function is:

$e^{(\mu + \sigma^2/2)}$ and the variance is

$e^{(2\mu + \sigma^2)}(e^{\sigma^2}-1)$

The parameters for the SIMSCRIPT function are μ and σ.

LET X = LOG.NORMAL.F (MU, SIGMA, I)

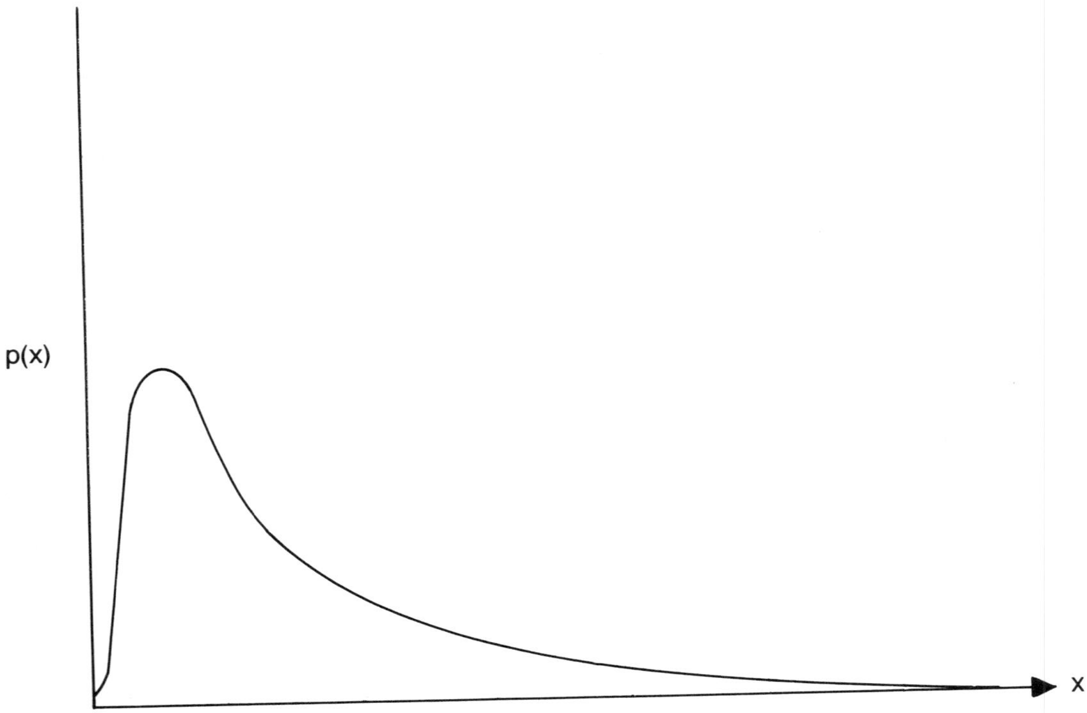

Figure 4.7 - LOG NORMAL Distribution

WEIBULL

The Weibull function is often used to generalize distribution function implementation. That is, by coding use of Weibull and then appropriately selecting the values of the parameters, one can represent several families of distributions. For example, if the shape parameter (α) = 1, the Weibull function is the same as the exponential with Mu = scale. Also note the similarity to the gamma distribution when α = 2.

```
LET X = WEIBULL.F (SHAPE, SCALE, I)
```

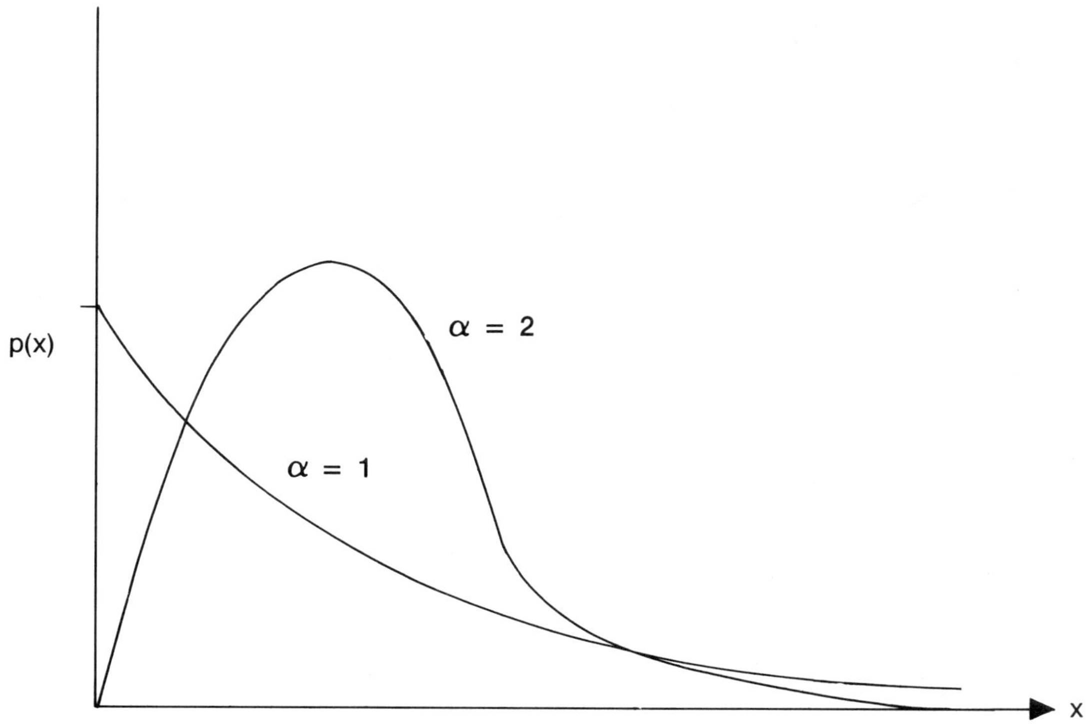

Figure 4.8 - WEIBULL Distribution

The remaining three distributions are discrete-valued.

INTEGER UNIFORM

RANDI is a variation of the uniform function which produces only integers.

```
LET N = RANDI.F (A, B, I)
```

where A is integer-valued lower limit
and B is integer-valued upper limit.

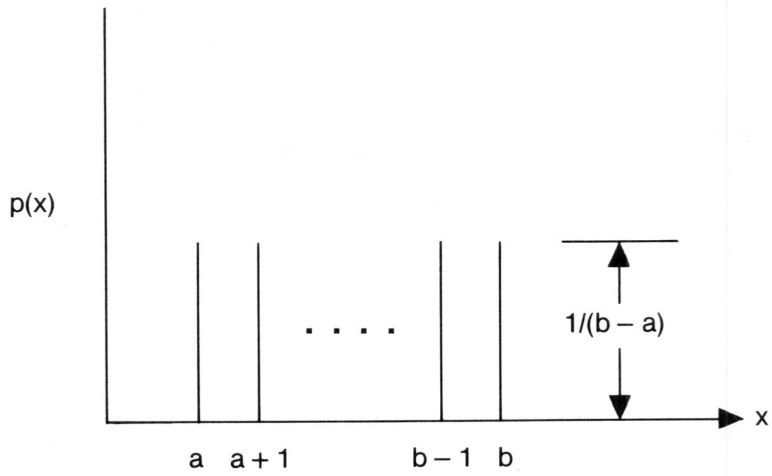

Figure 4.9 - INTEGER UNIFORM Distribution

POISSON

Poisson distributions are often used in modelling queueing situations when it is necessary to represent the number of arrivals (or occurrences of some event) in a given period of time. It is related to the exponential function, which is used for the interarrival times of Poisson-distributed arrivals.

```
LET N = POISSON.F (MEAN, I)
```

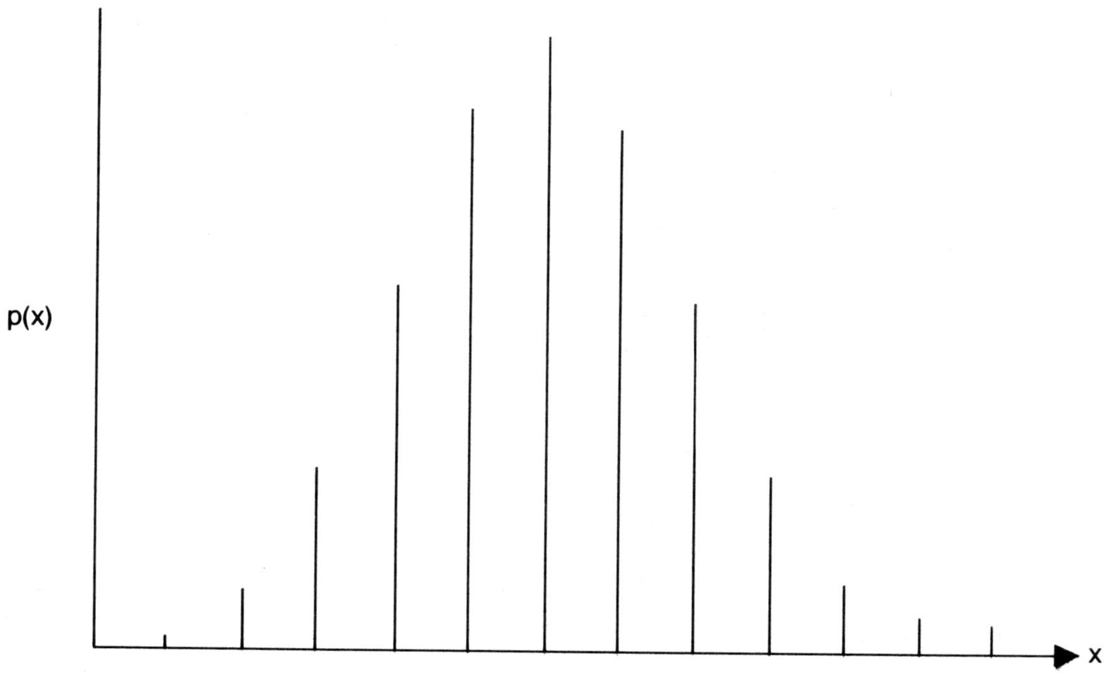

Figure 4.10 - POISSON Distribution

BINOMIAL

The binomial distribution represents the integer number of successes in n independent trials, each having probability of success p.

```
LET K = BINOMIAL.F (N, P, I)
```

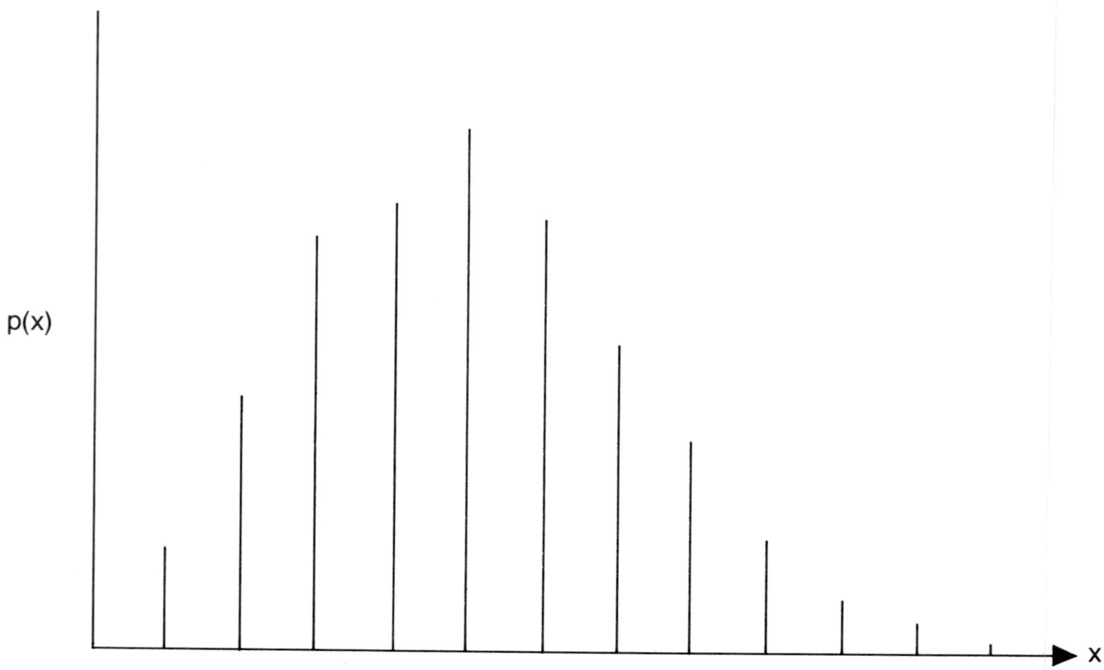

Figure 4.11 - BINOMIAL Distribution

4.3 Arbitrary Random Variables

More often than not, the modeller does not know which distribution in Section 4.2 best describes the situation at hand. We are usually given stacks of data and asked to derive some assumptions from them. We can do statistical analyses on these data and approximate their distribution with a function; but we can also prepare arbitrary distribution tables that summarize the observed data, and then sample from these tables in the same manner as with the functional representation. Two methods of sampling are available in SIMSCRIPT. They are designated STEP and LINEAR. The step sampling function will only choose samples from among the table data points, whereas the linear sampling function will linearly interpolate between data points. Neither method will include sample points outside the range of data in the table.

In order to use these random variables, it is necessary to declare and initialize them before attempting to sample from them.

For example, a random variable that can only take on certain discrete values could be described as follows:

```
THE SYSTEM HAS AN X RANDOM STEP VARIABLE
     DEFINE X AS AN INTEGER VARIABLE
```

In order to initialize X, data are prepared for input via a free-form READ as any number of pairs of values in which a probability is followed by the corresponding function value. The data are terminated by a special character (MARK.V), which by default is an asterisk (*). The probability values for step tables may be expressed as either individual probabilities or cumulative probabilities.

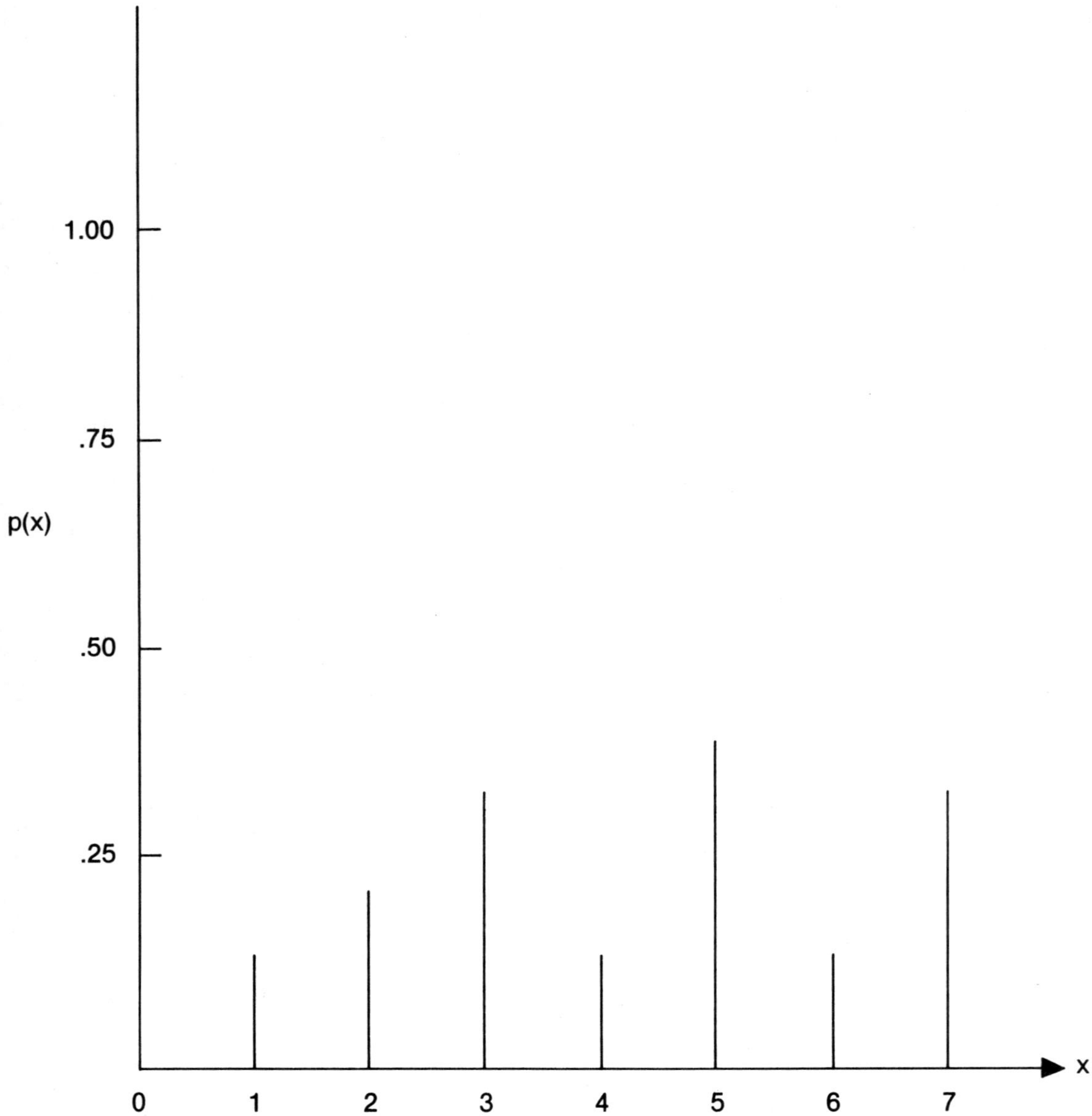

Figure 4.12 - Example of Discrete-Valued Random Variable

To initial X, include the statement,

```
READ X
```

and to match Figure 4.12 provide the data

```
0.2  2  0.25  3  0.33  5  0.22  7  *
```

Notice that the probabilities must sum to one. This variable may also be described in terms of a cumulative distribution by supplying the equivalent data:

```
0.0  0  0.2  2  0.45  3  0.78  5  1.0  7  *
```

where the first probability value must be 0 and the last must be 1.

To sample from X, we merely reference X like any variable or function, e.g.,

```
LET Y = X
```

Each time this statement is executed, a probability value is drawn from RANDOM.F using stream number 1 (by default). A table lookup procedure is then used to determine the corresponding sample value.

For example, assume .67 is drawn from RANDOM.F (1). Since .45< .67< .78, the corresponding value of X is 5.

A variable which is to assume values from a continuous population is described as follows:

```
THE SYSTEM HAS A Y RANDOM LINEAR VARIABLE
     DEFINE Y AS A REAL VARIABLE
```

The initialization procedure is the same except that the data must describe a cumulative probability distribution.

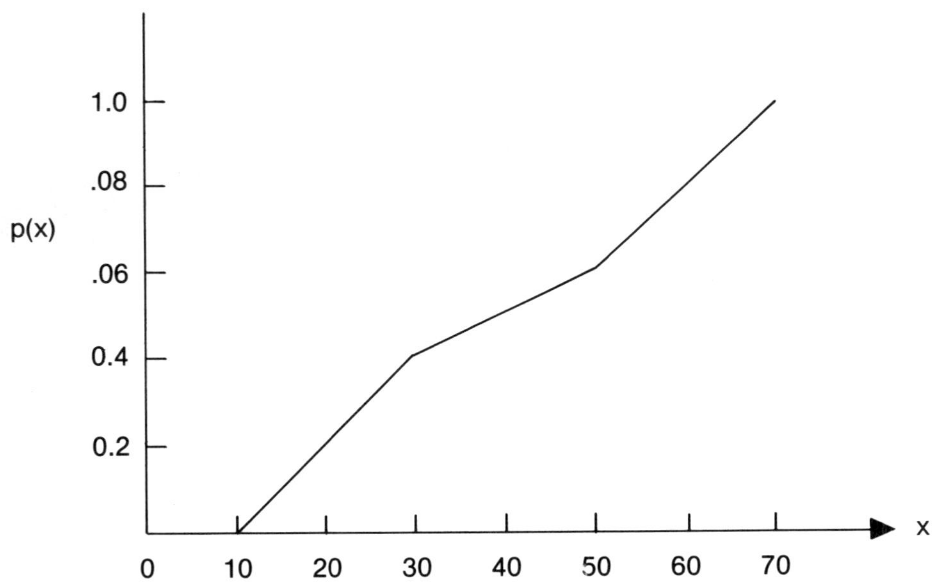

Figure 4.13 - Example of Continuous Random Variable

The data corresponding to Figure 4.13 are:

0.0 10 0.4 30 0.6 50 1.0 70 *

Whenever Y is sampled from, the probability is used to linearly interpolate between data points in the table.

For example, if a probability of .55 were drawn, the corresponding sample value of Y would be:

$$Y = 30 + \frac{(.55-0.4)}{(0.6-0.4)} \times (50-30)$$

$$= 45$$

These random variables may also be defined as attributes. For example, any entity such as a teller resource in a bank model might have such an attribute defined, for example, as:

```
RESOURCES
     EVERY TELLER HAS A SERVICE.RATE
          RANDOM LINEAR VARIABLE
     DEFINE SERVICE.RATE AS A REAL VARIABLE
```

Now a service.rate cumulative distribution must be established for each teller subgroup.

```
READ N.TELLER
CREATE EACH TELLER
FOR EACH TELLER,
     READ U.TELLER (TELLER) AND SERVICE.RATE (TELLER)
```

We might, for instance, be distinguishing between experienced tellers in one subgroup and trainees in another subgroup.

It is also possible to specify that a random number stream other than the first is to be used for drawing probabilities.

```
THE SYSTEM HAS AN X RANDOM STEP VARIABLE
DEFINE X AS A REAL, STREAM 7 VARIABLE
```

The stream specification must be an integer constant.

For an example of the use of random step variables, complete with a method of printing the input data, see Example 6 (A Job Shop Model).

4.4 Controlling Performance Measurements

Several features of SIMSCRIPT aid in the preparation of statistical results from simulations. In all the examples we have looked at thus far, the simplest sort of analysis has been performed -- e.g., specify some desired measures (mean, maximum, etc.) in an ACCUMULATE or TALLY statement, run the simulation, and print the results.

In a more general situation, it is often necessary to run a simulation for a while in a "warm-up" mode, to eliminate any initial atypical situation. Say we are to model traffic at an airport. Once it opens, there might never be a time at which no airplanes are there -- either landing, departing, or parked. To have a simulation warm-up period, or non-measurement-recording period, SIMSCRIPT provides a RESET statement. The RESET statement reinitializes all the statistical counters relative to the variable(s) listed in it.

For example,

```
RESET TOTALS OF CYCLE.TIME
```

where CYCLE.TIME is a global variable which appeared in a statement such as,

```
TALLY MEAN.WAITING.TIME AS THE MEAN
   AND MAX.WAITING.TIME AS THE MAXIMUM
   OF CYCLE.TIME
```

Both MEAN.WAITING.TIME and MAX.WAITING.TIME are reset as a consequence of the RESET statement. In fact, MEAN.WAITING.TIME is not actually implemented as a variable. Rather, it is a function and several variables are generated by the system for its use. These variables are automatically reset also.

Measurements made through the use of an ACCUMULATE statement involve several more system-generated variables which are also reset automatically. For example, consider a variable which has progressively taken on values as shown in Figure 4.14.

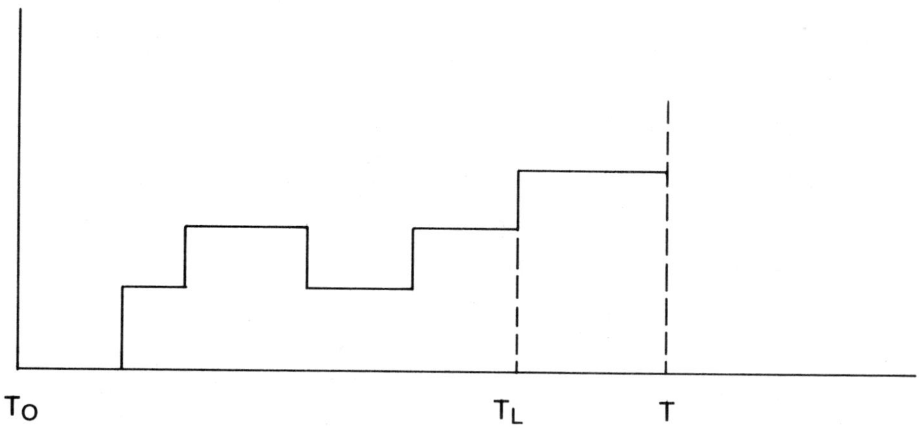

Figure 4.14 - RESET Example

If we reset the variable at time T, several system-generated variables will acquire non-zero re-initialized values. In particular, the system maintains the values of T_O and T_L, the beginning of the observation period and the time of last change in the variable, respectively. At reset, they both acquire the value of current time. Also, the maximum and minimum values of the variable are set to the current value.

Several variables may have statistics reset via a single RESET statement; however, if the observed variable is an attribute, each of its subscript values must be explicitly referenced for resetting.

Examples:

```
RESET TOTALS OF CYCLE.TIME, N.QUEUE
        AND N.DOCK


FOR EACH TELLER,
        RESET TOTALS OF N.Q.TELLER(TELLER)
```

Once we have the capability of resetting performance measures, it becomes natural to make several sets of experimental measures in a single simulation. For example, it may be desirable to make several consecutive measurement periods corresponding to hours, days, or months of operation of the system being studied. It may also be desirable to make several <u>concurrent</u> sets of such measurements, for example, to study daily, weekly and monthly cycles in a business system. All this can very conveniently be implemented in SIMSCRIPT using the concept of <u>qualified</u> statistics. Qualifying statistics allows for multiple, simultaneous gathering of measurements, and then selective resetting of some while not disturbing others. Qualifiers may be any word of the modeller's choosing.

Example:

```
ACCUMULATE WK.MEAN AS THE WEEKLY MEAN
     AND MON.MEAN AS THE MONTHLY MEAN
     AND GRAND.AVG AS THE AVERAGE
     OF N.QUEUE
```

We might include processes for printing results at the end of each week and month as follows:

```
PROCESS WEEKLY.REPORT
     UNTIL TIME.V > END.OF.SIMULATION
     DO
        WAIT 7 DAYS
        PRINT 1 LINE WITH TIME.V AND WK.MEAN THUS
        AT DAY    **.  WEEKLY.MEAN = *.**
        RESET THE WEEKLY TOTALS OF N.QUEUE
     LOOP
END
```

(and similarly for PROCESS MONTHLY.REPORT).

Note that the unqualified measurement (GRAND.AVG) is not affected by either reset. However, if a reset without a qualifier is executed, all statistics, whether qualified or not, are reset.

4.5 Additional Statistical Performance Measures

In our examples so far we have used ACCUMULATE and TALLY statements to compute averages, maxima, minima, and occasionally to count the number of samples (for TALLY). There are several more computations which can be specified in ACCUMULATE or TALLY statements. The complete list is as follows:

TABLE 4.1

ACCUMULATE/TALLY STATISTICS

STATISTIC	ACCUMULATE COMPUTATION	TALLY COMPUTATION
NUMBER	K = THE NO. OF CHANGES IN X	N = THE NO. OF SAMPLES OF X
SUM	$\Sigma(X(TIME.V - T_L))$	ΣX
MEAN	$\frac{SUM}{(TIME.V - T_O)}$	$\frac{SUM}{N}$
SUM.OF.SQUARES	$\Sigma(TIME.V - T_L)X^2)$	ΣX^2
MEAN.SQUARE	$\frac{SUM.OF.SQUARES}{(TIME.V - T_O)}$	$\frac{(\Sigma X^2)}{N}$
VARIANCE	$MEAN.SQUARE - MEAN^2$	$MEAN.SQUARE - MEAN^2$
STD.DEV	$\sqrt{VARIANCE}$	$\sqrt{VARIANCE}$
MAXIMUM	M = MAXIMUM (X) FOR ALL X	M = MAXIMUM (X) FOR ALL X
MINIMUM	m = MINIMUM (X) FOR ALL X	m = MINIMUM (X) FOR ALL X

NOTES:

TIME.V = current simulated time

T_L = simulated time at which variable was set to its current value

T_O = simulated time of last reset for this variable

x = sample value of variable before change occurs

In addition to these very useful performance measures, it is also possible to request a histogram of the variable. In the context of a TALLY statement, a histogram represents a distribution of the number of times the observed variable fell within certain limits, whereas in the ACCUMULATE context, it represents the total time the variable remained in each range.

The general form of a histogram specification is:

TALLY name_1, (r_1 TO r_2 BY r_3) AS THE

HISTOGRAM OF name_2

Name_2 must be either an unsubscripted global variable or system attribute, or an attribute of a resource or permanent entity. It is not (presently) possible to generate histograms for attributes of processes or temporary entities.

The histogram is implemented as a function which allocates its own internal storage and thus should only be referenced for "reading." The histogram is stored in an array, the size of which is determined by the formula,

$$n = (r_2 - r_3)/r_3 + 1$$

Thus samples are counted in the various array elements as follows:

Let $s_i < r_1 + r_3$	add 1 to $name_1$ (1)
$r_1 + r_3 \leq s_i , r_1 + 2r_3$	add 1 to $name_1$ (2)
.	
.	
.	
$r_2 - r_3 \leq s_i < r_2$	add 1 to $name_1$ (n-1)
$r_2 \leq s_i$	add 1 to $name_1$ (n)

For the accumulate type of histogram, the subdivision is the same; however, the quantity added to each cell is (TIME.V-T_L) from Table 4.1. The limits r_1 and r_2 and the increment r_3 are constants; their values need not be integer.

The references to a histogram ($name_1$) are made using the same subscripting appropriate for the observed variable ($name_2$) plus one additional subscript subscript for the cell of the histogram.

4.6 Example 5: The "Modern" Bank (Single-Queue-Multiple-Server)

Let us now illustrate some of the concepts of this chapter by rewriting Example 3 to model a bank with a single queue and a varying number of tellers. The task is to make a decision on the "optimum" number of tellers to employ. We wish to accomplish this by making multiple experimental runs in a single execution of the program. To increase our confidence in the results, we also wish to make several replications with each number of tellers, and report the results for each replication and as an average, over all the replications.

The measurements required are the average and maximum daily queues, the average utilization of tellers, and mean waiting time for all customers. The same statistics plus queue-length and cycle-time histograms should be generated for the composite (replicated) runs.

MODEL FORMULATION

The process/resource structure of this model parallels that of Example 3. The process CUSTOMER is considerably simplified by the reduction to a single queue. The resource TELLER is a single subgroup with the number in the subgroup as the control parameter of interest.

All of the replication and reporting operations are incorporated in the MAIN program. The daily and overall statistics are segregated by use of a qualifier "DAILY."

PROGRAM DISCUSSION

The process/resource logic of this model is actually a simplification of Example 3. Since only a single resource subgroup is used to model tellers, the customer-process teller-selection logic reduces to a single REQUEST statement.

The major interest in this model is concentrated in MAIN. There are two nested loops. The outer loop (lines 16-50) iterates over the range of tellers available. For each iteration the random-number seeds of the streams used are restored to their initial value. This, in effect, ensures that each bank configuration has the identical sequence of customer arrivals and customer service demands. Note that random stream 1 is dedicated to the arrival process and random stream 2 to the service process. The entire ensemble of statistics is reset at line 22 before each new experiment.

The inner loop (lines 26-37) iterates over the number of replications while holding the number of tellers constant. Note that each replication will start with different values of the random-number stream seeds. After reporting the results of a single replication, only the statistics qualified by the word "DAILY" are reset.

After all the replications for a single number of tellers are complete, the aggregated statistics for all the replications are printed (lines 39-49). Of particular interest are the examples of the forms of the histograms for a TALLY- and an ACCUMULATE-type measurement. Some extra effort was taken to print these with meaningful formats (lines 44-48).

```
''   EXAMPLE 5   THE MODERN BANK  (SINGLE-QUEUE-MULTIPLE-SERVER)

PREAMBLE
   PROCESSES INCLUDE GENERATOR AND CUSTOMER
   RESOURCES INCLUDE TELLER
   DEFINE MIN.TELLERS, MAX.TELLERS
      AND NO.OF.REPLICATIONS AS INTEGER VARIABLES
   DEFINE MEAN.INTERARRIVAL.TIME, MEAN.SERVICE.TIME,
      DAY.LENGTH AND WAITING.TIME AS REAL VARIABLES

   ACCUMULATE DLY.UTILIZATION AS THE DAILY AVERAGE OF N.X.TELLER
   ACCUMULATE DLY.AVG.QUEUE.LENGTH AS THE DAILY AVERAGE,
      DLY.MAX.QUEUE.LENGTH AS THE DAILY MAXIMUM OF N.Q.TELLER
   TALLY DLY.MEAN.WAITING.TIME AS THE DAILY MEAN OF WAITING.TIME
   ACCUMULATE UTILIZATION AS THE AVERAGE OF N.X.TELLER
   ACCUMULATE AVG.QUEUE.LENGTH AS THE AVERAGE,
      MAX.QUEUE.LENGTH AS THE MAXIMUM,
      AND QUEUE.HISTO (0 TO 20 BY 1) AS THE HISTOGRAM OF N.Q.TELLER
   TALLY MEAN.WAITING.TIME AS THE MEAN
      AND WAIT.HISTO(0 TO 100 BY 5) AS THE HISTOGRAM OF WAITING.TIME
END
```

```
MAIN
   DEFINE I, NO.OF.TELLERS AND REPLICATION AS INTEGER VARIABLES
   DEFINE SAVESEED1 AND SAVESEED2 AS INTEGER VARIABLES
   DEFINE START.TIME AS A REAL VARIABLE
   LET SAVESEED1 = SEED.V(1)
   LET SAVESEED2 = SEED.V(2)
   CREATE EVERY TELLER(1)
   READ MIN.TELLERS, MAX.TELLERS,
      NO.OF.REPLICATIONS, MEAN.INTERARRIVAL.TIME,
      MEAN.SERVICE.TIME AND DAY.LENGTH
   PRINT 9 LINES WITH MIN.TELLERS,
      MAX.TELLERS, NO.OF.REPLICATIONS,
      MEAN.INTERARRIVAL.TIME, MEAN.SERVICE.TIME
      AND DAY.LENGTH THUS
  SIMULATION OF A SINGLE-QUEUE BANK
     THE NO. OF TELLERS RANGES FROM  * TO   *
     (  * REPLICATIONS FOR EACH NO. OF TELLERS)
CUSTOMERS ARRIVE ACCORDING TO AN EXPONENTIAL DISTRIBUTION
  OF INTER ARRIVAL TIMES WITH A MEAN OF   *.**  MINUTES.
SERVICE TIME IS ALSO EXPONENTIALLY DISTRIBUTED
  WITH A MEAN OF   *.**  MINUTES.
THE BANK DOORS ARE CLOSED AFTER   *.**  HOURS (EACH DAY).
  (BUT ALL CUSTOMERS INSIDE ARE SERVED.)
```

Figure 4.15 - Example 5: The Modern Bank (Single-Queue-Multiple-Server)

```
    FOR NO.OF.TELLERS = MIN.TELLERS TO MAX.TELLERS,
    DO
       LET TIME.V = 0.
       LET SEED.V(1) = SAVESEED1
       LET SEED.V(2) = SAVESEED2
       LET U.TELLER(1) = NO.OF.TELLERS
       RESET TOTALS OF N.X.TELLER(1), N.Q.TELLER(1) AND WAITING.TIME
       SKIP 2 LINES

       PRINT 5 LINES WITH U.TELLER(1) THUS
NUMBER OF TELLERS =  *

FINISH     TELLER        QUEUE LENGTH             AVERAGE CUSTOMER
 TIME   UTILIZATION    AVERAGE  MAXIMUM            WAITING TIME
(HOURS)                                             (MINUTES)
       FOR REPLICATION = 1 TO NO.OF.REPLICATIONS,
       DO
          LET START.TIME = TIME.V
          RESET DAILY TOTALS OF N.X.TELLER(1), N.Q.TELLER(1),
             AND WAITING.TIME
          ACTIVATE A GENERATOR NOW
          START SIMULATION

          PRINT 1 LINE WITH (TIME.V - START.TIME) * HOURS.V,
             DLY.UTILIZATION(1)/U.TELLER(1),DLY.AVG.QUEUE.LENGTH(1),
             DLY.MAX.QUEUE.LENGTH(1) AND DLY.MEAN.WAITING.TIME THUS
  *.**        *.**         *.**       *                  *.**
       LOOP
       SKIP 1 LINE
       PRINT 1 LINE THUS
AVERAGE OVER ALL REPLICATIONS:
       SKIP 1 LINE
       PRINT 1 LINE WITH UTILIZATION(1)/U.TELLER(1),AVG.QUEUE.LENGTH(1),
          MAX.QUEUE.LENGTH(1) AND MEAN.WAITING.TIME THUS
              *.**         *.**       *                  *.**
       SKIP 3 LINES
       PRINT 3 LINES WITH WAIT.HISTO(1) AND QUEUE.HISTO(1,1)/TIME.V THUS
   WAITING TIME   NO. WHO WAITED        QUEUE LENGTH  PERCENTAGE
   (MINUTES)        THIS TIME                          OF TIME
      T <  5            *                   0          *.***
       FOR I = 2 TO 20,
          PRINT 1 LINE WITH 5 * (I-1), 5 * I, WAIT.HISTO(I),
             I-1 AND QUEUE.HISTO(1,I)/TIME.V THUS
   * <= T <  *          *                   *          *.***
       PRINT 1 LINE WITH WAIT.HISTO(21) AND QUEUE.HISTO(1,21)/TIME.V THUS
100 <= T                *                   20         *.***
       START NEW PAGE
    LOOP
 END
```

Figure 4.15 - Example 5 (continued)

```
PROCESS GENERATOR
   DEFINE TIME.TO.CLOSE AS A REAL VARIABLE
   LET TIME.TO.CLOSE = TIME.V + DAY.LENGTH / HOURS.V
   UNTIL TIME.V >= TIME.TO.CLOSE,
   DO
      ACTIVATE A CUSTOMER NOW
      WAIT EXPONENTIAL.F(MEAN.INTERARRIVAL.TIME,1) MINUTES
   LOOP
END
```

```
PROCESS CUSTOMER
   DEFINE ARRIVAL.TIME AS A REAL VARIABLE
   LET ARRIVAL.TIME = TIME.V
   REQUEST 1 TELLER
   LET WAITING.TIME = (TIME.V - ARRIVAL.TIME) * HOURS.V * MINUTES.V
   WORK EXPONENTIAL.F(MEAN.SERVICE.TIME,2) MINUTES
   RELINQUISH 1 TELLER
END
```

Figure 4.15 - Example 5 (continued)

SIMULATION OF A SINGLE-QUEUE BANK
THE NO. OF TELLERS RANGES FROM 1 TO 3
(5 REPLICATIONS FOR EACH NO. OF TELLERS)
CUSTOMERS ARRIVE ACCORDING TO AN EXPONENTIAL DISTRIBUTION
OF INTER ARRIVAL TIMES WITH A MEAN OF 5.00 MINUTES.
SERVICE TIME IS ALSO EXPONENTIALLY DISTRIBUTED
WITH A MEAN OF 10.00 MINUTES.
THE BANK DOORS ARE CLOSED AFTER 8.00 HOURS (EACH DAY).
(BUT ALL CUSTOMERS INSIDE ARE SERVED.)

NUMBER OF TELLERS = 1

FINISH TIME (HOURS)	TELLER UTILIZATION	QUEUE LENGTH AVERAGE	QUEUE LENGTH MAXIMUM	AVERAGE CUSTOMER WAITING TIME (MINUTES)
17.82	1.00	25.82	53	253.24
16.44	.99	21.66	44	227.24
19.28	1.00	32.25	58	373.17
14.56	1.00	22.80	44	209.70
14.03	.98	19.99	44	184.82

AVERAGE OVER ALL REPLICATIONS:

	TELLER UTILIZATION	QUEUE LENGTH AVERAGE	QUEUE LENGTH MAXIMUM	AVERAGE CUSTOMER WAITING TIME (MINUTES)
	1.00	24.97	58	251.57

WAITING TIME (MINUTES)	NO. WHO WAITED THIS TIME	QUEUE LENGTH	PERCENTAGE OF TIME
T < 5	13	0	.017
5 <= T < 10	2	1	.018
10 <= T < 15	1	2	.014
15 <= T < 20	4	3	.021
20 <= T < 25	2	4	.017
25 <= T < 30	2	5	.016
30 <= T < 35	6	6	.022
35 <= T < 40	5	7	.021
40 <= T < 45	6	8	.020
45 <= T < 50	4	9	.025
50 <= T < 55	5	10	.016
55 <= T < 60	10	11	.023
60 <= T < 65	7	12	.034
65 <= T < 70	6	13	.020
70 <= T < 75	9	14	.011
75 <= T < 80	2	15	.025
80 <= T < 85	12	16	.020
85 <= T < 90	4	17	.016
90 <= T < 95	5	18	.012
95 <= T <100	3	19	.027
100 <= T	381	20	.605

Figure 4.16 - Output from Example 5

NUMBER OF TELLERS = 2

FINISH TIME (HOURS)	TELLER UTILIZATION	QUEUE LENGTH AVERAGE	QUEUE LENGTH MAXIMUM	AVERAGE CUSTOMER WAITING TIME (MINUTES)
9.26	.96	3.61	13	18.38
9.11	.90	2.31	10	13.41
9.91	.97	12.27	28	72.95
8.05	.90	1.40	8	7.11
8.31	.83	2.23	9	12.23
AVERAGE OVER ALL REPLICATIONS:				
	.92	4.61	28	25.25

WAITING TIME (MINUTES)	NO. WHO WAITED THIS TIME	QUEUE LENGTH	PERCENTAGE OF TIME
T < 5	177	0	.281
5 <= T < 10	55	1	.139
10 <= T < 15	44	2	.093
15 <= T < 20	36	3	.077
20 <= T < 25	23	4	.074
25 <= T < 30	27	5	.053
30 <= T < 35	22	6	.049
35 <= T < 40	8	7	.035
40 <= T < 45	3	8	.022
45 <= T < 50	11	9	.023
50 <= T < 55	4	10	.013
55 <= T < 60	6	11	.013
60 <= T < 65	9	12	.019
65 <= T < 70	6	13	.020
70 <= T < 75	5	14	.013
75 <= T < 80	1	15	.010
80 <= T < 85	3	16	.010
85 <= T < 90	4	17	.002
90 <= T < 95	2	18	.001
95 <= T <100	2	19	.005
100 <= T	41	20	.047

Figure 4.16 - Simulation of a Single-Queue Bank (continued)

NUMBER OF TELLERS = 3

FINISH TIME (HOURS)	TELLER UTILIZATION	QUEUE LENGTH AVERAGE	QUEUE LENGTH MAXIMUM	AVERAGE CUSTOMER WAITING TIME (MINUTES)
8.27	.72	.65	5	2.96
8.34	.65	.35	4	1.87
8.17	.79	1.28	6	6.29
8.05	.60	.30	5	1.53
8.08	.57	.39	5	2.10

AVERAGE OVER ALL REPLICATIONS:

	TELLER UTILIZATION	QUEUE LENGTH AVERAGE	QUEUE LENGTH MAXIMUM	AVERAGE CUSTOMER WAITING TIME (MINUTES)
	.67	.60	6	2.99

WAITING TIME (MINUTES)	NO. WHO WAITED THIS TIME	QUEUE LENGTH	PERCENTAGE OF TIME
T < 5	384	0	.726
5 <= T < 10	36	1	.102
10 <= T < 15	45	2	.073
15 <= T < 20	15	3	.062
20 <= T < 25	7	4	.025
25 <= T < 30	1	5	.012
30 <= T < 35	1	6	.001
35 <= T < 40	0	7	0.
40 <= T < 45	0	8	0.
45 <= T < 50	0	9	0.
50 <= T < 55	0	10	0.
55 <= T < 60	0	11	0.
60 <= T < 65	0	12	0.
65 <= T < 70	0	13	0.
70 <= T < 75	0	14	0.
75 <= T < 80	0	15	0.
80 <= T < 85	0	16	0.
85 <= T < 90	0	17	0.
90 <= T < 95	0	18	0.
95 <= T <100	0	19	0.
100 <= T	0	20	0.

Figure 4.16 - Simulation of a Single-Queue Bank (continued)

Discussion of Results

Three experiments are performed. The first, with only one teller, shows an extreme situation since, effectively, customers are arriving twice as fast as they can be serviced.

The second run, while vastly improving the situation, still shows a great deal of congestion in the bank. This is due, primarily, to the large variance in the exponential distribution of both interarrival and service time. The third run, with three tellers, shows a much more acceptable situation in which, although there is still some congestion, over 75% (384 out of 489) of the customers receive service within five minutes of their arrival at the bank, while 98% are served within 20 minutes of arrival. Whether this is acceptable service is, of course, a bank management decision.

Chapter 5

MODELLING PASSIVE OBJECTS

5.0 Introduction

So far we have used only two types of SIMSCRIPT II.5 entities: processes and resources. These are relatively new additions (1975), considering that SIMSCRIPT originated in 1962.

The traditional SIMSCRIPT model has consisted of discrete events (to be discussed in Chapter 7) and entities, attributes and sets. This chapter described these latter concepts and shows how the process and resource constructs evolved from them.

In most small models, the concepts of processes and resources are adequate to describe the system. Processes either communicate directly with one another via INTERRUPT, RESUME, or ACTIVATE commands, or indirectly, via REQUEST and RELINQUISH commands for resources. As models become get more complex, so do their data structures.

For example, in our simple models, a process has requested a resource, used it for some time, and then relinquished the resource and terminated. In a more realistic situation, a process might require several resources, either sequentially or in parallel, and perform several sequential tasks with the resources. The order of the tasks might differ for different instances of the process, or might depend on the current availability of the resources.

To establish data structures for such models, we can use the SIMSCRIPT concepts of permanent and temporary entities and sets.

5.1 Permanent Entities

Resources are implemented as an extension of permanent entities. Thus the data structure to be shown here closely resembles that of Section 3.1.

Permanent entities may have attributes and either own or belong to sets. We define permanent entities in a section of the preamble of the same name.

```
PERMANENT ENTITIES
     EVERY JOB.TYPE HAS A NAME
          AND OWNS A TASK.LIST
```

The data structure for this permanent entity, JOB.TYPE would appear as shown in Figure 5.1 after execution of the statement,

```
CREATE EVERY JOB.TYPE (5)
```

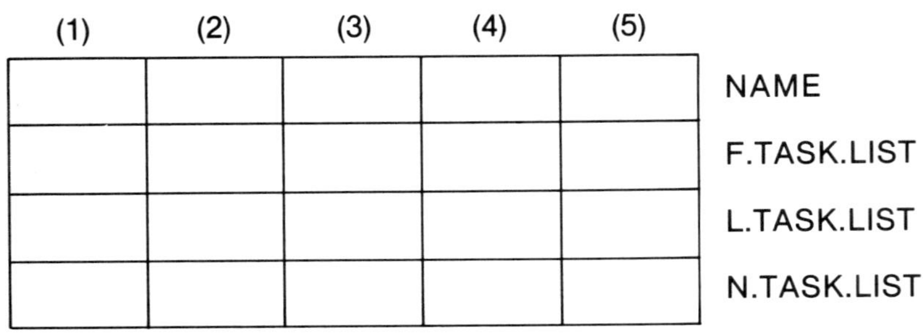

Figure 5.1 - Permanent Entity Data Structure

We need to declare a member entity for the set, TASK.LIST, or the compiler will produce a diagnostic message informing us that the set is incompletely specified.

These entities are called "permanent" for historical reasons. They can be eliminated during the execution of a model by use of the command,

```
DESTROY EACH JOB.TYPE
```

Thus, if we were conducting multiple simulations in which the number of JOB.TYPEs varied from one run to another, this statement should be used to release the old storage area before a new area of a different size is allocated.

As in the case of resources, there are two system-defined variables which are automatically generated for each permanent entity: the variable with the same name as the entity, and the N.entity variable which contains the maximum index value for the entity.

5.2 Compound Entities

The next logical extension to the data structure of SIMSCRIPT is to generalize the concept of a permanent entity to a multidimensioned structure (or a compound entity, as it is called in SIMSCRIPT).

Attributes of a permanent entity may be thought of as simple one-dimensional arrays or vectors. Attributes of a compound entity are multidimensioned.

A compound entity is declared as in the following example:

```
PERMANENT ENTITY
     EVERY JOB.TYPE, WORK.CENTER
          HAS A MEAN.TIME
          AND OWNS A TASK.LIST
```

This statement actually defines two permanent entities, JOB.TYPE and WORK.CENTER. These entities may have attributes of their own in addition to participating in the compound entity. When the entities are created, the attributes of the compound entity are automatically created when the last of the participating entities is created.

For example,

```
CREATE EVERY JOB.TYPE (2)
CREATE EVERY WORK.CENTER (3)
```

would yield four two-dimensional arrays of the form:

	W_1	W_2	W_3
J_1			
J_2			

(A row for each JOB.TYPE and a column for each WORK.CENTER.) Recall that attributes are automatically supplied for the ownership of the set, F.TASK.LIST, L.TASK.LIST, and N.TASK.LIST. In this case, these are also two-dimensional.

The references to attributes of compound entities are multi-subscripted in the same order as in the defining EVERY statement.

For example,

```
FOR EACH JOB.TYPE
     FOR EACH WORK.CENTER
          READ MEAN.TIME(JOB.TYPE, WORK.CENTER)
```

Accumulate and tally-type statistics may be collected on attributes of entities (either permanent or compound). When this is specified, additional array storage is automatically allocated by the compiler.

5.3 Temporary Entities

Just as resources are an extension of the permanent entity concept, we shall now see that processes have a similar relationship to temporary entities. A temporary entity is used to model an object or data-item which is short-lived in the model or for which the number of copies varies within the execution of the model.

Temporary entities may have attributes and either belong to or own sets. There are no automatically defined attributes for temporary entities nor is there a dynamic description for them (like the process routine). That is, temporary entities are purely passive data structures which are manipulated explicitly by the user-written code.

We define temporary entities in a section of the preamble of the same name,

```
TEMPORARY ENTITIES
     EVERY TASK HAS A MACH.ID
          AND A PROCESSING.TIME
          AND BELONGS TO A TASK.LIST
```

The data structure for this temporary entity would appear as shown in Figure 5.2 after execution of the statement,

```
CREATE A TASK
```

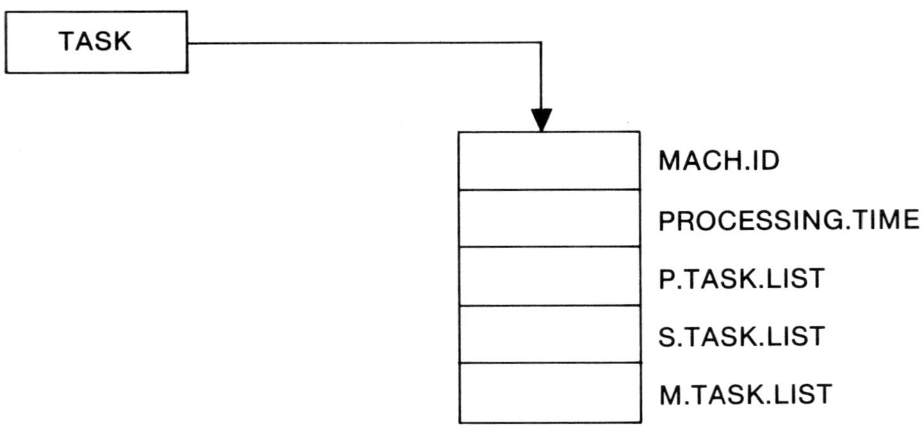

Figure 5.2 - Temporary Entity Data Structure

Like the process structure described in Chapter 3, a temporary entity has a reference variable which has the same name as the entity (as in Figure 5.2). Since this single variable can only reference one copy of the entity at a time, we need a scheme for referencing multiple copies. Actually there are two possibilities in SIMSCRIPT. One is to name reference variables explicitly in the CREATE statement; e.g.,

```
CREATE A MAN CALLED TOM
CREATE A MAN CALLED DICK
CREATE A MAN CALLED HARRY
```

After execution of these three statements, we have three different instances of the temporary entity MAN (assuming, of course, we have declared MAN as a temporary entity in the preamble). These are illustrated in Figure 5.3. Note that no entity is referenced by the variable name MAN.

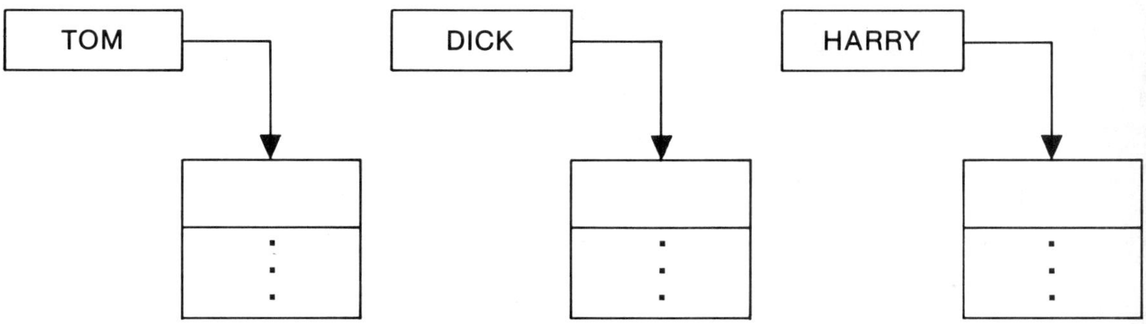

Figure 5.3 - Multiple Instances of a Temporary Entity

Instead of simple variables (TOM, DICK, HARRY) it is equally permissible to store the reference variables in the attributes of other entities, e.g.,

```
CREATE A MAN
CREATE A CAR CALLED VEHICLE (MAN)
```

where we might have two entities defined as:

```
TEMPORARY ENTITIES
     EVERY MAN HAS A VEHICLE
               AND A HOME
     EVERY CAR HAS A HORSEPOWER
               AND AN EPA.MILEAGE
```

The two entities would be linked as shown in Figure 5.4.

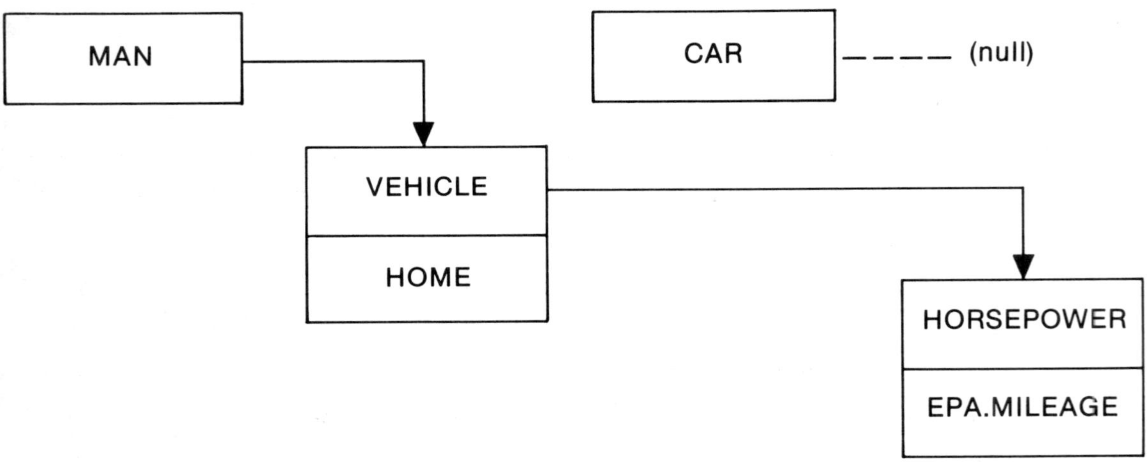

Figure 5.4 - "Linked" Entities

These same relationships can also be established between any types of entities (processes, resources, permanent or temporary).

When an individual copy of a temporary entity is no longer needed, it may be eliminated from the model by executing the DESTROY statement; for example:

```
DESTROY THIS CAR
```

or,

```
DESTROY THE CAR CALLED X
```

Again CAR or X must contain a valid reference to an instance of the temporary entity CAR.

Compound entity structures which include at least one temporary entity are treated quite differently from the previous example, which involved only permanent entities.

When at least one temporary entity is involved, the attributes automatically become functions. They have no storage allocated to them. A routine must be written for each attribute of a compound entity of this type. This routine must accept the entity references as arguments (in preamble order). The attribute "value" is the result of the function.

5.4 A Second Look At Sets

In Section 3.14, the concept of a set was introduced for the purpose of modelling a queue of processes. Sets are often used to model queues but they also have many other applications. Any type of entity (or "THE SYSTEM") may own a set, and any type of entity (except a compound entity and "THE SYSTEM") may belong to a set.

Sets of entities are used to describe data structures which either change rapidly in the model or vary widely from one instance to another. For example, we may choose to describe a network in terms of nodes and links. The nodes might best be modelled as permanent entities and the links as temporary entities. Then a set could be defined to describe the path from every node to every other node. Some of these paths would be empty, indicating no path between the two nodes; others would have a single link, while some might have very long paths (many links). Such a structure could be declared as follows:

```
PREAMBLE
   PERMANENT ENTITIES
      EVERY NODE, NODE
         OWNS A PATH
   TEMPORARY ENTITIES
      EVERY LINK BELONGS TO A PATH
         AND HAS A TO.NODE
```

Thus we use a compound entity to describe this collection of sets. It is represented pictorially in Figure 5.6 for the three-node situation described in Figure 5.5.

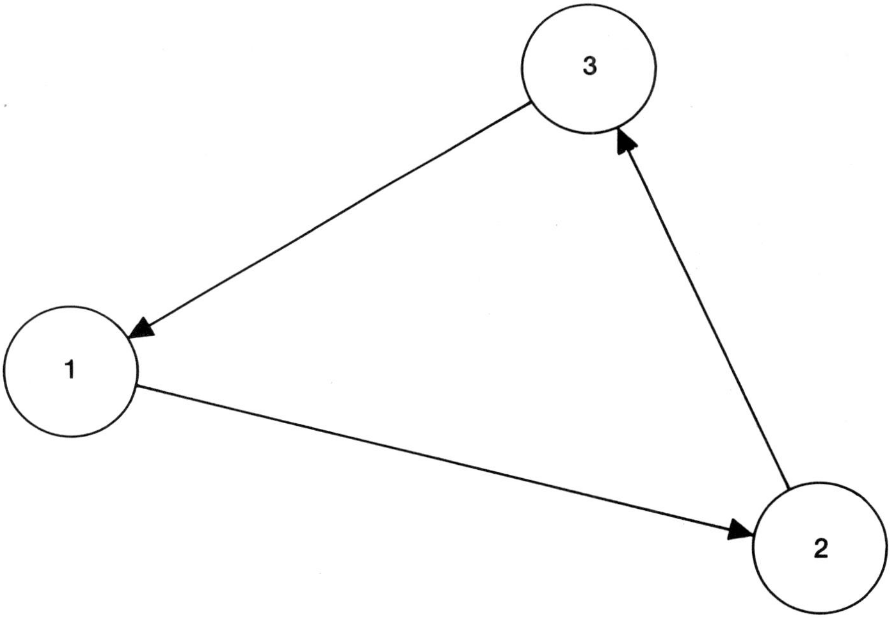

Figure 5.5 - A Unidirectional Network

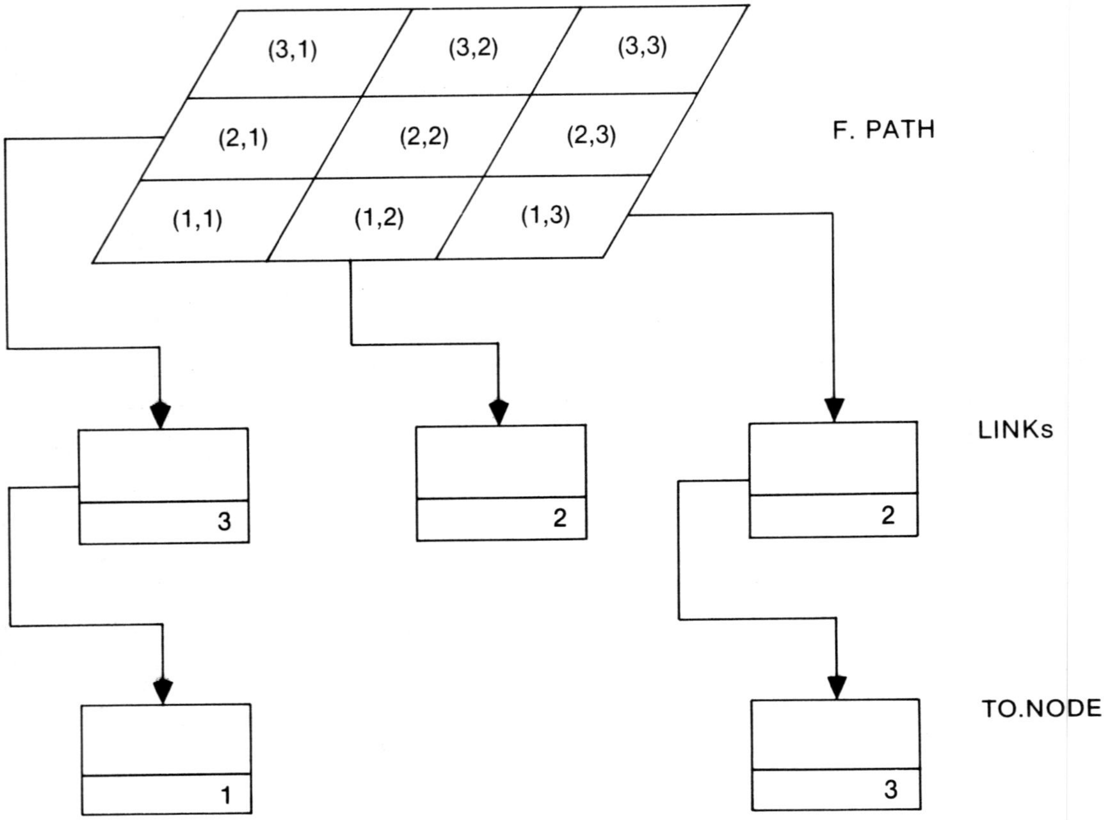

Figure 5.6 - Network Structure

In our discussion of sets, so far, we have used the default set discipline of first-in-first-out or FIFO. Two other set disciplines are available in SIMSCRIPT. They are the so-called LIFO or last-in-first-out discipline and the _ranked_ set.

In a purely LIFO set, all of the manipulations are performed at the top or first member end of the set. That is, new members filed into the set go to the head of the line and remove operations are always of the "REMOVE FIRST" variety. This is sometimes referred to as a push-down stack.

In a ranked set, the filing operation initiates a search to insert the new member in its proper place based on the value of its ranking attribute(s). The attributes to be considered in ranking the set are specified when defining the set in the preamble. The only filing operation allowed for a ranked set is merely

FILE _entity_ IN _set_

Because an attempt to specify placement of the member entity would possibly destroy the ranking of the set, it is not permitted. However, with a LIFO or FIFO set, the modeller may specify a position for placement of the new member. This placement may be FIRST, LAST, or BEFORE or AFTER an entity which is already known to be a member of the set.

In order to specify a set discipline other than the default FIFO, it is necessary to include a statement defining the set in the preamble. For example,

```
DEFINE STACK AS A LIFO SET
```

or,

```
DEFINE QUEUE AS A FIFO SET
```

or,

```
DEFINE INPUT.QUEUE AS A SET
   RANKED BY HIGH PRIORITY,
   THEN BY LOW EXECUTION.TIME
```

This last example specifies a ranked set with two ranking criteria. PRIORITY and EXECUTION.TIME must be declared as attributes of the entity which belongs to INPUT.QUEUE. The EVERY statement defining the entity must precede the DEFINE statement for the set. For example,

```
TEMPORARY ENTITIES
   EVERY JOB HAS A PRIORITY
      AND AN EXECUTION.TIME
      AND BELONGS TO THE INPUT.QUEUE
THE SYSTEM OWNS THE INPUT.QUEUE
DEFINE INPUT.QUEUE AS A SET
   RANKED BY HIGH PRIORITY,
   THEN BY LOW EXECUTION.TIME
```

In this ranked set, filing occurs in the following fashion:

(1) The PRIORITY attribute of the JOB to be filed is compared with that of each of the members of the set, starting from the first, until one is found with lower value. The new member is then inserted in front of the first one with lower PRIORITY attribute value.

(2) If a current member has a PRIORITY attribute value equal to that of the new member, their EXECUTION.TIME attributes are compared. The one with a lower value is placed in front of the one with a higher value. (If there are several "ties," the appropriate searching occurs.)

(3) Finally, if the new entity compares in all specified attributes with one or more existing members, it is placed after them in the set (effectively, then, the final tie-breaking rule is FIFO).

5.5 Additional Set Manipulations

We saw in Section 3.14 the possibility of looping over all the members of a set, possibly with selectivity or termination phrases built into the control structure. Several more operations can also be specified:

IN REVERSE ORDER

This phrase, when appended to a "FOR EACH OF" _set_ phrase, specifies that execution will begin with processing of the _last_ member of the set. Explicitly, this is the entity referenced by the last-in-set attribute of the owner. It may, of course, be the most recent addition to the set (pure FIFO), the oldest member (pure LIFO), or the member with the least desirable combination of ranking attributes (a ranked set).

FILE FIRST and FILE LAST

It is possible to specify where to place a new member in a set. (Does not apply to ranked sets.)

REMOVE FIRST and REMOVE LAST

Similarly, one may specify the entity to remove by position.

REMOVE entity

It is possible to specify which individual entity to remove from a set by reference variable name rather than by position as above. Two important aspects of this operation should be noted:

1) entity must be a member of the set.

2) The syntax of the language is such that if the words FIRST or LAST are inadvertently omitted from a REMOVE FIRST or REMOVE LAST statement, the "specific" form is implied. This will cause an error if the entity referenced is not presently a member of the set.

FILE BEFORE and FILE AFTER

It is possible to insert new entities into a set at positions other than the ends by specifying a position relative to a present member of the set.

A great deal of error checking is automatically done for set operations. Among the error conditions diagnosed are:

1) Attempts to file an entity in a set of which it is already a member. This includes the situation of attempting to file an entity in two different sets with the same name, for example, QUEUE(I) and QUEUE(J) where I and J are indices for a permanent entity which owns a QUEUE.

2) Attempts to remove something from an empty set.

3) Attempts to destroy an entity which is a member of any set. This would, if permitted to occur, destroy the set because of the use of the attributes of the entity as links in the set.

5.6 Example 6: A Job Shop Model

To illustrate the very general nature of the entity-attribute-set structure, we shall now model a typical job shop in which several types of jobs are done. The system is described as follows:

> There are any number of different "machines" in the shop. There may be several copies of identical machines clustered in groups. There are any number of prototype jobs. Jobs arrive according to a Poisson process at which time their types are randomly chosen according to an arbitrary distribution. Each job prototype consists of a sequence

of tasks. Each task has a specified machine group and mean completion time. The actual task times are sampled from exponential distributions using the given mean.

The purpose of the study is to evaluate the performance of the shop for a particular workload, measuring the utilization of each machine group, the delays experienced by jobs at each machine group, and overall delays in the shop. Experiments which might typically be conducted with such a model include evaluating the impact of reconfiguring the machines in the shop (adding or deleting), deciding whether the system could handle additional job types, whether reordering the tasks for a certain job type would improve turnaround, etc.

Model Formulation

The machines can be modelled as a single resource comprising several subgroups. Each subgroup has a number of units representing the number of identical machines in the group. The various types of jobs can be described by the permanent entity JOB.TYPE, and the sequence of tasks for each type of job can be represented as a set of temporary entities (TASKs) called SEQUENCE. Jobs are represented as processes which are randomly assigned a job type from the system-owned random step variable, JOB.MIX.

There is a second process, EXPERIMENT, to insert jobs into the shop and print results after a specified time.

To improve the readability of the output and to simplify the preparation of the input, we shall specify alphanumeric names for the machines and the tasks, and then perform a matching operation as the input is read, assigning tasks to proper machines.

The performance measurements desired are collected through ACCUMULATE and TALLY statements on the attributes of the resource, N.Q.MACHINE and N.X.MACHINE. The aggregate delay through the shop is recorded separately for each job type by tallying the statistics on the DELAY.TIME attribute of JOB.TYPE.

```
''   EXAMPLE 6   A JOB SHOP MODEL

PREAMBLE
   RESOURCES
      EVERY MACHINE HAS A MCH.NAME
         AND A NO.OF.UNITS
      DEFINE MCH.NAME AS AN TEXT VARIABLE
      DEFINE NO.OF.UNITS AS AN INTEGER VARIABLE
   PROCESSES INCLUDE EXPERIMENT AND JOB
   PERMANENT ENTITIES
      EVERY JOB.TYPE HAS A JT.NAME
         AND HAS A DELAY.TIME
         AND OWNS A SEQUENCE
      DEFINE JT.NAME AS AN TEXT VARIABLE
      DEFINE DELAY.TIME AS A REAL VARIABLE
   TEMPORARY ENTITIES
      EVERY TASK HAS A TK.NAME
         AND A TK.MEAN.TIME
         AND A TK.MACH.ID
         AND BELONGS TO A SEQUENCE
      DEFINE TK.MEAN.TIME AS A REAL VARIABLE
      DEFINE TK.MACH.ID AS AN INTEGER VARIABLE
      DEFINE TK.NAME AS AN TEXT VARIABLE
  THE SYSTEM HAS A MEAN.JOB.INTERARRIVAL.TIME
      AND A STOP.TIME
      AND A JOB.MIX RANDOM STEP VARIABLE
   DEFINE MEAN.JOB.INTERARRIVAL.TIME AND STOP.TIME AS REAL VARIABLES
   DEFINE JOB.MIX AS AN INTEGER, STREAM 9 VARIABLE
   DEFINE SEQUENCE AS A FIFO SET
   ACCUMULATE AVG.QUEUE.LENGTH AS THE AVERAGE
      AND MAX.QUEUE.LENGTH AS THE MAXIMUM OF N.Q.MACHINE
   ACCUMULATE UTILIZATION AS THE AVERAGE OF N.X.MACHINE
   TALLY NO.COMPLETED AS THE NUMBER,
      AND AVG.DELAY AS THE AVERAGE OF DELAY.TIME
   DEFINE HOURS TO MEAN UNITS
END
```

Figure 5.7 - Example 6: A Job Shop Model

```
MAIN
    READ N.MACHINE
    CREATE EVERY MACHINE
    FOR EACH MACHINE,
    DO
        READ NO.OF.UNITS(MACHINE), MCH.NAME(MACHINE)
        START NEW CARD
        LET U.MACHINE(MACHINE) = NO.OF.UNITS(MACHINE)
    LOOP
    READ N.JOB.TYPE
    CREATE EVERY JOB.TYPE
    FOR EACH JOB.TYPE,
    DO
        READ JT.NAME(JOB.TYPE)
        START NEW CARD
        UNTIL MODE IS ALPHA,
        DO
            CREATE A TASK
            READ TK.MEAN.TIME(TASK) AND TK.NAME(TASK)
            START NEW CARD
            FOR EACH MACHINE,
                WITH MCH.NAME(MACHINE) = TK.NAME(TASK)
            FIND THE FIRST CASE
            IF FOUND,
                LET TK.MACH.ID(TASK) = MACHINE
                FILE TASK IN SEQUENCE(JOB.TYPE)
            ELSE
                PRINT 1 LINE WITH TK.NAME(TASK) AND JT.NAME(JOB.TYPE) THUS
TASK ******************** FOR JOB TYPE ******************** IS NOT DEFINED
                DESTROY THIS TASK
            ALWAYS
        LOOP
    LOOP
```

Figure 5.7 - Example 6 (Continued)

```
33     START NEW CARD
34     READ MEAN.JOB.INTERARRIVAL.TIME, STOP.TIME AND JOB.MIX
35     PRINT 1 LINE THUS
          E X A M P L E   J O B   S H O P   S I M U L A T I O N
36     SKIP 1 LINE
37     PRINT 1 LINE THUS
   THE JOB TYPE DESCRIPTIONS
38     FOR EACH JOB.TYPE,
39     DO
40        PRINT 3 LINES WITH JT.NAME(JOB.TYPE) THUS
      JOB NAME ********************
                   TASK SEQUENCE
                          MACHINE                    MEAN TIME
41        FOR EACH TASK IN SEQUENCE(JOB.TYPE)
42           PRINT 1 LINE WITH TK.NAME(TASK) AND TK.MEAN.TIME(TASK) THUS
                          ********************       *.**
43     LOOP
44     SKIP 1 LINE
45     PRINT 2 LINES THUS
   THE JOBS WERE DISTRIBUTED AS FOLLOWS:
      NAME                         PROBABILITY
46     FOR EACH RANDOM.E IN JOB.MIX,
47        PRINT 1 LINE WITH JT.NAME(IVALUE.A(RANDOM.E)) AND PROB.A(RANDOM.E) THUS
      ********************          *.***
48     ACTIVATE AN EXPERIMENT NOW
49     START SIMULATION
50  END
```

Figure 5.7 - Example 6 (Continued)

```
PROCESS EXPERIMENT
    UNTIL TIME.V >= STOP.TIME,
    DO
       ACTIVATE A JOB NOW
       WAIT EXPONENTIAL.F(MEAN.JOB.INTERARRIVAL.TIME,10) HOURS
    LOOP
    SKIP 1 LINE
    PRINT 3 LINES WITH TIME.V THUS
RESULTS AFTER     *.** HOURS OF CONTINUOUS OPERATION
   JOB TYPE                       NO. COMPLETED       AVERAGE DELAY
                                                         (HOURS)
    FOR EACH JOB.TYPE,
       PRINT 1 LINE WITH JT.NAME(JOB.TYPE), NO.COMPLETED(JOB.TYPE)
          AND AVG.DELAY(JOB.TYPE) THUS
   ********************                *                  *.**
    SKIP 1 LINE
    PRINT 4 LINES THUS
   DEPARTMENT INFORMATION

NAME                    NO.OF MACHINES   UTILIZATION   AVG. NO. OF JOBS   MAXIMUM
                                                        IN BACKLOG         BACKLOG
    FOR EACH MACHINE,
       PRINT 1 LINE WITH MCH.NAME(MACHINE), NO.OF.UNITS(MACHINE),
          UTILIZATION(MACHINE) / NO.OF.UNITS(MACHINE),
          AVG.QUEUE.LENGTH(MACHINE), MAX.QUEUE.LENGTH(MACHINE) THUS
********************          *           *.**           *.**              *
END

PROCESS JOB
    DEFINE TASK AND JOB.TYPE AS INTEGER VARIABLES
    DEFINE JOB.DELAY AND START.DELAY AS REAL VARIABLES
    LET JOB.TYPE = JOB.MIX
    LET JOB.DELAY = 0.
    FOR EACH TASK IN SEQUENCE(JOB.TYPE)
    DO
       LET START.DELAY = TIME.V
       REQUEST 1 UNIT OF MACHINE(TK.MACH.ID(TASK))
       ADD TIME.V - START.DELAY TO JOB.DELAY
       WORK EXPONENTIAL.F(TK.MEAN.TIME(TASK),TK.MACH.ID(TASK)) HOURS
       RELINQUISH 1 UNIT OF MACHINE(TK.MACH.ID(TASK))
    LOOP
    LET DELAY.TIME(JOB.TYPE) = JOB.DELAY
END
```

Figure 5.7 - Example 6 (Continued)

```
6
14 CASTING_UNITS
 5 LATHES
 4 PLANES
 8 DRILL_PRESSES
16 SHAPERS
 4 POLISHING_MACHINES
 3
 FIRST
 2.0833 CASTING_UNITS
 0.5833 PLANES
 0.3333 LATHES
 1.0    POLISHING_MACHINES
 SECOND
 1.75 SHAPERS
 1.5  DRILL_PRESSES
 1.0833 LATHES
 THIRD
 3.9166 CASTING_UNITS
 4.1666 SHAPERS
 0.8333 DRILL_PRESSES
 0.5    PLANES
 0.4166 POLISHING_MACHINES
 END
 0.16 40
 .241 1  .44 2  .32 3  *
```

Figure 5.8 - Input for Example 6

EXAMPLE JOB SHOP SIMULATION

THE JOB TYPE DESCRIPTIONS

JOB NAME FIRST

TASK SEQUENCE

MACHINE	MEAN TIME
CASTING_UNITS	2.08
PLANES	.58
LATHES	.33
POLISHING_MACHINES	1.00

JOB NAME SECOND

TASK SEQUENCE

MACHINE	MEAN TIME
SHAPERS	1.75
DRILL_PRESSES	1.50
LATHES	1.08

JOB NAME THIRD

TASK SEQUENCE

MACHINE	MEAN TIME
CASTING_UNITS	3.92
SHAPERS	4.17
DRILL_PRESSES	.83
PLANES	.50
POLISHING_MACHINES	.42

THE JOBS WERE DISTRIBUTED AS FOLLOWS:

NAME	PROBABILITY
FIRST	.241
SECOND	.681
THIRD	1.000

RESULTS AFTER 40.01 HOURS OF CONTINUOUS OPERATION

JOB TYPE	NO. COMPLETED	AVERAGE DELAY (HOURS)
FIRST	51	.18
SECOND	94	.32
THIRD	47	.18

DEPARTMENT INFORMATION

NAME	NO.OF MACHINES	UTILIZATION	AVG. NO. OF JOBS IN BACKLOG	MAXIMUM BACKLOG
CASTING_UNITS	14	.57	.01	2
LATHES	5	.60	.47	6
PLANES	4	.38	.04	2
DRILL_PRESSES	8	.59	.39	8
SHAPERS	16	.73	1.24	13
POLISHING_MACHINES	4	.44	.06	2

Figure 5.9 - Output From Example 6

Program Discussion

Each entity of this model has an attribute of TEXT mode (MCH.NAME, JT.NAME and TK.NAME) to allow for more readable output. In the input section of MAIN (lines 2-34), these names are read together with numeric data required to configure a shop. In order to use the free-form READ statement, the names must consist of a contiguous sequence of characters, or the "extra" words will not be read. Consequently, by placing name data last on a data card and executing "START NEW CARD" after reading the name, any superfluous words will be skipped over.

Rather than require the user to count the number of tasks for each job type, lines 16-31 execute repetitively until the next data field to be read is of the alpha mode (i.e., not numeric). The sample data in Figure 5.8 illustrate the intended form. Each job type has a name which delimits the list of tasks for its predecessor. The word END delimits the last task sequence.

Although the JOB.MIX random step variable data are input as individual probabilities, note that they are printed as a cumulative distribution in the output (Figure 5.9). This is because of the automatic conversion which occurs on input of random variables.

The output of JOB.MIX (lines 46-47) treat the random variable as if it were a set. The internal storage of a random variable is a set structure in which system-defined temporary entities, RANDOM.E by name, are stored. These entities have system-defined attributes for the probability (PROB.A) and value (RVALUE.A or IVALUE.A for the real or integer value of the variable). In our example, the table value corresponds to an index of the permanent entity job type.

The basic time units are chosen to be hours and the appropriate redefinition appears at line 33 of the preamble.

In the process JOB, the job type is sampled from JOB.MIX and stored as a <u>local</u> variable. Similarly, TASK is defined as a local variable and used as an index to the SEQUENCE of tasks for the particular type of job. This is very important! If TASK and JOB.TYPE were not explicitly defined in this routine, they would refer to the global variables of the same name. This would be disastrous since no job would "remember" where it was from one REQUEST/WORK to the next.

Job delays are computed by job type. Delays are defined as "time in queue" and do not include processing time. Since a job is (or may be) multi-task, the delays at all its processing steps are accumulated in the local variable, JOB.DELAY, and finally passed to the DELAY.TIME attribute for its job type at completion of its task sequence.

The assignment of random streams is arbitrary. The index of the resource MACHINE is used to choose a stream for each machine's work time distribution. Stream 9 is used for the job-mix random variable (line 28 of preamble) and stream 10 for job interarrival times (line 5 of process EXPERIMENT). This scheme would require modification if more than ten machine subgroups were required.

Sample data are shown in Figure 5.8 and the corresponding output is in Figure 5.9.

5.7 More Efficient Use of Data Storage

As models grow in complexity, their storage requirements also tend to grow. In SIMSCRIPT a considerable amount of storage can be saved through the use of data packing.

All the changes described in this section are accomplished by making changes to the preamble only. In practice, packing and other assignments are usually omitted until the program logic is fairly complete and the program is operational.

Attributes may be packed according to several different schemes. Only attributes whose mode is alpha or integer may be packed. Packing reduces the range of allowable values for a variable. The actual range of values depends on the packing chosen and on the computer word size.

The two most widely applicable forms of packing are designated field packing and bit packing. In field packing, we assign an attribute to a particular fraction of a word. For example,

1/4 specifies the first quarter of a word
3/4 specifies the third quarter of a word
2/2 specifies the second half of a word
5/6 specifies the fifth sixth of a word

The allowable fractions are machine-dependent, although half and quarter packing are universal. The 32-bit word size does not permit 1/3 or 1/6 packing, while the 36-bit word on Honeywell and Univac machines and the 60-bit word on CDC machine do permit more flexibility in packing. The complete specification of allowable packing factors is found in each system SIMSCRIPT User Manual.

Bit packing is specified by an expression of the form:

$(n_1 - n_2)$ where $0 < n_1 \leq n_2 \leq$ word size

For example,

(1-7) specifies the first 7 bits

(13-17) specifies bits 13, 14, 15, 16, and 17

(32-32) specifies a single bit

All of this is of no value unless we can specify that several different attributes are to be packed into the same word. We can do this in two ways: either by grouping attribute specifications with parentheses, or by specifying a "word number" for each attribute.

These concepts will now be illustrated:

```
TEMPORARY ENTITIES
     EVERY CAR
          HAS A (WEIGHT.CLASS(1/2),ECONOMY.CLASS(2/2))
          AND A (HORSEPOWER(1/4),WHEELBASE(2/4),
                 DISPLACEMENT(2/2))
```

Or, equivalently:

```
TEMPORARY ENTITIES
     EVERY CAR
          HAS A WEIGHT.CLASS(1/2)IN WORD 1
          AND AN ECONOMY.CLASS(2/2)IN WORD 1


          AND A HORSEPOWER(1/4) IN WORD 2
          AND A WHEELBASE(2/4) IN WORD 2
          AND A DISPLACEMENT(2/2) IN WORD 2
```

The storage allocation is pictured in Figure 5.10.

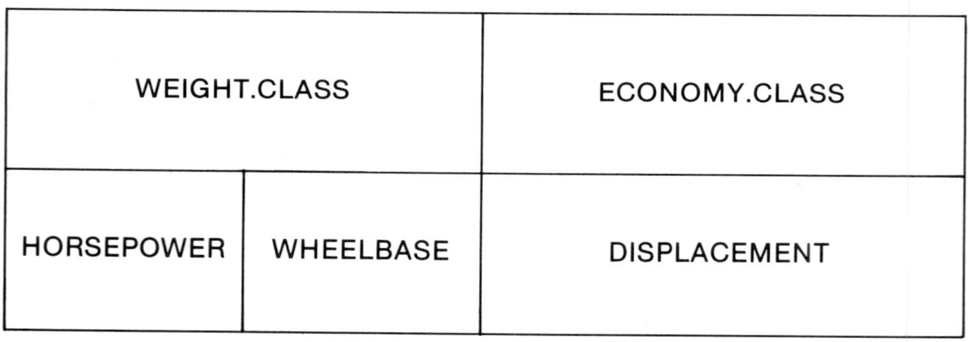

Figure 5.10 - Packed Temporary Entity

The use of "IN WORD" phrases has several non-obvious effects. In particular, it is sometimes desirable to have the same attributes on different entities. These are referred to as "common attributes" and must be specified using the IN WORD phrase. Each entity declaration must specify the common attribute(s) in the same word(s). Note: Common attributes are not allowed for permanent entities or resources.

Secondly, in some implementations, in the compilation of a SIMSCRIPT program, certain external names are constructed by the compiler and used by the system loader. These names are produced by truncating the user-supplied names, sometimes producing duplication in the truncation process. When attributes are allocated to specific words via the IN WORD mechanism, this external name problem is circumvented.

If some attributes are assigned word numbers and others are not, the unassigned attributes will be automatically assigned to available words, filling in spaces between assigned attributes if available. Word numbers should be assigned consecutively starting from one. A large number (e.g., 100) would cause the entity block to be unnecessarily large.

When packing is specified for attributes of permanent entities or resources, the data structure appears quite different. For example, if we repeat the previous example, but change to a permanent entity, the structure is as follows:

```
PERMANENT ENTITIES
     EVERY CAR
          HAS A (WEIGHT.CLASS(1/2),ECONOMY.CLASS(2/2))
          AND A (HORSEPOWER(1/4),WHEELBASE(2/4),
                 DISPLACEMENT(2/2))
```

If we then create this entity with six elements as in

```
CREATE EVERY CAR (6)
```

the data structure appears as:

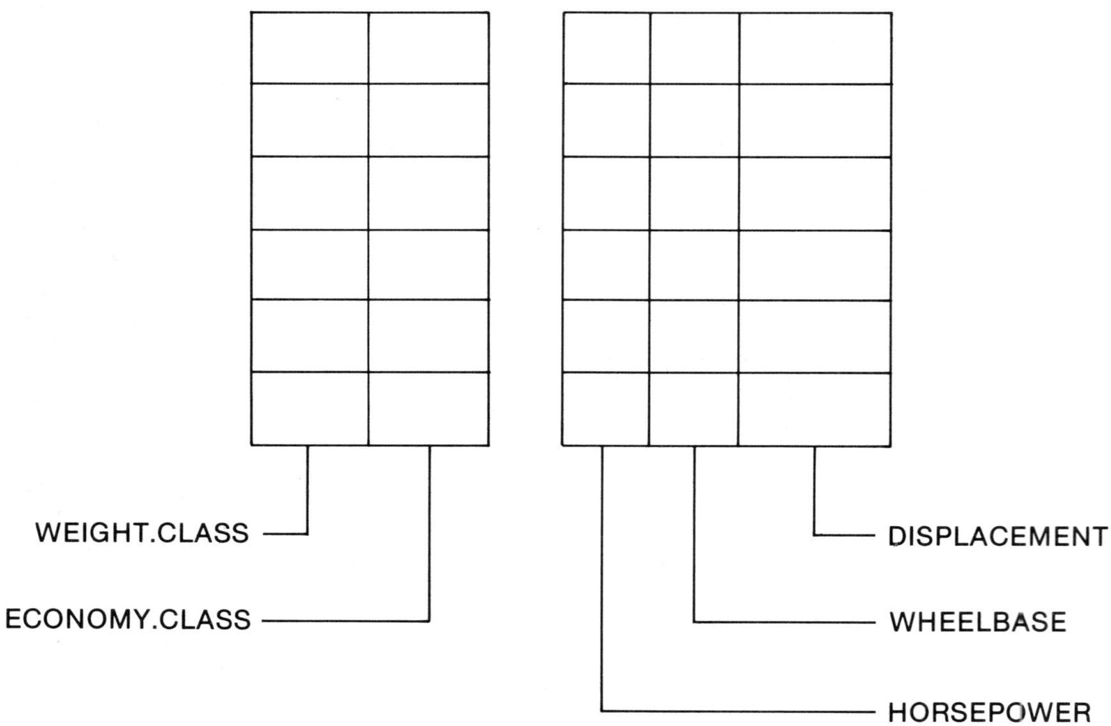

Figure 5.11 - Packed Permanent Entity

From Figure 5.11 we observe that the storage requirement for six car entities is now 12 words instead of 30.

Another form of packing which applies only to attributes of permanent entities is intra-packing. Intra-packing is specified separately for each attribute. For example,

```
PERMANENT ENTITIES
     EVERY CAR HAS A HORSEPOWER(*/4)

CREATE EVERY CAR (6)
```

HORSEPOWER

(1)	(2)	(3)	(4)
(5)	(6)	x	x

Figure 5.12 - Intra-Packed Permanent Entity

The IN WORD concept may be used with attributes of permanent entities to overcome the unique-name problem as with temporary entities. However, a unique IN WORD number must be assigned to each attribute of any permanent entity or system attribute. If this is not done, the two attributes having the same IN WORD number are effectively equivalenced and assigned to the same storage area. This can be disastrous because they may be of different size (attributes of different permanent entities, for example).

5.8 Efficiency Improvements for Set Structures

By default, six attributes and seven routines are defined for every set. Three are attributes of the owner and three are attributes of each member. They may be packed according to the techniques of the previous section. Further, if there are to be common sets, i.e., more than one owner or member entity for a single set, the set-related attributes become common attributes and must be assigned "IN WORD" numbers.

Common set membership is a dangerous modelling technique. Once an entity is placed in a set, it is indistinguishable from other set members except by position in the set. For example,

```
TEMPORARY ENTITIES
     EVERY LION
          HAS A P.CAGE IN WORD 1
          AND A S.CAGE IN WORD 2
          AND A M.CAGE IN WORD 3
          AND BELONGS TO A CAGE
     EVERY TIGER
          HAS A P.CAGE IN WORD 1
          AND A S.CAGE IN WORD 2
          AND A M.CAGE IN WORD 3
THE SYSTEM OWNS THE CAGE
```

Now as lions and tigers are created and filed in the cage, there is no way to tell what they are. A possible solution would be to add another common attribute, for example ANIMAL.TYPE and code the two types differently.

Another, and perhaps more general, solution is as follows:

```
TEMPORARY ENTITIES
     EVERY ANIMAL HAS A TYPE
          AND BELONGS TO A CAGE
THE SYSTEM OWNS THE CAGE
```

Set attributes may also be eliminated when not needed. A purely FIFO set requires only the F, S and L attributes, whereas a purely LIFO set requires only the F and S attributes. The N attribute is never required by the system but is often used for statistical measurements. The M attribute is primarily used for diagnostic purposes and should not be deleted until a program is "fully debugged."

One advantage of eliminating the unneeded attributes for LIFO and FIFO sets is to enforce proper discipline in the set. Because of the default general structure of both, as we have seen, it is possible to remove other than the next in order from the set.

To delete attributes or processing routines associated with a set, the set definition in the preamble is augmented thus:

```
DEFINE STACK AS A LIFO SET,
     WITHOUT P AND N ATTRIBUTES
     AND WITHOUT FL, FB, FA, RL AND RS ROUTINES
```

or,

```
DEFINE QUEUE AS A FIFO SET,
     WITHOUT P AND N ATTRIBUTES
     AND WITHOUT FF, FB, FA, RL AND RS ROUTINES
```

The attributes required for various set operations are listed in Table 5.1.

TABLE 5.1

REQUIRED SET ATTRIBUTES AND ROUTINES

	Attributes Required						Routines Required						
	F	L	P	S	M	N	FF	FL	FB	FA	RF	RL	RS
FILE in a ranked set	X			X			X						
FILE FIRST	X			X			X						
FILE LAST	X	X		X				X					
FILE BEFORE	X		X	X					X				
FILE AFTER	X			X						X			
REMOVE FIRST	X			X							X		
REMOVE LAST	X	X	X	X								X	
REMOVE specific	X		X	X									X
IS EMPTY	X												
IS IN set					X								
Automatic checking					X								
FOR EACH V IN set	X			X									
FOR EACH V IN set in REV.		X	X										
FOR EACH V FROM W IN set				X									
FOR EACH V FROM W IN set IN REV.			X										
FOR EACH V AFTER W IN set				X									
FOR EACH V AFTER W IN set IN REV.			X										

5.9 System Attributes and Arrays

All that has been said about packing of attributes of permanent entities applies equally well to attributes of THE SYSTEM. However, all the system attributes we have used thus far have been unsubscripted and packing would be of dubious value if applied only to a single word of storage!

It is, however, possible to declare attributes of the system as arrays and then to specify IN WORD or packing for them. It is also possible to declare arrays which are not system attributes. In this latter case, neither packing nor IN WORDing is applicable. Arrays may even be local to a routine.

Permanent entities are a preferred data structure to either dimensioned system attributes or arrays for several reasons. First, the structure is more "cohesive" in the sense that if a change is made in the number of elements in a permanent entity, that change is automatically reflected in the storage allocation for all associated attributes. Whereas with arrays, the modeller must remember to make the proper association. This is particularly evident when new attributes are added.

Secondly, it is not possible to specify ACCUMULATE or TALLY statistics on dimensioned system attributes or arrays.

Even in spite of these negative factors, some useful applications can be found, so we shall now detail the use of these features.

```
THE SYSTEM HAS A CALLS.BY.TYPE(*/4)
DEFINE CALLS.BY.TYPE
     1-DIM, INTEGER VARIABLE
```

In order to allocate storage for this system attribute, a RESERVE statement is required:

```
RESERVE CALLS.BY.TYPE AS 20
```

would yield a data structure as shown in Figure 5.13.

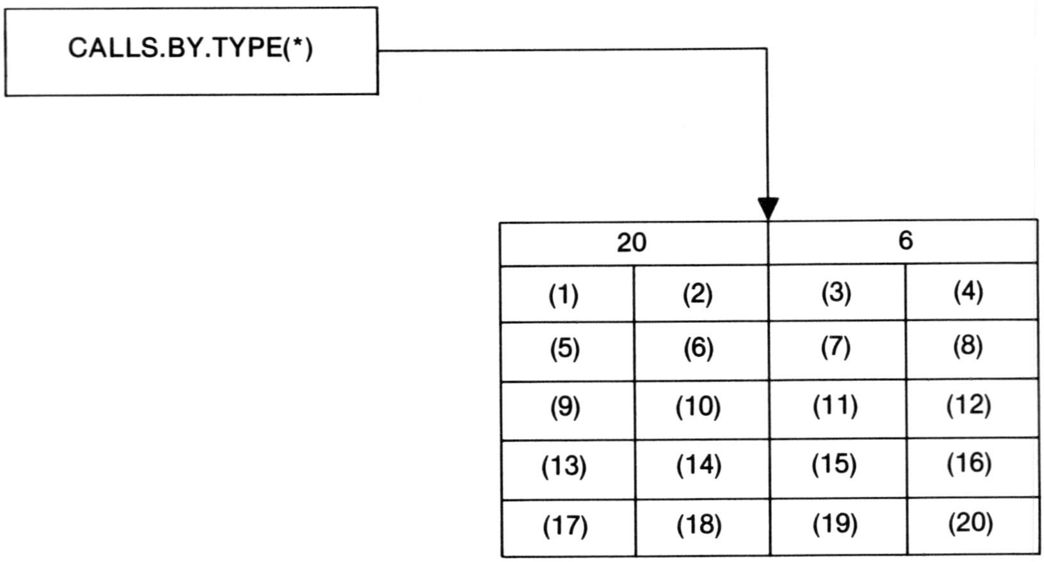

Figure 5.13 - Intra-Packed System Attribute

This is the "real" implementation of array structures. Name(*) is referred to as the base pointer of the array. After the reserve occurs, it contains the address of the block of storage assigned to the array. The first word of the block contains system information. In one half of the word is the size of the block (6 in our example). In the other half is the maximum subscript value (20 in our example). This latter value may be accessed by means of a system-defined function DIM.F. For example,

```
FOR I = 1 TO DIM.F(CALLS.BY.TYPE(*))
     LET CALLS.BY.TYPE(I) = 1
```

would initialize this array to one in place of the default zeroes.

Arrays (or system attributes) may be multi-dimensioned and need not be rectangular. For example,

```
DEFINE TRIANGLE AS A REAL, 2-DIM ARRAY
RESERVE TRIANGLE(*,*) AS 3 BY *
FOR I = 1 TO DIM.F(TRIANGLE(*,*)),
     RESERVE TRIANGLE(I,*) AS I
```

would yield an array as shown in Figure 5.14.

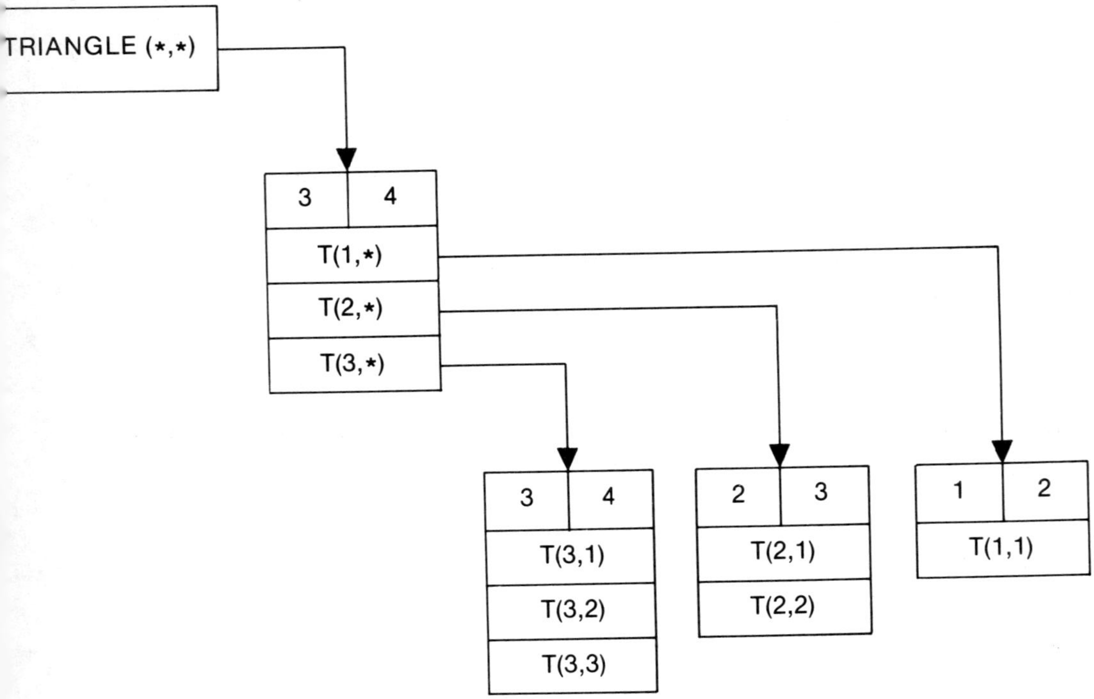

Figure 5.14 - Ragged Array Storage Allocation

Whenever array storage is to be deallocated, the statement to use is:

```
RELEASE name
```

or,

```
RELEASE name (*)
```

For example, one row of the TRIANGLE array above could be released and re-reserved with

```
RELEASE TRIANGLE (2,*)
RESERVE TRIANGLE (2,*) AS 3
```

Note that a reserve operation on an existing array is ignored.

Arrays may be defined locally as mentioned above. However, it is very important to observe that the base pointer for such an array becomes a local variable and is destroyed when control passes back from the routine to its calling routine (MAIN, timing routine, etc.) <u>without</u> automatically releasing the array storage. This is often a source of wasted storage to the unsuspecting modeller.

Chapter 6
MISCELLANEOUS SIMULATION TOPICS

6.0 Introduction

This chapter discusses an entirely different mechanism for initiating processes, that of the direct stimulus from data -- or external processes, as they are called in SIMSCRIPT. We then elaborate on the implementation of the mechanisms for handling processes, showing, for example, exactly what happens when two processes are supposed to occur at exactly the same time.

As an example of the flexibility of SIMSCRIPT, we describe the implementation of priority queueing for resources as it is currently implemented, and then discuss how it might be modified to implement a preemptive process.

Finally, to complete our detailed discussion of process concepts, we discuss the handling of process attributes as they relate to the arguments of a process routine, and complete the discussion of SIMSCRIPT subroutine linkage in general.

6.1 External Processes

Sometimes data are available about an explicit sequence of process activations to be included in a simulation. Sources for such data might be:

Observations of an actual system
Tapes generated from a computer performance measurement system
Historical files such as weather records

Two procedures for incorporating such data into a model have previously been discussed: either to find an existing distribution function to approximate the data, or to transform the data into an empirical distribution to be represented as a SIMSCRIPT random variable.

A third possibility is to introduce the sequence of process activations directly into the model as data. These are known as _external_ (or _exogenous_) _processes_. An external process differs from other processes, which we shall now refer to as _internal_ (or _endogenous_) processes in two aspects:

The mechanism for its activation
The method of initializing its attributes

External processes are activated from external data which are automatically read by the SIMSCRIPT system. Each external process activation record must contain the name of the process and the absolute simulated time at which the activation is to occur. Following this there may be any amount of additional data to be read by the corresponding process routine when the process actually activates. The order of the external records determines the order of the process activations. These records must be in order of ascending activation time.

In order to use external processes, three steps must be taken:

(1) Declare which processes might be triggered externally;

(2) Declare where the data to activate the processes are to be found;

(3) Prepare the data.

The declaration of external processes and the location of the data are declared in the preamble. For example,

```
EXTERNAL PROCESS IS SPECIAL.JOB

EXTERNAL PROCESS UNIT IS 7
```

The only type of process which may be triggered externally in this example is SPECIAL.JOB and the data for activating SPECIAL.JOBs are to be found on logical unit 7 (SIMSCRIPT I/O devices are described more fully in Chapter 8).

Several special situations may arise. First, if external processes are declared but no unit is declared, the standard system input device becomes the external process unit by default. Second, multiple units may be declared, in which case the sequences of process activations are automatically merged. Finally, even though external processes are declared, they need not be activated. Merely omitting the data will accomplish this. For example, we might use this technique in checking out a new model, supply a known sequence of process activations externally to verify proper execution, and then let the model be driven internally for normal execution.

The data for initiating an external process consist of the following:

(1) The process name;

(2) The process activation time in one of several formats described below;

(3) Any data to be read by the process routine upon activation;

(4) A termination character.

Process Name

This must be one of the processes defined as being external in the preamble.

Process Activation Time

There are three formats for the representation of the absolute time at which the process activation is to occur.

Decimal time corresponds to an absolute time expression in an ACTIVATE statement such as,

```
ACTIVATE A SPECIAL.JOB AT 12.25
```

As an external process, this same activation would be caused by the following data card:

```
SPECIAL.JOB    12.25     *
```

where * is the termination character required at the end of each external process activation description. This character is the default value of a system-defined variable, MARK.V, which may be changed by the modeller.

The day-hour-minute format consists of three consecutive integer fields, for example,

```
SPECIAL.JOB   12   6   0   *
```

would be equivalent to the above 12.25, i.e., on the 12th day at 6AM (assuming the default value of 24 hours per day).

The third format extends the day-hour-minute format by replacing the integer day representation by a calendar date of the form

```
MM/DD/YY
```

For example,

```
SPECIAL.JOB    5/12/79   3   10   *
```

where month and day may be one or two-digit integers, and year may be two or more digits. If year is two digits, it is assumed to mean a year in the current century. The entire month-day-year expression must not contain any blanks.

Before calendar dates can be used, an origin must be established. This is accomplished by a call to a system routine, ORIGIN.R, of the form:

```
CALL ORIGIN.R (MM,DD,YY)
```

Internally, TIME.V records elapsed time from this arbitrary origin, where TIME.V=0 corresponds to the start of the day of origin.

To facilitate time conversions between the internal and external representations, several system variables and functions are available.

HOURS.V -- the number of hours in a day (by default 24).

MINUTES.V -- the number of minutes in an hour (by default 60).

DATE.F (MM,DD,YY) -- converts this triple into a time relative to the origin.

YEAR.F (T) -- computes the year corresponding to the given time expression, T, regarding T as elapsed time relative to the origin.

MONTH.F (T) -- computes the month corresponding to the given time.

DAY.F (T) -- computes the day of the month corresponding to the given time.

DATE.F, YEAR.F, MONTH.F, and DAY.F all properly account for leap years.

HOUR.F (T) -- computes the hour of the day corresponding to the given time.

MINUTE.F (T) -- computes the (rounded) minute corresponding to the given time.

WEEKDAY.F (T) -- computes the day modulo 7 corresponding to the given time.

NOTE: HOUR.F, MINUTE.F and WEEKDAY.F do not require a time origin to have been previously established, whereas the remainder of the above functions do.

As an example of how these functions are used, consider the following:

```
CALL ORIGIN.R (1,1,76)
```

After some time has passed in the simulation, assume we wish to print the (then) current date:

Assume TIME.V has advanced to 552.5

Then,

```
PRINT 1 LINE WITH MONTH.F (TIME.V),
   DAY.F(TIME.V), YEAR.F(TIME.V),
   HOUR.F(TIME.V) AND MINUTE.F(TIME.V) THUS
THE CURRENT TIME IS **/**/****   **:**
```

would yield

```
THE CURRENT TIME IS  7/5/1977  12:00
```

In Chapter 3, we illustrated the possibility of setting process attributes in an ACTIVATE statement. In an externally activated process the analogous concept is the reading of the optional data on the external process card (record). Let us assume a process STORM with two attributes, location and duration. In the internal process activation scheme, the attributes are set as follows:

```
PROCESSES
     EVERY STORM HAS A LOCATION
          AND A DURATION

ACTIVATE A STORM GIVING 1500 AND 5 AT 23.5 DAYS
```

The external equivalent of this mechanism is:

```
PROCESSES
     EVERY STORM HAS A LOCATION
          AND A DURATION
EXTERNAL PROCESS IS STORM
```

and the data card:

```
STORM  1/24/79  12 00 1500  5  *
```

assuming an origin of 1/1/79.

Then in the process routine for storm, we must explicitly read the data for the attributes, as in:

```
PROCESS STORM
    READ LOCATION(STORM) AND DURATION(STORM)
```

The sequence of execution of external processes is so automatic as to seem mysterious to the uninitiated. The detailed sequence is as follows:

(1) When the START SIMULATION statement is executed, the timing routine initiates the reading of each external process unit.

(2) For each unit, the first external process record is read and a process notice of the corresponding type is created.

(3) The activation time of the process is read and converted to internal time format.

(4) The process notice is then placed on the pending list in chronological order (merged in with any other existing notices, either internal or external).

(5) The current record of each external unit is stored in a buffer so that at the time the process notice is selected for execution (by the timing routine), the input conditions are automatically restored; thus any reading done in the process routine will commence with the next field after the activation record time field.

(6) When an externally activated process returns control to the timing routine for the first time (upon encounter of a WORK, WAIT, SUSPEND, unsatisfied REQUEST, etc.), the timing routine automatically scans the input file for the MARK.V character, ignoring any intervening data. It then reads the next process name and activation time and schedules the activation of that process.

(7) If an end of data is encountered after a MARK.V, the system automatically suspends any further reading from that particular unit.

It is possible to activate the same type of process either internally or externally. Sometimes it becomes important to be able to ascertain which method was used to activate the process. For example, if attributes of the process are to be used, they could have been set by an internal activation but not by an external activation. Our previous example of the storm process can now be modified to include both methods of activation.

```
PROCESS STORM

    IF PROCESS IS EXTERNAL,
        READ LOCATION(STORM) AND DURATION(STORM)
    ALWAYS
    .
    .
    .
```

If the process is activated internally, the attributes are set from the given arguments of the ACTIVATE statement, whereas if the process is externally activated they will be read as shown above.

It is important to note that, because of the variable nature of the data to be read by an external process upon activation, only one activation record from each external process unit is represented in the pending list at a time. Only after that process is executed is the next activation record for that unit read. Processes of different types may have activation records in the same external process unit file.

6.2 Priority and Tie-Breaking Among Processes

Occasionally, process (re)activations are scheduled to occur at exactly the same simulated time. It is important to understand exactly what happens in these circumstances. There are some default precedence rules in the SIMSCRIPT system. We shall present these rules and then show how they may be explicitly overridden.

By default, if two instances of the same process are scheduled to (re)activate at exactly the same time, they are treated in FIFO fashion, i.e., the one which was scheduled first will be selected for execution first. However, in the case of two processes of different types which have a time tie, the situation is handled quite differently. The preference is given to the process which was declared first in the preamble.

We have occasionally activated a process "NOW." This is handled separately from the above scheme and forces the process to occur before any other process which might happen to be scheduled for the current time. If more than one process is scheduled "NOW," they are prioritized among themselves by the above rules.

There are two statements which may be included in the preamble to override the default rules. To break ties among different instances of the same process, the statement is:

BREAK process TIES BY HIGH attribute

This statement allows the system to compare the attribute values of the two instances of the process and order their reactivations based on the relative values of their specified attributes. This ranking is static in the sense that the attribute values must be established before the process is placed in the pending list. It will be rank-ordered among the other processes already in the list at the time of activation. Changing the attribute values would not automatically change the position in the pending list. However, when a process is active, it may change its attribute values so that the next time it is placed on the pending list, it is ranked (again only in case of time-tie) by these new values.

To override the rather arbitrary default priority rule for ties between processes of different types, the statement is:

PRIORITY ORDER IS $process_1$, $process_2$, . . .

That is, the processes are listed by name in the order of decreasing precedence. This is also a PREAMBLE statement and the order of precedence is static. If only some of the processes are included in the PRIORITY ORDER statement, those which are not included are, in effect, included after those which do appear, in the order of their appearance in the preamble.

These concepts can be summarized and perhaps crystallized by explaining the mechanism by which these features are implemented. For historical reasons, which we shall discuss in a subsequent section, the pending list in SIMSCRIPT is named EV.S and referred to as "the event set." This set is actually several separate ranked sets, one for each type of process. It is illustrated in Figure 6.1. In the figure, we see an instantaneous picture of the processes which are either awaiting initial activation or are in the middle of a WORK or WAIT statement delay. Processes which have either been interrupted, suspended or delayed due to unavailable resources, do not appear in this set. The event set might represent an instant in a simulation for which the following statements describe the processes:

```
PREAMBLE
    PROCESSES INCLUDE HARBOR.MASTER, CLOSING AND EMERGENCY
        EVERY SHIP HAS A TONNAGE
            AND A CARGO.TYPE
    BREAK SHIP TIES BY LOW CARGO.TYPE
        THEN BY HIGH TONNAGE
    PRIORITY ORDER IS EMERGENCY,
        SHIP, HARBOR.MASTER AND CLOSING
```

The processes are assigned to the columns in priority order. Thus, we observe that at the time of this snapshot, there are no emergencies pending, three ships, one harbor master, and one closing. The three instances of the ship process are scheduled to (re)activate at times 15, 17, and 17, indicating that a scheduling tie has occurred and been resolved by the tie-breaking rule for ships: "Give precedence to a ship with low cargo type, and then if two tied ships also have the same cargo type, give the preference to the one with higher value of tonnage." (The attribute values have not been shown in the figure.) If all the tie-breaking rules do not resolve the tie, the final decision is FIFO.

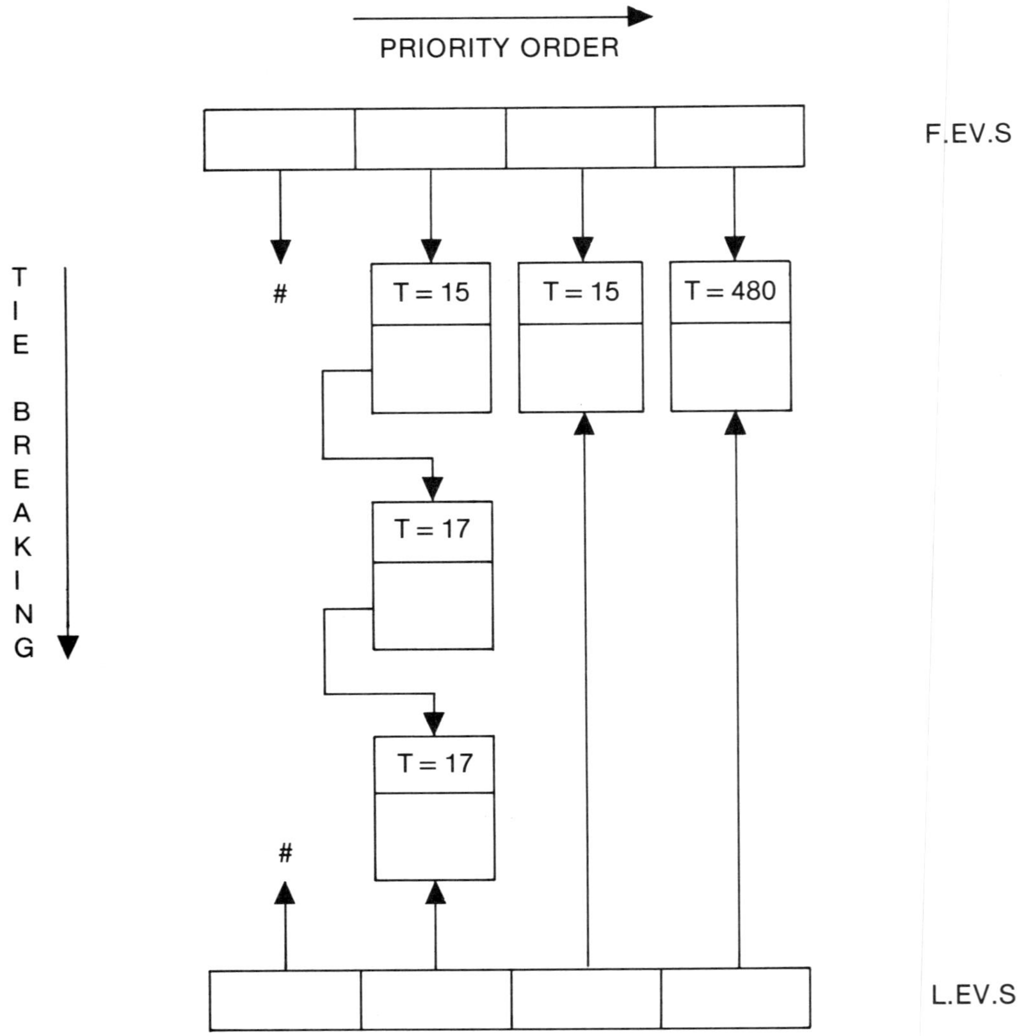

Figure 6.1 - Event Set

The timing routine scans the event set each time a new process is to be selected for execution. The sequence is:

(1) Start with the process class of priority 1 (leftmost column in Figure 6.1).

(2) If there are no pending processes in this class, skip it.

(3) For a non-empty class, compare the reactivation time with that of the "current candidate."

(4) If the time is less than the current candidate, this process becomes the current candidate.

(5) Record the priority class of the new current candidate.

(6) After examining all priority classes, remove the current candidate from the event set.

(7) If there are no members in the event set, the simulation is finished.

This description refines somewhat the algorithm presented in Chapter 2 (Figure 2.1).

Several variables associated with the event set are useful in various modelling situations. Each process class has a variable associated with it which contains the process priority. The name of this variable is derived from the process name by prefixing "I.". For example, I.EMERGENCY = 1 and I.SHIP = 2 in the preceding example.

The number of process classes for a particular model is recorded in the system-defined variable, EVENTS.V.

After the timing routine has selected the next process for execution, two variables are set in order to facilitate reference to the variable:

(1) A global variable, EVENT.V, contains the priority of the selected process.

(2) The global variable which has the same name as the selected process class contains the reference value for the particular process notice.

Finally, N.EV.S is a function which may be interrogated at any time to determine the number of pending processes of a certain class. It requires, as an argument, the priority of the process class in question. For example,

```
LET NO.OF.SHIPS = N.EV.S (I.SHIP)
```

will count the number of ship process notices in the event set and store this value in NO.OF.SHIPS.

6.3 Priority Queueing for Resources

In a manner which is analogous to the tie-breaking rules of processes, it is possible to specify a priority for a particular request of a resource. For example,

```
REQUEST 8000 UNITS OF MEMORY(1) WITH PRIORITY 10
```

If the requested resource is available in the amount requested, it is allocated as usual. If that amount is not available, the request is filed in the queue for the resource (Q.MEMORY). This set is actually a ranked set in which the ranking attribute is set from the "WITH PRIORITY" phrases in the REQUEST statement. If the phrase is omitted, the default priority of zero is used. The priority values may be any integer value (positive or negative). The higher values take precedence in determining queue position.

It is important to observe that this priority request mechanism is non-preemptive. That is, a request which is currently being satisfied is not preempted by a high-priority request. Many modelling situations do require such preemption but a number of non-obvious questions arise when preemption is considered:

(1) If an overhead is associated with a preemption, should it be charged to the preemptor or preemptee?

(2) Should the overhead be assessed at the time of preemption or resumption?

(3) Processes which hold several resources concurrently may lose some more while having already been preempted from others. A preemption counter is needed to indicate the number of preemptions a process is experiencing simultaneously.

The present implementation of SIMSCRIPT lays the foundation for the preemption of resources, but is not complete. Presently, each request for a resource causes an internal (system-defined) entity to be created. This entity, QC.E, has a pointer to the requesting process, WHO.A, the number of units requested, QTY.A, and the priority of the request, PTY.A.

QC.E is filed in the resource set for the process, RS.S and either in the queue or working set for the resource (Q.resource or X.resource, respectively).

An example of this structure is shown below.

Assume the following code fragments have been executed:

```
MAIN
   CREATE EVERY CPU(1)
   LET U.CPU(1) = 1
   CREATE EVERY STORAGE(1)
   LET U.CPU(1) = 12000
   FOR I = 1 to 3
      ACTIVATE A JOB NOW
   START SIMULATION
END
PROCESS JOB
   REQUEST 1 CPU(1)
   REQUEST 5000 UNITS OF STORAGE(1)
   WORK ...
   .
   .
   .
```

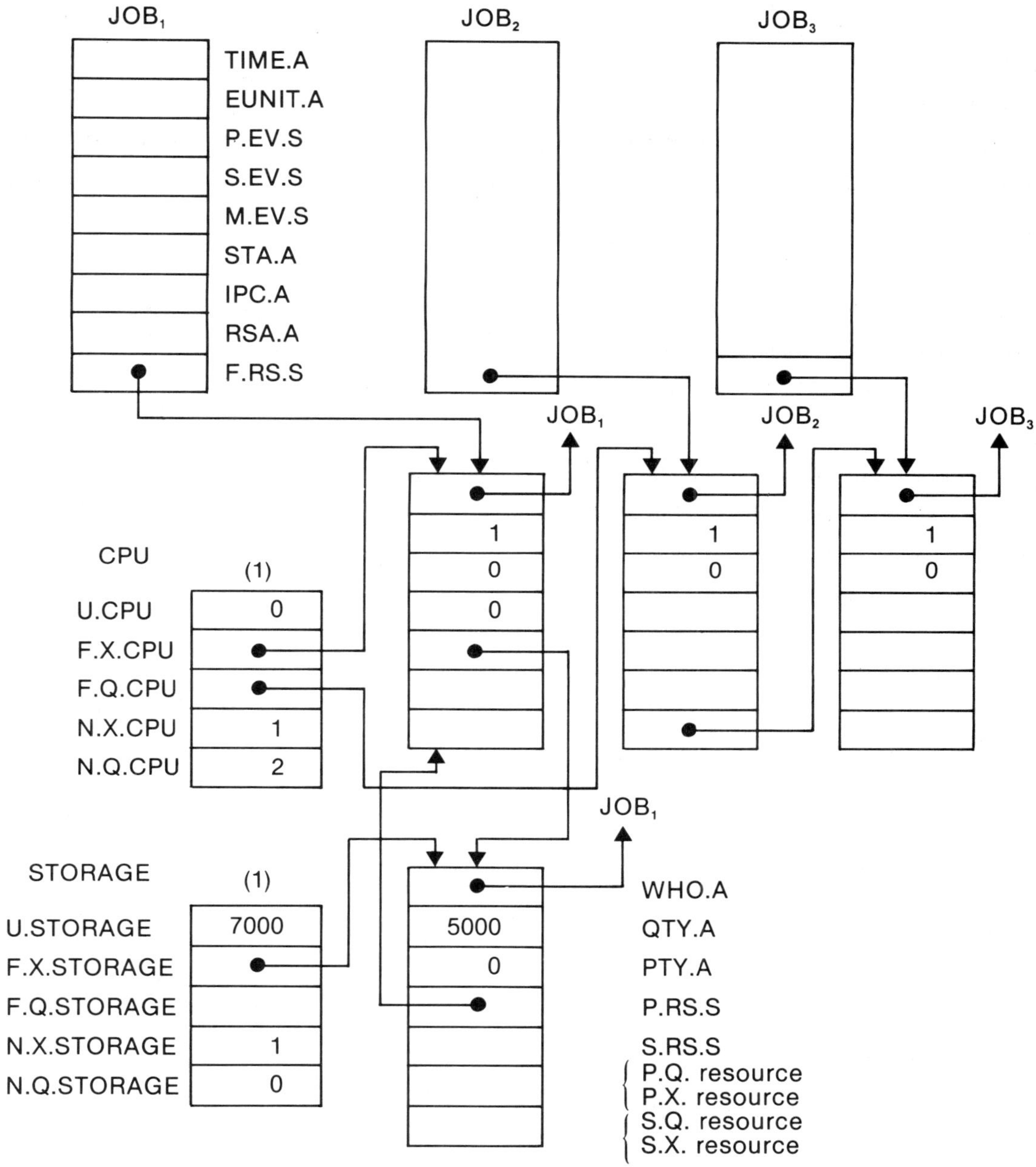

Figure 6.2 - Detailed Resource Mechanism

JOB_1 holds one unit of CPU(1) and 5000 units of STORAGE(1). JOB_2 and JOB_3 are enqueued for CPU(1).

When allocation of a resource can be made, after queueing has occurred, the system automatically moves the appropriate QC.E from the Q.resource set to the X.resource set.

A user wishing to implement a simple preemption scheme could move QC.E entities appropriately before making a normal request. This would also require interrupting the preempted process and preventing it from proceeding until the preemption was ended.

Until the preemption feature is fully implemented, the user might best be advised to proceed as in Example 4, using processes to represent preemptable resources.

6.4 Example 7: A Computer Center Study

To illustrate the features of this chapter, let us now model a computer center in which jobs are processed on a priority basis according to a priority chosen by the user. Higher-priority jobs are processed sooner, but at a premium in cost. Small interactive jobs arrive very frequently and have a short execution time. These will be modelled as internally generated according to the assumptions of a Poisson arrival process and exponential service time (truncated to the prespecified limit on small interactive jobs). Larger jobs will be completely specified through data.

Let us assume that contention for storage is also a problem, and that each job requires a prespecified amount of storage. If the storage is available, the program can run immediately. If not, the program will be enqueued according to its priority. For multiple jobs with the same priority, the amount of storage required will be used to break the tie (i.e., smaller jobs run sooner).

Model Formulation

Small jobs will be generated by a GENERATOR process. Large jobs will be represented as external processes. The same JOB process can be used to represent both large and small jobs. The CPU and the storage will be modelled as resources. We shall not allow preemption of resources; however, we shall specify priority queueing for the CPU based on job priority.

We shall run the model for an arbitrary period of time and stop abruptly to produce the desired measurements.

Desired measurements are:

- number of jobs processed
- average job dwell time
- utilization of each resource
- average queue for each resource

The program listing for this example is shown in Figure 6-3. Sample input for the program is shown in Figure 6-4, and corresponding results are shown in Figure 6-5.

```
''EXAMPLE 7  A COMPUTER CENTER STUDY

PREAMBLE
   RESOURCES INCLUDE CPU AND MEMORY
   PROCESSES INCLUDE GENERATOR AND STOP.SIM
      EVERY JOB HAS A JB.PRIORITY
                AND A JB.MEMORY.REQUIREMENT
      DEFINE JB.PRIORITY AND JB.MEMORY.REQUIREMENT
         AS INTEGER VARIABLES
      DEFINE JOB.DELAY.TIME AS A REAL VARIABLE
   EXTERNAL PROCESS IS JOB
   EXTERNAL PROCESS UNIT IS 7
   DEFINE SMALL.JOB.INTERARRIVAL.TIME,
      MEAN.SMALL.JOB.PROCESSING.TIME, RUN.LENGTH
         AND STOP.TIME AS REAL VARIABLES
   DEFINE NO.CPU AND MAX.MEMORY AS INTEGER VARIABLES
   DEFINE MAX.MEMORY.QUEUE TO MEAN 1MAX.MEMORY.QUEUE

   ACCUMULATE CPU.UTILIZATION AS THE AVG OF N.X.CPU
   ACCUMULATE MEMORY.UTILIZATION AS THE AVERAGE
      OF N.X.MEMORY
   ACCUMULATE AVG.CPU.QUEUE AS THE AVG AND
      MAX.CPU.QUEUE AS THE MAXIMUM OF N.Q.CPU
   ACCUMULATE AVG.MEMORY.QUEUE AS THE AVG
      AND MAX.MEMORY.QUEUE AS THE MAXIMUM OF N.Q.MEMORY
   TALLY AVG.JOB.TIME AS THE AVERAGE AND NO.JOBS.PROCESSED AS
      THE NUMBER OF JOB.DELAY.TIME

   DEFINE HOURS TO MEAN UNITS
END  ''PREAMBLE
```

Figure 6.3 - Example 7: A Computer Center Study

```
MAIN
   LET HOURS.V = 1
   CREATE EVERY CPU(1) AND MEMORY(1)
   READ U.CPU(1) AND U.MEMORY(1)
      LET NO.CPU = U.CPU(1)
      LET MAX.MEMORY = U.MEMORY(1)
   READ SMALL.JOB.INTERARRIVAL.TIME,
      MEAN.SMALL.JOB.PROCESSING.TIME, AND RUN.LENGTH
   LET STOP.TIME = RUN.LENGTH / HOURS.V
   PRINT 6 LINES WITH U.CPU(1), U.MEMORY(1),
      60/SMALL.JOB.INTERARRIVAL.TIME, MEAN.SMALL.JOB.PROCESSING.TIME
      AND RUN.LENGTH THUS
      A   C O M P U T E R   C E N T E R   S T U D Y
NO. OF CPU'S    **    STORAGE AVAILABLE   ****
SMALL JOBS ARRIVE AT THE RATE OF  *** / HOUR
   AND HAVE A MEAN PROCESSING TIME OF   ***.*** SECONDS
LARGE JOBS ARE SUPPLIED AS EXTERNAL DATA
THE SIMULATION PERIOD IS   **.**  HOURS
   ACTIVATE A GENERATOR NOW
   ACTIVATE A STOP.SIM IN STOP.TIME HOURS
   START SIMULATION
END  ''MAIN
```

```
PROCESS GENERATOR
   UNTIL TIME.V >= STOP.TIME
   DO
      ACTIVATE A JOB NOW
      LET JB.PRIORITY.. = RANDI.F(1,10,1)
      LET JB.MEMORY.REQUIREMENT.. = RANDI.F(1,MAX.MEMORY,2)
      WAIT EXPONENTIAL.F(SMALL.JOB.INTERARRIVAL.TIME,3) MINUTES
   LOOP
END
```

Figure 6.3 (Continued)

```
PROCESS JOB
    DEFINE ARRIVAL.TIME AND PROCESSING.TIME
        AS REAL VARIABLES
    IF PROCESS IS EXTERNAL
        READ JB.PRIORITY..,JB.MEMORY.REQUIREMENT.. AND
            PROCESSING.TIME
    ELSE
        LET PROCESSING.TIME = MIN.F(EXPONENTIAL.F
            (MEAN.SMALL.JOB.PROCESSING.TIME,4),2 *
            MEAN.SMALL.JOB.PROCESSING.TIME)
    ALWAYS
    LET ARRIVAL.TIME = TIME.V
    REQUEST JB.MEMORY.REQUIREMENT.. UNITS OF MEMORY(1)
        WITH PRIORITY JB.PRIORITY..
    REQUEST 1 CPU(1) WITH PRIORITY JB.PRIORITY..
    WORK PROCESSING.TIME MINUTES
    RELINQUISH JB.MEMORY.REQUIREMENT.. UNITS OF MEMORY(1)
    RELINQUISH 1 CPU(1)
    LET JOB.DELAY.TIME = TIME.V - ARRIVAL.TIME
END
```

```
PROCESS STOP.SIM
    SKIP 6 LINES
    PRINT 9 LINES WITH TIME.V, CPU.UTILIZATION(1)*100/NO.CPU,
        MEMORY.UTILIZATION(1)*100/MAX.MEMORY,
        AVG.MEMORY.QUEUE(1), MAX.MEMORY.QUEUE(1),
        AVG.CPU.QUEUE(1), MAX.CPU.QUEUE(1),
        NO.JOBS.PROCESSED AND AVG.JOB.TIME * MINUTES.V
        THUS
A F T E R      **.**  HOURS
THE CPU UTILIZATION WAS          *.** %
THE MEMORY UTILIZATION WAS       *.** %
THE AVG QUEUE FOR MEMORY WAS     *.** JOBS
THE MAX QUEUE FOR MEMORY WAS     *.** JOBS
THE AVG QUEUE FOR A CPU WAS      *.** JOBS
THE MAX QUEUE FOR A CPU WAS      *.** JOBS
THE TOTAL NUMBER OF JOBS COMPLETED WAS      ***
WITH AN AVERAGE PROCESSING TIME OF     *.***   MINUTES
    STOP
END
```

Figure 6.3 (Continued)

```
1 6 2.0 0.8 12



JOB 1.00 3 1 5.00 *
JOB 2.46 1 2 7.00 *
JOB 3.78 3 3 10.00 *
JOB 9.28 2 2 30.00 *
JOB 10.48 1 4 40.00 *
JOB 24.22 1 5 60.00 *
```

Figure 6.4 - Input for Example 7

```
     A   C O M P U T E R   C E N T E R   S T U D Y
NO. OF CPU'S    1   STORAGE AVAILABLE     6
SMALL JOBS ARRIVE AT THE RATE OF   30 / HOUR
   AND HAVE A MEAN PROCESSING TIME OF       .800 SECONDS
LARGE JOBS ARE SUPPLIED AS EXTERNAL DATA
THE SIMULATION PERIOD IS   12.00  HOURS



A F T E R     12.00  HOURS
THE CPU UTILIZATION WAS          47.74 %
THE MEMORY UTILIZATION WAS       10.28 %
THE AVG QUEUE FOR MEMORY WAS      1.17 JOBS
THE MAX QUEUE FOR MEMORY WAS     19.00 JOBS
THE AVG QUEUE FOR A CPU WAS        .14 JOBS
THE MAX QUEUE FOR A CPU WAS       2.00 JOBS
THE TOTAL NUMBER OF JOBS COMPLETED WAS      364
WITH AN AVERAGE PROCESSING TIME OF     3.535    MINUTES
```

Figure 6.5 - Output from Example 7

6.5 Monitored Actions

SIMSCRIPT provides a mechanism for intervening just before or just after certain actions are taken. The actions include creating and destroying entities, scheduling and cancelling events (including the corresponding process actions of ACTIVATE, INTERRUPT, WORK, WAIT, RESUME), filing in and removing from sets.

In order to use this mechanism, it is necessary to declare the intention in the preamble with a BEFORE or AFTER statement. These statements reference a subroutine which must also be supplied. Arguments are automatically supplied to this routine by the system in accordance with Figure 6.6.

ACTION	SYSTEM-SUPPLIED ARGUMENTS
CREATE*	entity reference
DESTROY*	entity reference
SCHEDULE	event (or process) reference, time
CANCEL	event (or process) reference, time
FILE	entity reference, owner subscripts
REMOVE	entity reference, owner subscripts

* BEFORE CREATE and AFTER DESTROY are not allowed.

Figure 6.6 - BEFORE and AFTER Arguments

The action cannot be avoided by the BEFORE routine, although it may be altered or even undone by the AFTER routine.

For example, if one were interested in collecting information on the amount of time entities spend in several different sets, one could specify:

```
        BEFORE FILING IN QUEUE, CALL CHECK.IN
        AFTER REMOVING FROM QUEUE, CALL CHECK.OUT

    ROUTINE CHECK.IN GIVEN JOB AND MACHINE
        DEFINE JOB AND MACHINE AS INTEGER VARIABLES
        LET JOB.START.DELAY(JOB) = TIME.V
        RETURN
    END

    ROUTINE CHECK.OUT GIVEN JOB AND MACHINE
        DEFINE JOB AND MACHINE AS INTEGER VARIABLES
        LET JOB.DELAY (TYPE(MACHINE)) = TIME.V - JOB.START.DELAY(JOB)
        RETURN
    END
```

If sets other than QUEUE are to be included in this measurement, additional BEFORE/AFTER statements for those sets referencing these same routines could be added to the preamble.

After addition of the BEFORE/AFTER statements, all FILE and REMOVE statements will be modified to call CHECK.IN or CHECK.OUT respectively. Note that routines containing FILE/REMOVE must be recompiled to be affected by the BEFORE/AFTER statements.

6.6 Monitored Variables

The mechanism of the preceding section can be extended to apply to actions performed on any global variable. When this is desired, the mechanism to use is "MONITORING ON THE LEFT" or "MONITORING ON THE RIGHT." A left-monitored variable has actions which would change the value of the variable intercepted, whereas a right-monitored variable has actions which would access the variable intercepted.

Monitored variables have data storage as well as programs associated with them. As such their storage is allocated in the usual manner (CREATE, RESERVE, or initialization for unsubscripted global variables). Monitoring applies only to preamble-defined variables or attributes.

As an example of the use of monitored variables, consider a situation in which one variable changes value continuously dependent on another variable, its rate. For instance, the current inventory in an oil refinery is a function of the refinery production rate and the rate at which tankers are unloading oil into the storage tank. We can represent this situation with two monitored variables, or rather attributes, of the entity TANK.

A fragment of the program is shown in Figure 6.7.

```
PREAMBLE
   PROCESSES
      EVERY TANK
         HAS A TK.NET.RATE
         AND A TK.INVENTORY
         AND A TK.TIME.LAST.UPDATE
      DEFINE TK.NET.RATE  AS  A  REAL  VARIABLE  MONITORED  ON  THE  LEFT
      DEFINE TK.INVENTORY  AS  A  REAL  VARIABLE  MONITORED  ON  THE  RIGHT
      DEFINE TK.TIME.LAST.UPDATE AS A DOUBLE VARIABLE
END

LEFT ROUTINE TK.NET.RATE GIVEN TANK
   DEFINE TANK AS AN INTEGER VARIABLE
   DEFINE INCREMENT AND NET.RATE AS REAL VARIABLES
   ENTER WITH NET.RATE
   LET INCREMENT = TK.NET.RATE..*(TIME.V - TK.TIME.LAST.UPDATE..)
   LET TK.TIME.LAST.UPDATE.. = TIME.V
   MOVE FROM NET.RATE
   ADD INCREMENT TO TK.INVENTORY..
   RETURN
END

RIGHT ROUTINE TK.INVENTORY GIVEN TANK
   DEFINE TANK AS AN INTEGER VARIABLE
   DEFINE INVENTORY AS A REAL VARIABLE
   MOVE TO INVENTORY
   ADD TK.NET.RATE..*(TIME.V - TK.TIME.LAST.UPDATE..) TO INVENTORY
   RETURN WITH INVENTORY
END
```

Figure 6.7 - Example of Monitored Variables

Program Discussion

When a change in TK.NET.RATE(TANK) occurs -- for example, at the arrival or departure of an oil tanker, or when the inventory in the tank is exhausted, or the tank is full -- the LEFT ROUTINE TK.NET.RATE is automatically invoked. The routine executes as follows:

(1) At line 4, the new value of TK.NET.RATE is stored in a local variable, NET.RATE.

(2) At line 5, the change in inventory since the last change in net rate is computed using the old value of TK.NET.RATE.

(3) At line 6, the time of last update is made current.

(4) At line 7, the new value of TK.NET.RATE is established by copying from the local variable, NET RATE.

(5) At line 8, the additional increment of inventory is added to TK.INVENTORY. NOTE: This statement, which compiles as LET TK.INVENTORY.. = TK.INVENTORY.. + INCREMENT invokes the right-monitoring routine for TK.INVENTORY, but a careful examination of that routine will show that no additional change in inventory will occur, since TK.TIME.LAST.UPDATE.. has already been set to TIME.V.

Whenever the value of the inventory is required, the RIGHT ROUTINE TK.INVENTORY is automatically invoked. It executes as follows:

(1) At line 4, the old value of TK.INVENTORY is placed in a local variable, INVENTORY.

(2) At line 5, this local value of INVENTORY is updated to the current time.

(3) At line 6, this local value is returned to the calling routine as current (updated) inventory.

Particular attention should be paid to the ENTER WITH, MOVE FROM, and MOVE TO statements in these routines.

ENTER WITH must be the first executable statement in a LEFT-monitoring routine since it captures the new value of the monitored variable (which is currently computed but not stored anywhere).

The MOVE statements, which may appear only in LEFT- (FROM) or RIGHT- (TO) monitoring routines, are actually the equivalent of LET statements. However, they are used in place of LET statements within monitoring routines to avoid the problem of infinite recursion.

For example, if we wrote,

```
LET TK.NET.RATE.. = NET.RATE
```

in place of line 7 of the preceding LEFT ROUTINE TK.NET.RATE, this would require that the LEFT routine itself be called in the execution of line 7 and we would quickly exceed a "recursion limit" in the execution of the program.

These routines could be used in a program that includes REFINERY and SHIP processes, which change the TK.NET.RATE and are, in turn, governed by the TK.INVENTORY. The intended use is illustrated in Figure 6.8.

Assuming some positive value for TK.INVENTORY at time zero, the net rate also is zero to start with. When a ship arrives (at time a), the net rate becomes positive and the inventory starts to increase. When a second ship arrives (at time b), the rate doubles and the inventory increases more rapidly. When a ship leaves (at time c), the rate is reduced correspondingly. Finally, when the second ship leaves, the refinery continues to withdraw oil, thus leaving a negative net rate and a declining inventory.

The inventory is updated by the left routine TK.NET.RATE at times a, b, c, and d. If the inventory were desired at, say, time e (when no net rate change occurs, the right routine, TK.INVENTORY, would be called to update the inventory since time d.

TK.INVENTORY and TK.NET.RATE could also be used to govern the processes with statements such as:

```
PROCESS REFINERY
WHILE TIME.V < END.SIMULATION
DO
   IF TK.INVENTORY > 0,
      SUBTRACT REFINERY.RATE FROM TK.NET.RATE
      WORK TK.INVENTORY/REFINERY.RATE HOURS
   ELSE
      SUSPEND
   ALWAYS
   .
   .
   .
```

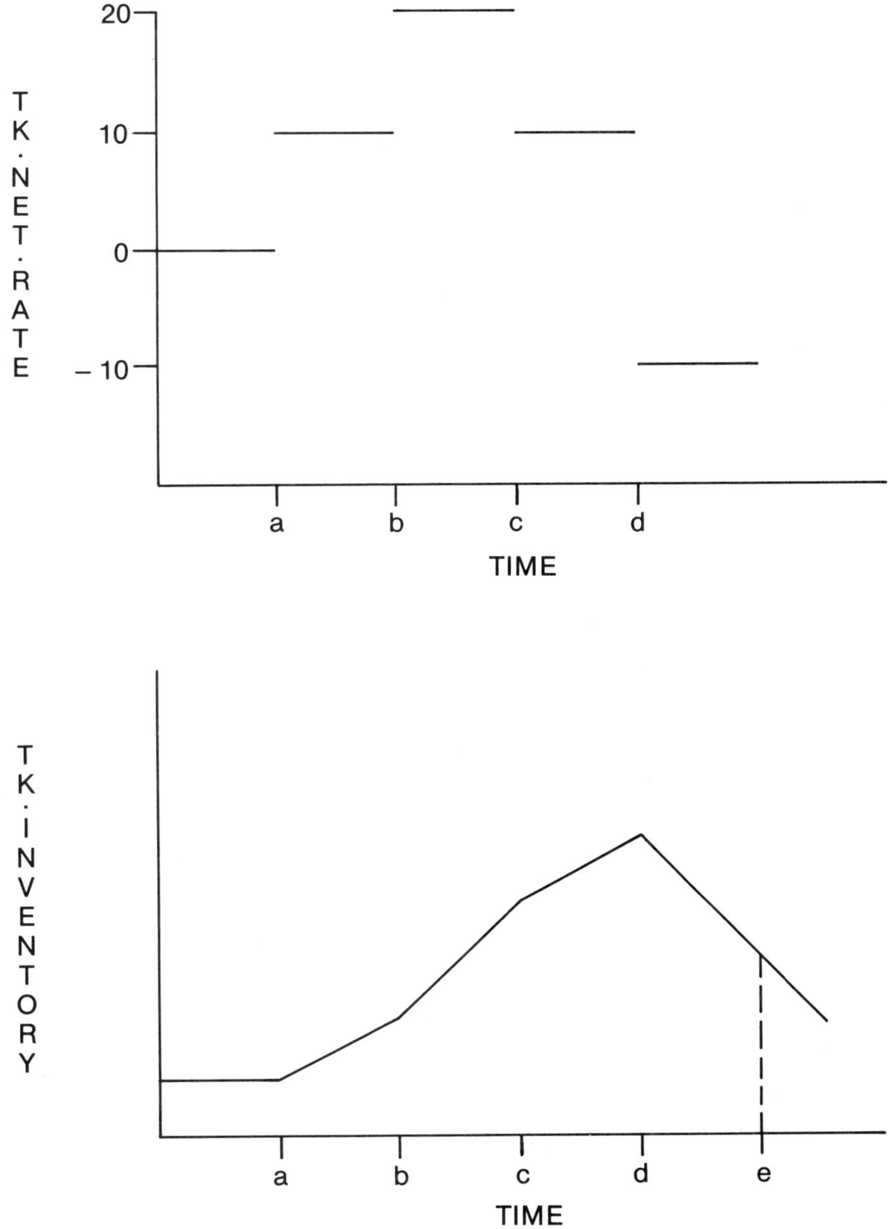

Figure 6.8 - Example: Inventory Measurements Using Monitored Variables

One may note a strong similarity between the monitored variable concept and the implementation of the performance measuring statements, ACCUMULATE and TALLY. In fact, these statements are implemented using automatically generated monitoring routines. As a consequence, a variable may not be both left-monitored and appear as the object of ACCUMULATE or TALLY measurements.

Chapter 7

MODELLING WITH DISCRETE EVENTS

7.0 Introduction

Historically, SIMSCRIPT has been a discrete-event simulation language. In a sense, discrete events are the atomic elements of discrete simulation. An event occurs at an instant in simulated time. Since processes have evolved from events, there is a strong resemblance in the nomenclature.

7.1 Analogy Between Processes and Events

An event, in SIMSCRIPT, is described by the same triple as a process:

(1) An event "notice" -- the data block containing pertinent information about a particular copy of (or instance of) the event.

(2) An event routine -- the program describing the logic of the event, how it responds to its environment, and how it changes the environment.

(3) A global variable with the same name as the event -- used to identify a particular instance of the event, either at creation time or during execution.

A process may be thought of as a sequence of events -- which in fact it is. If we wish to replace even the most elementary process by the equivalent event code, it will require at least two events whenever we wish to represent a simulated time delay.

Since events are instantaneous, the treatment of attributes and local variables is quite different from processes. It may be recalled that attributes and/or local variables of a process are preserved until the process finally self-destructs (at a RETURN or END statement). In the case of events, the local variables are initialized to zero each time the event occurs, but in addition, the event notice self-destructs on entry into the event routine (after copying user-defined attributes to user-defined given arguments).

It is quite common to find temporary entities used to pass information from one event in a sequence to the next.

A small example may serve to clarify these concepts:

A process might be used to represent a telephone call; for example,

```
PROCESS CALL
   ADD 1 TO BUSY.LINES
   WORK 5 MINUTES
   SUBTRACT 1 FROM BUSY.LINES
END
```

representing the simplest sort of process model.

An equivalent event model might be,

```
EVENT BEGIN.CALL
   ADD 1 TO BUSY.LINES
   SCHEDULE AN END.CALL IN 5 MINUTES
END
```

```
EVENT END.CALL
   SUBTRACT 1 FROM BUSY.LINES
END
```

The portion of the process CALL preceding the WORK statement is modelled as one event (BEGIN.CALL) and the portion after the WORK statement is modelled as another event (END.CALL). The SCHEDULE statement is analogous to the process ACTIVATE statement.

If it is necessary to pass information from one event to another, a temporary entity is introduced. For example, since resources cannot be used except by processes, we might proceed as shown in Section 7.2 to extend our simple example to include queueing for available lines.

7.2 Example 8: Gas Station 1A Revisited

This program, shown in Figure 7.1, is exactly equivalent to Example 1A. The important implementational differences are:

(1) The generation of new ARRIVAL events has been included in the ARRIVAL event itself although this could have been put in a separate event.

(2) The CUSTOMER entity created in ARRIVAL is disposed of either by filing in the QUEUE or passing to END.SERVICE. Otherwise it would be lost to the system when the next call was created.

```
''   EXAMPLE 8   GAS STATION MODEL 1A USING DISCRETE EVENT LOGIC

PREAMBLE
    EVENT NOTICES INCLUDE ARRIVAL
        EVERY END.SERVICE HAS AN ES.CUSTOMER
    TEMPORARY ENTITIES
        EVERY CUSTOMER HAS AN TIME.OF.ARRIVAL
            AND MAY BELONG TO THE QUEUE
    THE SYSTEM OWNS THE QUEUE
    DEFINE NO.BUSY AND NO.CUSTOMERS AS INTEGER VARIABLES
    ACCUMULATE AVG.QUEUE.LENGTH AS THE AVERAGE
        AND MAX.QUEUE.LENGTH AS THE MAXIMUM
        OF N.QUEUE
    ACCUMULATE UTILIZATION AS THE AVERAGE OF NO.BUSY
END
```

```
MAIN
    SCHEDULE A ARRIVAL NOW
    START SIMULATION
    PRINT 4 LINES WITH AVG.QUEUE.LENGTH, MAX.QUEUE.LENGTH,
        AND UTILIZATION * 100 / 2 THUS
SIMPLE GAS STATION MODEL WITH 2 ATTENDANTS
    AVERAGE CUSTOMER QUEUE LENGTH IS     *.***
    MAXIMUM CUSTOMER QUEUE LENGTH IS     *
    THE ATTENDANTS WERE BUSY    *.** PER CENT OF THE TIME.
END
```

Figure 7.1 - Example 8: Gas Station 1A Revisited

```
EVENT ARRIVAL
   IF NO.CUSTOMERS < 1000,
      ADD 1 TO NO.CUSTOMERS
      CREATE A CUSTOMER
      LET TIME.OF.ARRIVAL(CUSTOMER) = TIME.V
      IF NO.BUSY = 2,
         FILE CUSTOMER IN QUEUE
      ELSE
         ADD 1 TO NO.BUSY
         SCHEDULE AN END.SERVICE GIVING CUSTOMER
            IN UNIFORM.F(5.0, 15.0, 2) MINUTES
      ALWAYS
      SCHEDULE A ARRIVAL IN UNIFORM.F(2.0, 8.0, 1) MINUTES
   ALWAYS
END
```

```
EVENT END.SERVICE GIVEN CUSTOMER
   DEFINE CUSTOMER AS AN INTEGER VARIABLE
   LET SERVICE.TIME = TIME.V - TIME.OF.ARRIVAL(CUSTOMER)
   DESTROY CUSTOMER
   IF QUEUE IS NOT EMPTY,
      REMOVE THE FIRST CUSTOMER FROM QUEUE
      SCHEDULE AN END.SERVICE GIVING CUSTOMER
         IN UNIFORM.F(5.0, 15.0, 2) MINUTES
   ELSE
         SUBTRACT 1 FROM NO.BUSY
   ALWAYS
END
```

Figure 7.1 - Example 8 (Continued)

(3) The event END.SERVICE must have an attribute (ES.CUSTOMER) to store the pointer to the CUSTOMER with which it is associated.

(4) More global variables are required than in the process-equivalent model (i.e., NO.BUSY, and NO.CUSTOMERS.)

The output, which is identical to that of Example 1A, is shown in Figure 7.2.

```
SIMPLE GAS STATION MODEL WITH 2 ATTENDANTS
   AVERAGE CUSTOMER QUEUE LENGTH IS      7.809
   MAXIMUM CUSTOMER QUEUE LENGTH IS     21
   THE ATTENDANTS WERE BUSY  98.64 PER CENT OF THE TIME.
```

Figure 7.2 - Output from Example 8

7.3 Additional Event Commands

Continuing the comparison of processes and events, the following should be noted:

(1) Events and processes may be intermingled in a model.

(2) Events may ACTIVATE or INTERRUPT processes.

(3) Processes may SCHEDULE or CANCEL events.

(4) Internally, event notices and process notices cohabit in the event set or "pending list" (EV.S). But, of course, each has a unique priority class.

(5) Events may be scheduled via the EXTERNAL route (i.e., external data).

The CANCEL Statement

In order to prevent the occurrence of an event known to be currently scheduled (i.e., on the pending list), the statement to execute is

CANCEL event

where event must point to an event awaiting execution. The CANCEL statement merely removes the event notice from the event set. It does not change the value of its TIME.A attribute as INTERRUPT does with a process.

Chapter 8
INPUT AND OUTPUT

8.0 Introduction

Until this point we have used only the most rudimentary input and output commands. Many very powerful input/output concepts are incorporated in SIMSCRIPT. These include automatic page titling, character string manipulations, formatted input/output, ability to process multiple files, and generalized reports (multi-page in width as well as length). All these concepts will be addressed in this chapter.

8.1 Review: Free-Form READ and the PRINT Statement

The simplest input statement is the free-form READ. The requirements for using this statement lie mainly with the data preparation. Each variable in the statement will be filled in order from successive data fields, where a data field is delimited by blanks or the end of a record. Mode conversions are performed automatically in those combinations which are permitted (refer to Figure 3.2). Data fields are the primary organizational entity in free-form input. A single READ statement may read several records. Or conversely, several separate READ statements may read data from the same record.

For example,

```
DEFINE X AND Y AS REAL VARIABLES
DEFINE M AND N AS INTEGER VARIABLES
DEFINE NAME AS AN ALPHA VARIABLE
```

then,

```
READ X, Y, NAME, M, AND N
```

will accept any of the following sets of input records and produce identical results:

```
1)  5.0    6     ABC    9    99

2)  5     6.0    ABC
    9     99

3)  5
    6.0
    ABC
    9
    99
```

Two observations should be made:

(1) INTEGER variables must be filled with integer data, whereas REAL variables will permit integer data (and convert them).

(2) Alpha variables have a peculiar implementational dependency, i.e., the number of characters read varies from one implementation to another. The number of characters read is exactly the number that can be stored in one computer word. If more characters appear in the data than can fit in one word, only the exact number are read and the input mechanism is left positioned to read the next character. Of course, if the data field length is less than or equal to the number of characters in one computer word, normal processing occurs. Because of the nuisance this feature introduces, the TEXT variable has been introduced to allow complete machine independence (see Section 8.2).

It is possible to skip unwanted free-form data with either of the following statements:

```
SKIP e FIELDS
```

or,

```
START NEW RECORD
```

For example, to create a "user-friendly" input routine, one which forgives mispunches at the terminal, the following sequence might be used:

```
UNTIL MODE IS NOT ALPHA,
DO
   PRINT 1 LINE THUS
   PLEASE ENTER NUMERIC DATA ONLY
   SKIP 1 FIELD
LOOP
READ X
```

Using the "look ahead" feature of the "MODE IS" expression, this program will reject all alpha mode input data with a message to the user. Only when a purely numeric field of data is encountered will its value be recorded in the variable X.

Two more tests may be used in conjunction with free-form input for determining whether data have been exhausted, either on the current record or entirely. The tests are:

```
IF DATA IS [NOT] ENDED
```

and,

```
IF CARD IS [NOT] NEW
```

Each is a "look ahead" feature which does not cause any actual data to be read. They merely determine whether any data remain to be read, or whether the next data to be read is the first field of a record, respectively.

The only output statement used thus far is the PRINT statement. A PRINT statement, it may be recalled (Section 2.6), is composed of a list of variables (or expressions) and a format for the variables.

For instance,

```
        PRINT 3 LINES WITH M,X,N,Y AND NAME THUS
    FOR M = * X is *.***
        N = * Y is *.***
    CASE NAME ****
```

Recall the following properties of PRINT statements:

(1) There must be a 1-to-1 correspondence between expressions in the list and formats ("pictures" composed of asterisks in the format).

(2) The numeric in PRINT n LINES governs the number of successive input records to be processed as format.

(3) Record boundaries are significant in this context (in order to count LINES).

(4) In numeric formats, blanks preceding an asterisk serve to extend the field to the left.

(5) If the value cannot be printed meaningfully in the allotted space, an error condition will be printed but will not stop program execution.

Finally, there are several commands for controlling the spacing of output:

```
SKIP n LINES
```

will introduce blank lines into output up to one full page;

```
START NEW PAGE
```

will move the output position to the beginning of a new page (unless already there); and

```
PAGE IS [NOT] NEW
```

is a logical test which may be used to determine where next output will be printed.

8.2 The TEXT Mode

To relieve the problems caused by truncation of ALPHA mode variables to the word size of the various computers, a more general and machine-independent TEXT mode has been introduced. TEXT variables contain strings of characters of virtually any length. They may be read from data, printed, compared, and changed by concatenation or by extraction.

Global variables, attributes of any type of entity, and local variables may all be of TEXT mode.

Text literals may be used in assignment statements and as arguments to subroutines.

Free-Form Input

A variable of TEXT mode may be initialized by a READ statement. The data field to be read may contain any number of alphanumeric characters, but will terminate at either the first blank or the end of the record (whichever comes first).

For example:

```
DEFINE TYPE AND NAME AS TEXT VARIABLES
READ TYPE AND NAME
```

with data as,

```
PORT VALDEZ
```

The assignment is equivalent to the statements,

```
LET TYPE = "PORT"
LET NAME = "VALDEZ"
```

CONCAT.F(A, B)

Two TEXT variables can be combined via the CONCAT.F function. The CONCAT.F function requires two TEXT mode arguments. For example,

```
LET LONG.NAME = CONCAT.F(TYPE, "_")
LET LONG.NAME = CONCAT.F(LONG.NAME,NAME)
```

produces, first, "PORT_"
then "PORT_VALDEZ"

This example illustrates the use of a TEXT literal, the underscore enclosed in quotation marks.

Each TEXT variable in a program is stored as a separate string, even though several variables may have exactly the same character representation. Before a TEXT variable is changed (as in line 2 of the above example), the old character string is automatically erased.

Null strings are supported as legal TEXT strings. Some of the following TEXT support functions may, on occasion, produce null strings.

LENGTH.F (A)

The LENGTH.F function returns the integer value of the number of characters in the TEXT character string pointed to by A. If A is the null string, the result is a zero.

MATCH.F (A, B, I)

The MATCH.F function scans the character string pointed to by the TEXT variable A, starting at the I + 1st location in A. If a string matching the TEXT variable B is found, the location of the first character of the first occurrence of that string is returned as an integer result. If no matching string is found, a zero is returned. Both A and B are unchanged.

If either A or B is the null string, a zero is returned. Also, if I = 0, the search starts at the beginning of the string A.

For example,

```
LET SPACE = MATCH.F (LONG.NAME,"_",0)
```

will return a value of 5 when the value of LONG.NAME is "PORT_VALDEZ."

SUBSTR.F (A, I, J)

There are actually two different functions referenced by the name SUBSTR.F. One is used for extracting a substring from an existing string and the other is used for replacing part of a string. Which function to reference is determined solely by the context in which the function name appears.

Example: LET C = SUBSTR.F(A,I,J)

This "right-handed" reference to SUBSTR.F extracts a character string of length J starting from the I-th position in A. A new character string is formed; A remains unchanged.

Second Example: LET SUBSTR.F(A,I,J) = C

This "left-handed" reference to SUBSTR.F replaces characters in the character string pointed to by A by characters from the character string pointed to by C. The first J characters of C replace the J characters of A starting from the I-th character of A.

If A is the null string, or if I or J is zero, or if I points beyond the end of A, this function does nothing. If the right-hand string, C, is the null string, the portion of A specified by I and J is replaced with blanks. If J specifies a length longer than that of C, trailing blanks are supplied. The value of J is automatically adjusted so that writing does not extend beyond the end of the character string pointed to by A. (I.e., this function cannot be used to change the length of the character string A.)

<u>TTOA.F(A)</u>

This function returns the first n characters of the text variable A in ALPHA format. The number of characters returned (n) is computer dependent, i.e., the number of characters in an ALPHA variable for the specific implementation.

<u>ATOT.F(A)</u>

This function returns the pointer to a character string TEXT variable representation of the ALPHA variable A. The number of characters in A is implementation dependent (never more than one computer word).

<u>ITOT.F(I)</u>

This function returns the pointer to a character string TEXT variable representation of the INTEGER variable I.

TEXT Comparisons

Comparisons between text variables or literals are treated as comparisons on a character-by-character basis after a shorter string has been extended with blanks. Usual comparisons are for equality or inequality, but, other comparisons are permitted (greater than or less than). The result of these comparisons (<, >) depends on the host computer collating sequence and thus may produce different results on different computers.

Storage Considerations

Since each TEXT variable is stored as a separate string, the amount of storage used for TEXT variables can become large. However, the allocation and deallocation of storage is handled automatically, consistent with other data structures in SIMSCRIPT.

For example, all unsubscripted local variables of the TEXT mode are automatically erased on return from the routine. Also, when an entity with a TEXT attribute is DESTROYed, the character string is erased. Finally, when a TEXT array is RELEASEd, the individual character strings are automatically erased.

Should the user wish to erase a TEXT variable explicitly, the statement

```
ERASE variable
```

may be used. This statement deallocates the character string storage and sets the variable to the null string. It is equivalent to:

```
LET variable = "".
```

8.3 The Report Generator

The PRINT statement, which has been employed in every example so far, has been quite adequate for producing output either of messages or the values of variables.

The goal of simulation is to produce information about the system being studied. Such information should be in a form easily read by someone who is not familiar with the details of the program, much less the programming language in which the model was written!

We shall now introduce additional features of the PRINT statement which contribute to a generalization of output generation. These features are available only within a REPORT section. A REPORT section in SIMSCRIPT is contained within a pair of delimiters, BEGIN REPORT and END. A REPORT section is not a routine, hence it must be contained within a routine (process, event, MAIN, etc.). REPORT sections allow for automatic page titling, automatic pagination, and an easy expansion of columnar output to multi-pages in width as well as length. A report may be forced to begin on a new page by adding the phrase "ON A NEW PAGE" to the BEGIN REPORT statement.

Automatic Page Titling

Within a report section, a HEADING section is used to specify titling information. The flow of control within a report follows normal conventions except for the HEADING section. A HEADING section is executed the first time it is encountered. After that, and while control remains within the REPORT section, the system automatically counts output lines. Each time the maximum number of lines on a page is reached, the system automatically issues a new page command and executes the HEADING section.

As an example,

```
 1   MAIN
 2      BEGIN REPORT
 3         PRINT 2 LINES THUS
              TABLE OF
     SQUARES SQUARE-ROOTS AND RECIPROCALS
 4         SKIP 1 LINE
 5         BEGIN HEADING
 6            PRINT 1 LINE WITH PAGE.V THUS
        N        N**2          SQRT(N)         1/N
 7            SKIP 1 LINE
 8         END
 9      FOR N = 1 TO 1000,
10         PRINT 1 LINE WITH N, N**2, SQRT.F(N), AND 1/N THUS
        *        *.            *.****          *.****
11      END
12   END
```

The execution of this program is as follows:

1. The PRINT statement (line 3) is executed once and one blank line is "printed" (line 4).

2. The PRINT and SKIP in the HEADING section are executed.

3. Assuming a standard of 55 lines per page, the PRINT statement (line 10) is executed for N = 1,2,...50.

4. The system detects a full page, increments PAGE.V and re-executes the HEADING section.

5. The HEADING section consumes two lines of the new page; therefore, the remainder of the second page is filled with output from the PRINT statement (line 10) for N = 51,52...,103.

6. The cycle (steps 4-5) repeats until N = 1000.

7. When control passes out of the REPORT section, the HEADING is deactivated.

System Variables Related to Output

Several system-maintained variables were referred to in the above example either explicitly or implicitly. They are:

LINES.V -- The number of lines to be printed on a page. The default value is installation-dependent.

LINE.V -- The current line number (ranges from 1 to LINE.V).

PAGE.V -- The current page number. Starts at 1 by default, but may be initialized by this user. Each time a page is filled, PAGE.V is incremented by one.

Two more system variables serve to generalize the features of a REPORT section and allow them to be used throughout a program, whereas a REPORT is confined within a single routine.

PAGECOL.V -- When not set to zero (its default value), this variable serves to specify the printing of a page number on every page of output from the program. The value of the variable is the column number of the first letter of the phrase "PAGE ***."

HEADING.V -- When not zero (its default value), this variable serves to request execution of a routine every time a new page of output is started. The value of the variable is the name of the routine.

For example,

```
LET HEADING.V = 'TITLE'
```

The user must then supply a routine named TITLE.

Before concluding this section, we introduce two more features of the PRINT statement.

Until now, our use of PRINT has been confined to producing output lines no longer than the lines of source in our program (usually 80 columns). However, since printers are usually wider than 80 columns (typically 132 columns), a means is provided for specifying these long formats.

```
PRINT i DOUBLE LINES THUS
```

followed by 2i format lines will print i lines of 132-column output. The "long" lines of output will be formed from 80 columns of the first of each successive pair of cards and 52 columns of the following card in each pair. Variables and formats may be used as "single" lines. For input devices with other than 80 columns, adjustment is made by the compiler through installation or compile-time parameters. For instance, if 72-column input is the norm, then 72 + 60 columns would be used to form a double line.

On occasion it is necessary to print two or more fields of data contiguously. To accomplish this, the first asterisk of the second and successive contiguous formats is replaced by a single parallel (|). If this is not done, two contiguous formats merge into one.

```
PRINT 1 LINE WITH A AND B THUS **|*
```

assuming A and B are ALPHA (or TEXT) variables,

```
A = "AAAA" and B = "BBBB"
```

The resulting output line is

```
AABB
```

Multiple Page-width Reports (Column Repetition)

As models become more complex, it is often desirable to specify fairly general reports and allow the specific output generated to be dictated by the data structures of the program (at run time). One such possibility in SIMSCRIPT is the column repetition feature. To use this feature one specifies the format of a single page of output, and the indexing control, which (may) extend the output to multiple pages (in width). Optionally, certain information may be suppressed to be printed only on the last or right-hand page.

As an example, consider the printing of a two-dimensional matrix of a size determined during program execution. S(I,J) is a matrix of size M by N.

```
1    BEGIN REPORT PRINTING FOR J = 1 TO N,
        IN GROUPS OF 5 PER PAGE
2       BEGIN HEADING
3          PRINT 1 LINE WITH A GROUP OF
              J FIELDS THUS
           *    *    *    *    *
4          SKIP 1 OUTPUT LINE
5       END
6       FOR I = 1 TO M,
7          PRINT 1 LINE WITH I AND
              A GROUP OF X(I,J) FIELDS THUS
     *    *    *    *    *    *
8    END
```

If M is less than 54 and N is less than 6, a single page of output is produced as illustrated in Figure 8.1.

```
        1    2    3    4    5
   1    *    *    *    *    *
   2    *    *    *    *    *
   3    *    *    *    *    *
   .
   .
   .
```

Figure 8.1 - Column Repetition Illustration

However, if N were 7, an additional page of output would be produced as shown in Figure 8.2.

```
             6         7
   1         *         *
   2         *         *
   3         *         *
   .
   .
```

Figure 8.2 - Column Repetition Continuation Page

If it is desirable to print two variables intermingled, one might write:

```
PRINT 1 LINE WITH I AND A GROUP
   OF X(I,J),Y(I,J) FIELDS THUS
*  **  *.*  ** *.*  **  *.*  **  *.*  **  *.*
```

A format must be given for each output value. Furthermore, all repeated formats must agree in mode, although the width (number of characters) may differ.

It is not possible to write:

```
PRINT 1 LINE WITH A GROUP OF I FIELDS THUS
*  *.*  *  *.*
```

A final feature makes it possible to generate attractively labeled reports that have row, as well as column, summarizations, even if the reports use column repetition. This is accomplished by adding a clause to the PRINT statement that suppresses some output until all column repetition data have been printed. Our previous example, if modified as shown here, would produce a second page as shown in Figure 8.3, rather than that of Figure 8.2.

```
PRINT 1 LINE WITH I, A GROUP OF
   X(I,J) FIELDS AND SUMX(I)
   SUPPRESSING FROM COLUMN 70 THUS
*  **  **  **  **  **  ****
                       ↑
                       COLUMN 70
```

```
        6          7

1      * *        * *        ****
2      * *        * *        ****
3      * *        * *        ****
.
.
```

Figure 8.3 - Illustration of Column Suppression

8.4 Formatted Input/Output

The input/output requirements of the majority of programs can be satisfied with the free-form READ statement, the PRINT statement, and the REPORT features of the previous section.

There are occasions, however, when more elaborate mechanisms are required. For input, this would include situations where data are available, but in a form not compatible with the free-form specifications (for instance, not separated by blanks).

It is possible to specify a format for the reading of input data. It is equally possible to use the same formatting mechanism to specify the writing of output rather than to use PRINT statements.

The general form of the statements for these actions is

READ variable list AS format list

or,

WRITE arithmetic expression list AS format list

where format list is composed of the individual specifications of each data field plus any number of positioning directives.

There are six data field descriptors for describing integer (I), decimal (D), scientific (E), computer-dependent (C), alpha (A), and text (T) formats.

In addition, there are five descriptors for positioning the "pointer" to the data. These are beginning column (B), skip columns (S), start new record (/), start new page (*), and character-string delimiters (""). The later two descriptors apply only to output formats.

It is important to know the actual length of the input/output record. An attempt to read beyond the end of a record with a formatted read will cause a fatal error. An attempt to write past the end of a record will cause a new record to be started. As in the case of free-form READ statements, both formatted READ and WRITE statements start their operations at the current position in the input/output. That is, neither automatically moves to the beginning of the next record.

The data format descriptors are as follows:

The general form of the data descriptors is,

n X e

where n is an integer value specifying a number of consecutive fields. If omitted, n is understood to be 1.

X is one of the letters A, C, D, E, I, or T.

e is an expression describing the specific format.

There must be at least one blank before and after X. However, n and e may be enclosed in parentheses, in which case no space is required, i.e., (n)X(e).

The specific requirements are:

n A e (Alpha Format)

1. e may be an expression. It specifies the width of the field.
2. Characters are left-justified in a word with trailing blanks.
3. On input, if more characters are specified than can be stored, the left-most are stored and the remainder are skipped.

n C e (Computer Representation)

1. e may be an expression. It specifies the width of the field.
2. The C format is Computer-dependent (hexadecimal, octal, etc.).

n D(a,b) (Decimal Format)

1. a and b may be expressions.
2. a is the total width of the field.
3. b is the number of fractional digits.
4. A decimal point is optional in the input data field. If it is present it overrides the location implied by D. If the decimal point is omitted (on input), a decimal point is implied before the first digit of the b field.
5. The scientific format can be used for input to a D format.

n E(a,b) (Scientific Notation)

1. a and b may be expressions.
2. a is the total width of the field.
3. b is the number of fractional digits.
4. The general form of input data is

   ±XXX.XXXE±XX
5. The E format is similar to the D format. However, on input, either the E or the sign of the scale factor (power of ten) must be present.

n I e (Integer Format)

1. e may be an expression. It specifies the total width of the field.
2. On input, the system treats leading, embedded, and trailing blanks as zeros.

n T e (Text Formats)

1. e may be an expression or an *.
2. e expresses the width of the field.
3. If e is an * it specifies a special form of input, in which the next input character read is to be used as a character string delimiter.
4. e may express a format which extends over multiple input (or output) records.

The Positioning Descriptors are:

B e (Begin Column)

1. e may be an expression.
2. e is the column number at which to position the input/output device.
3. B descriptors need not be in ascending order in a format list.

S e (Skip Columns)

1. e may be an expression.
2. e is evaluated as the number of columns to skip from the present position.
3. e must be positive.

/ (Start New Record)

1. Each / skips to a new record.

* (Start New Page)

1. On output only, ejects one page.
2. In other circumstances, this descriptor is disregarded.

" " (Character String)

1. On output only, all characters are written exactly as they appear in the quotation marks.
2. A character string format must be contained within one record.

Some examples may help to clarify this maze of formats:

```
READ X, Y, AND Z AS I 3, 2 I, 2
```

Column number

```
0  0  0  0  0  0  0  0  0  1
1  2  3  4  5  6  7  8  9  0

1  6  0     3     8
```

Will assign X = 160, Y = 3, and Z = 8.

```
READ X, Y, AND Z AS I 2, 2 D(10,3)
```

Column number

```
0 0 0 0 0 0 0 0 0 0 1 1 1 1 1 1 1 1 2 2 2
1 2 3 4 5 6 7 8 9 0 1 2 3 4 5 6 7 8 9 0 1 2

- 5         1 6.8 2       2 3 6 9 3 4 9
```

will result in X = -5.0

Y = 16.82

Z = 2369.349

Note that it is assumed X, Y, and Z are of mode REAL. The integer value, 5, is converted to real on input. The value assigned to Y has an overriding decimal point punched, and the data for Z uses the format to locate the decimal point.

```
READ TEXT1 and TEXT2 as T 1, B 1, T *

Column number
0  0  0  0  0  0  0  0  0  1
1  2  3  4  5  6  7  8  9  0
$     N  A  L  I  N  $
```

This operation results in

```
TEXT1 = "$"
TEXT2 = "_NALIN"
```

Sometimes it is desirable to repeat a format a specified number of times and then start a new record. The following form permits this:

```
START NEW CARD
FOR I = 1 TO N,
   READ A(I) AS (4) I 6
```

or,

```
FOR I = 1 TO N
   READ A(I) AND B(I) AS (10)I 2, D(6,2)
```

In both examples, the reading is assumed to begin in the first column of a record. After the format has been used the number of times specified in the preceding parenthetical expression, a new record is read. The statement can terminate in the middle of a record of input.

This same concept can be applied to output. Note that the input/output statement must be under the control of a FOR phrase.

8.5 Multiple Input/Output Devices

The default conditions of SIMSCRIPT are such that we have not been concerned with the identification of input/output units. Units actually do have "logical" numbers. By default, Unit 5 is the system input device and Unit 6 is the system listing device. What physical devices these logical units are associated with is of no importance to this discussion. The actual association is made either by the system at installation or at run-time through job control parameters.

When it is necessary to address units other than the standards, the change is made thus:

```
USE e FOR INPUT
```

or,

```
USE e FOR OUTPUT
```

Several actions are taken by these statements. First, all the unit information regarding the current device is preserved. Then the previously preserved unit information for the specified device is made accessible. Unit information includes the following:

For each device,

1. The current record, contained in a buffer.

2. The last column accessed within the buffer; RCOLUMN.V for input, WCOLUMN.V for output.

3. The end-of-file flag, EOF.V (meaningful only for input).

   For an output unit, the following additional information is preserved:

4. The current line number (LINE.V).

5. The number of lines per page (LINES.V).

6. The current page number (PAGE.V).

7. The current heading routine (HEADING.V).

8. The current pagination column (PAGECOL.V).

Only the unit information about the current input or output device can be accessed by the user. When a device is selected, the information is made available by setting the system variable READ.V (for input) or WRITE.V (for output).

1. The current record:

   On input, the existence of this buffer makes it possible to "look ahead" with commands such as IF MODE IS

ALPHA or WHILE DATA IS NOT ENDED. There are also two functions which can be used to determine where the next data field starts (SFIELD.F) or ends (EFIELD.F). It is also possible to reread data contained in the buffer via the READ format "B" (setting the next column to be read back to previously read information. Note that a slash (/) format or START NEW CARD statement reinitializes the buffer to all blanks).

On output, the buffer may be modified after writing either by rewriting (via the B format) or explicitly, character by character, through use of the OUT.F function.

```
LET OUT.F(7) = "A" changes the seventh character
in the output buffer to an A.
```

```
FOR I = 1 TO 132,
   WITH OUT.F(I) = "b"
LET OUT.F(I) = "."
```

This loop will test each position in the current output buffer for existence of a blank. Each blank found will be replaced by a period.

2. The last column indicator RCOLUMN.V and WCOLUMN.V are moved by operations either of free-form or formatted input/output. They may be tested and/or changed via statements such as IF CARD IS NEW or WRITE AS B 32.

3. The end-of-file indicator.

It is possible to exercise control over end-of-file conditions via the EOF.V variable. By default, encountering an end-of-file during a READ operation is a fatal error. However, the user may specify that an end-of-file is to be processed differently. If EOF.V = 0 when an end-of-file is reached, the error condition is reported. However, if EOF.V is not zero, it is set to 2, the variables which have yet to be read are set to zero, and control passes to the statement following the READ. By testing EOF.V, the user can determine whether an end-of-file has been encountered.

4. LINE.V, LINES.V, PAGE.V

In order to change or test the values of these variables, WRITE.V must currently address the unit of interest. For example,

```
USE 8 FOR OUTPUT
LET LINES.V = 43
LET PAGE.V = 500
```

would cause output to go to unit 8 at 43 lines per page and be paginated starting from page number 500. Also, all succeeding output would be directed to unit 8.

5. HEADING.V and PAGECOL.V

A separate copy of these variables is maintained for each output unit.

A single unit can be used only for input or output at one time. If the current input unit is USEd for output, the current input unit reverts to the standard input unit (5). Similarly, USING the current output unit for input will cause the current output unit to revert to the standard output unit (5 or 6, depending on the implementation). In some implementations, more than one logical unit may address a single physical device (e.g., the terminal may be addressed as both unit 5 and unit 6 simultaneously).

8.6 Miscellaneous Input/Output Features

The REWIND statement

In order to reposition a unit at its first record, the REWIND statement is used:

```
REWIND e
```

After a unit has been rewound, it is logically disconnected, thus requiring a USE statement before subsequent input/out to (from) that unit.

The USING phrase

It is possible to specify a temporary change in input/output unit (for the duration of one statement), by appending the phrase USING UNIT e to any input/output statement. For example,

```
READ  A  USING UNIT 7
```

would cause a temporary switch to unit 7 for input and revert to the previously specified input unit afterward. If we assume unit 5 is the current input unit, this single statement is equivalent to:

```
USE 7 FOR INPUT
READ A
USE 5 FOR INPUT
```

As a matter of efficiency, this phrase should not be used excessively. For example,

```
FOR I = 1 TO 1000,
   READ A(I) USING UNIT 7
```

is much more costly than:

```
USE 7 FOR INPUT
FOR I = 1 TO 1000,
   READ A (I)
USE 5 FOR INPUT
```

since the input unit information is switched only twice rather than 2,000 times!

THE BUFFER

There are situations when input/output operations are convenient to use for data conversion, compression or expansion, even though no actual transmission to or from the program is desired. When this is desired, a virtual input/output device called "THE BUFFER" may be used. For example,

```
FOR I = 1 TO 4,
   WRITE A(I) AS A 1 USING THE BUFFER
READ NAME USING THE BUFFER
```

Assuming A and NAME are alpha variables, if the array A contains the letters, "A,B,C,D" then after execution of the above code, NAME contains the string "ABCD".

A much more exotic use of this feature is in conjunction with the initialization of random variables. In Example 6, we illustrated the use of a random step variable to select a job type from a distribution of job types (JOB.MIX). In the example, the data for initializing the random variable were read as input. If the data were either "builtin" to the program, or possibly to be derived from other data by some data reduction technique, a very simple means of initializing the final random variable is to write these data to THE BUFFER and then read them from there to form the probability distribution. For example,

```
WRITE AS ".241 1 .44 2 .32 3 *" USING THE BUFFER
READ JOB.MIX USING THE BUFFER
```

will accomplish the JOB.MIX random variable initialization.

Similarly, if the values of probability and variable were derived from computation and stored in arrays P and V, the following code would initialize the random variable:

```
USE THE BUFFER FOR OUTPUT
WRITE AS /
FOR I = 1 TO N,
   WRITE P(I) AND V(I) AS S 1, D(6,3), S 2,I 4
WRITE AS S 2, "*"
READ JOB.MIX USING THE BUFFER
```

In this example, one possible problem exists in that the BUFFER is a single "record" of a given size; if that size is exceeded on output, it "wraps around," overwriting previously inserted data. The length of the buffer is contained in a system variable, BUFFER.V. By default, this variable is initialized to 132. In order to have a different buffer size, one must assign a different value to BUFFER.V prior to its first use (READ, WRITE, or USE statement).

Input/Output of BINARY Information

When data are to be recorded for later processing, and no "human readable" form is required, a very efficient mechanism exists for writing to and reading from input/output units which store binary information (tapes, discs, etc.). In place of a format, the phrase "AS BINARY" in a READ or WRITE statement is all that is required. Of course, the physical device must be capable of storing information in this form. (Not the terminal, card reader, or printer!)

The EXTERNAL Process or Event

In light of the preceding discussion of input/output, it is relatively simple to see now how data are preserved ror externally triggered processes or events.

Each EXTERNAL EVENT UNIT is a logical input unit. Thus it has its own buffer, EOF.V, RCOLUMN.V, and all the other previously specified unit information.

When a process or event is selected for execution, the system examines an attribute of the process notice to determine how the process was triggered. If this attribute, EUNIT.A, is not zero, the process has been triggered externally. The value of EUNIT.A is transferred to READ.V, thus automatically reestablishing the input conditions which existed when the externally triggered process was created. After the first return to the system (timing routine), the EUNIT.A attribute is used to read the next process name and activation time, then EUNIT.A is set to zero, so that subsequent reactivations will be treated as internally generated.

Chapter 9

MODEL VERIFICATION AND DEBUGGING

9.0 Introduction

There comes a time when one must say that the computer program is "finished," make it perform as it is intended to, and then convince oneself (and perhaps others) that it actually does perform correctly.

In a high-level language, such as SIMSCRIPT, the user is quite far removed from the details of machine instruction/hardware. This is as it should be. The purpose of this chapter is to aid the user in taking advantage of all the information available from the SIMSCRIPT compiler, the loader, the run-time library, and other special mechanisms that are convenient for general "debugging."

9.1 Compiler Aids to Debugging

The first (and perhaps foremost) debugging aid produced by the compiler is a complete listing of the source program. Embedded in this listing are messages describing errors detected by the compiler. These errors range from simple spelling mistakes to fairly complex modelling logic flaws.

Along with the source listing of each routine is a local variable or cross-reference listing. This listing should always be scanned for any surprises. In some contexts, a misspelled variable is not recognized as such and becomes a local variable. The compiler will recognize this fact and flag the variable in the cross-reference as a "stray name" or "sole reference" (assuming it appears only once in the program). In other cases, the cross-reference map helps to clarify how a name has been understood -- for example, as an entity reference, the global variable with the same name as the entity or a local variable with the same name as the entity. Even the references that do not appear, i.e., the implied subscripts, are cross-referenced.

An example of a source listing, complete with errors and cross-references is shown in Figure 9.1.

The routine (lifted from Example 4) has four error messages. The first message is a syntax error caused by the misspelling of a symbol from a DEFINE TO MEAN. (.DOCK.IS.NOT.FULL had a missing period.) When an error is detected in a statement, that statement is removed from the program and compilation/error scanning continues. When an error is detected, however, it is not necessarily obvious where the next statement begins! This is the consequence of two aspects of SIMSCRIPT. First, the lack of an explicit statement delimiter, and second, the fact that keywords are not reserved words. If the user has variables with the same spelling as some key word, additional extraneous error messages can be expected until the keyword which begins the next statement is found. Since the statement in error is removed, other statements which depend on it may now be erroneous also. In our example (Figure 9.1), the ELSE and ALWAYS (lines 18 and 33) depended upon the IF at line 4. But the ALWAYS at line 17 (which should have matched the IF at line 5) was taken as the end of the IF at line 4. Therefore, lines 18 and 33 were dropped erroneously! The final error message comes at the end of the program because a DO (line 8) was never matched with a LOOP.

In addition to the source listing, three more listings are available.

```
                                   CACI SIMSCRIPT II.5 IBM S/370 R9.1        PAGE     2
OPTIONS  TERM                                                 09-NOV-1982 14:59 (   1)

    1  ROUTINE HARBOR.MASTER GIVEN ACTION YIELDING STATUS
    2     DEFINE ACTION AND STATUS AS INTEGER VARIABLES
    3     DEFINE NEW.SHIP AND OTHER.SHIP AS INTEGER VARIABLES
    4     IF ACTION = .ARRIVING
    5        IF .DOCK.IS.NOT FULL,
**** ERROR OF TYPE 1001 INVOLVING 'IF' AT STATEMENT     5.
    6           IF DOCK IS NOT EMPTY,
    7              FOR EACH OTHER.SHIP AT DOCK,
    8              DO
    9                 INTERRUPT SHIP CALLED OTHER.SHIP
   10                 LET TIME.A(OTHER.SHIP) = TIME.A(OTHER.SHIP) * 2.0
   11                 RESUME SHIP CALLED OTHER.SHIP
   12           ELSE
   13              LET UNLOADING.TIME(SHIP) = UNLOADING.TIME(SHIP) / 2.0
   14           ALWAYS
   15           FILE THIS SHIP IN DOCK
   16           LET STATUS = .OK
   17        ALWAYS
   18     ELSE
**** ERROR OF TYPE 1008 AT STATEMENT    18.
   19        IF QUEUE IS NOT EMPTY,
   20           REMOVE THE FIRST SHIP FROM QUEUE
   21           FILE THIS SHIP IN DOCK
   22           REACTIVATE THIS SHIP NOW
   23        ELSE
   24           IF DOCK IS NOT EMPTY,
   25              FOR EACH OTHER.SHIP AT DOCK,
   26              DO
   27                 INTERRUPT SHIP CALLED OTHER.SHIP
   28                 LET TIME.A(OTHER.SHIP) = TIME.A(OTHER.SHIP) / 2.0
   29                 RESUME SHIP CALLED OTHER.SHIP
   30              LOOP
   31           ALWAYS
   32        ALWAYS
   33     ALWAYS
**** ERROR OF TYPE 1008 AT STATEMENT    33.
   34     RETURN
   35  END
**** ERROR OF TYPE 1022 AT STATEMENT     8.
```

Figure 9.1 - A Routine from Example 4 (with Compilation Errors)

```
ROUTINE HARBOR.MASTER          CACI SIMSCRIPT II.5 IBM S/370 R9.1        PAGE    3
OPTIONS   TERM                                              09-NOV-1982 14:59 (   1)
```

C R O S S - R E F E R E N C E

NAME	TYPE			MODE	LINE NUMBERS OF REFERENCES					
.ARRIVING	DEFINE TO MEAN				4					
.OK	DEFINE TO MEAN				16					
ACTION	ARGUMENT	NO.	1	INTEGER	1	2	4			
DOCK	SET				6	7	15	21	24	25
HARBOR.MASTER	ROUTINE			INTEGER	1					
NEW.SHIP	RECURSIVE VARIABLE	WORD	1	INTEGER	3					
OTHER.SHIP	RECURSIVE VARIABLE	WORD	2	INTEGER	3	7*	9*	10*	11*	25*
					28*	29*				
QUEUE	SET				19	20				
SHIP	PROCESS NOTICE				9	11	22	27	29	
	+ GLOBAL VARIABLE			INTEGER	13*	15	20	21	22*	
STATUS	ARGUMENT	NO.	2	INTEGER	1	2	16			
TIME.A	TEMPORARY ATTRIBUTE	WORD	3	DOUBLE	10*	11	28*	29		
TIME.V	PERMANENT ATTRIBUTE	SYS	41	DOUBLE	11	29				
UNLOADING.TIME	TEMPORARY ATTRIBUTE	AUTO		REAL	13*					

```
                 0 WARNINGS,     4 ERRORS IN ROUTINE HARBOR.MASTER
                                       DISTRIBUTED AS FOLLOWS...
1 INSTANCES OF TYPE 1001: WORD DOES NOT CONFORM TO STATEMENT SYNTAX,
                          OR STATEMENT IS NOT ALLOWED IN THIS PART OF THE PROGRAM
2 INSTANCES OF TYPE 1008: ELSE OR ALWAYS STATEMENT WITHOUT A MATCHING IF.
1 INSTANCES OF TYPE 1022: DO WITHOUT A MATCHING LOOP.

 1 ROUTINES CONTAIN ERRORS
```

Figure 9.1 - A Routine from Example 4 (Continued)

The STAR listing (Figure 9.2) is produced after the compiler has performed the substitutions dictated by any DEFINE TO MEAN or SUBSTITUTE statements (a very handy listing if you must debug someone else's program). In addition, the computer instruction address (offset from beginning of routine) is printed on each line. This is not often used by modellers.

The ALLSTARS listing (Figure 9.3) illustrates how the SIMSCRIPT compiler works. Lines with multiple asterisks are generated from the preceding single asterisk (star) line until the sequence consists only of IF, CALL, LET, and GO TO statements. The compiler then generates the assembly language of the target computer (shown in Figure 9.4). The ALLSTARS and LIST listings are rarely used by modellers. They might be of interest to those who wish to understand compiler operation better, or in some circumstances when it is unclear exactly how a certain sequence of statements is compiled. Another use might be to compare the code generated by two equivalent sequences for efficiency considerations.

9.2 Resolving Loader Name Conflicts

The next step after producing a "clean compile" is to load and run the program. The Loader (variously called linkage editor, collector, mapper, ...) is an operating system-supplied mechanism and differs somewhat for the various implementations of SIMSCRIPT. In this section, our main interest is the error messages the loader produces for either duplicate or missing routines. Missing routines can be detected either when a routine name has been spelled incorrectly (e.g., in a CALL statement) or when a routine really has been omitted. The compiler can detect many inconsistencies such as a reference to a process not defined in the preamble, but it cannot detect a missing process or subroutine because separate compilation of routines is supported, and therefore it is not possible to detect the absence of a properly referenced routine until "load time."

```
*   ROUTINE HARBOR.MASTER GIVEN ACTION YIELDING STATUS
*   DEFINE ACTION AND STATUS AS INTEGER VARIABLES
*   DEFINE NEW.SHIP AND OTHER.SHIP AS INTEGER VARIABLES
*   IF ACTION = 1
*   IF N.DOCK < 2,
*   IF DOCK IS NOT EMPTY,
*   FOR EACH OTHER.SHIP AT DOCK,
*   DO
*   INTERRUPT SHIP CALLED OTHER.SHIP
*   LET TIME.A(OTHER.SHIP) = TIME.A(OTHER.SHIP) * 2.0
*   RESUME SHIP CALLED OTHER.SHIP
*   LOOP
*   ELSE
*   LET UNLOADING.TIME(SHIP) = UNLOADING.TIME(SHIP) / 2.0
*   ALWAYS
*   FILE THIS SHIP IN DOCK
*   LET STATUS = 1
*   ALWAYS
*   ELSE
*   IF QUEUE IS NOT EMPTY,
*   REMOVE THE FIRST SHIP FROM QUEUE
*   FILE THIS SHIP IN DOCK
*   REACTIVATE THIS SHIP NOW
*   ELSE
*   IF DOCK IS NOT EMPTY,
*   FOR EACH OTHER.SHIP AT DOCK,
*   DO
*   INTERRUPT SHIP CALLED OTHER.SHIP
*   LET TIME.A(OTHER.SHIP) = TIME.A(OTHER.SHIP) / 2.0
*   RESUME SHIP CALLED OTHER.SHIP
*   LOOP
*   ALWAYS
*   ALWAYS
*   ALWAYS
*   RETURN
*   END
```

Figure 9.2 - The "STAR" Listing of Example 4 (Extract)

```
*    ROUTINE HARBOR.MASTER GIVEN ACTION YIELDING STATUS
*    DEFINE ACTION AND STATUS AS INTEGER VARIABLES
*    DEFINE NEW.SHIP AND OTHER.SHIP AS INTEGER VARIABLES
*    IF ACTION = 1
*    IF N.DOCK < 2,
*    IF DOCK IS NOT EMPTY,
**   THEN IF F.DOCK NE 0
*    FOR EACH OTHER.SHIP AT DOCK,
**   LET OTHER.SHIP = F.DOCK
**   GO L.3
**   ' L.1 '
**   DEFINE L.4 AS RECURSIVE 0 - DIM INTEGER VARIABLE
**   LET OTHER.SHIP = L.4
**   ' L.3 '
**   IF OTHER.SHIP ZERO
**   GO L.2
**   ENDIF
**   LET L.4 = S.DOCK(OTHER.SHIP)
*    DO
*    INTERRUPT SHIP CALLED OTHER.SHIP
**   CANCEL THE SHIP CALLED OTHER.SHIP
***  CALL Z.EV.S(INT.F(OTHER.SHIP), I.SHIP)
**   LET TIME.A(OTHER.SHIP) = TIME.A(OTHER.SHIP) - TIME.V
**   LET STA.A(OTHER.SHIP) = 3
*    LET TIME.A(OTHER.SHIP) = TIME.A(OTHER.SHIP) * 2.0
*    RESUME SHIP CALLED OTHER.SHIP
**   CAUSE THE SHIP CALLED OTHER.SHIP AT TIME.V + TIME.A(OTHER.SHIP)
***  LET TIME.A(INT.F(OTHER.SHIP)) =(TIME.V + TIME.A(OTHER.SHIP))
***  CALL T.EV.S(INT.F(OTHER.SHIP), I.SHIP)
**   LET STA.A(OTHER.SHIP) = 1
*    LOOP
**   GO L.1
**   ' L.2 '
*    ELSE
*    LET UNLOADING.TIME(SHIP) = UNLOADING.TIME(SHIP) / 2.0
*    ALWAYS
*    FILE THIS SHIP IN DOCK
**   CALL U.DOCK(INT.F(SHIP))
*    LET STATUS = 1
*    ALWAYS
```

Figure 9.3 - The "ALLSTARS" Listing of Example 4 (Extract)

```
ALLSTARS LISTING

EXTERNALS
OFFSET  EXT.NAME  FULL NAME
     0  GN$DOCK   GN$DOCK
     4  GF$DOCK   GF$DOCK
     8  GS$DOCK   GS$DOCK
    12  GI$SHIP   GI$SHIP
    16  HZ$EV$S   HZ$EV$S
    20  HT$EV$S   HT$EV$S
    24  GSHIP     GSHIP
    28  GUNLOADI  GUNLOADING$TIME
    32  RU$DOCK   RU$DOCK
    36  GF$QUEUE  GF$QUEUE
    40  RX$QUEUE  RX$QUEUE
    44  HU$EV$S   HU$EV$S

                        RHARBOR$  CSECT
0000 902F B008                    STM    2,15,    8(11)
0004 47F0 F020                    BC    15,  32( 0,15) ; 01$
0008 D9C8C1D9                     DC    CL4'RHAR'
000C C2D6D95B                     DC    CL4'BOR$'
0010                    $ADTCONS  EQU   *
0010 00107A00                     DC    X'00107A00'
0014 000003D8                     DC    F'          984'
0018 00000448                     DC    F'         1096'
001C 00000000                     DC    F'            0'
0020                    01$       EQU   *
0020 18AF                         LR    10,15
0022 5890 A014                    L      9,  20( 0,10) ; $ADTCONS
0026 18CB                         LR    12,11
0028 41B0 C058                    LA    11,  88( 0,12)
002C 59B0 D168                    C     11, 360( 0,13)
0030 4720 D16C                    BC     2, 364( 0,13)
0034 2F66                         SWR    6, 6
0036 7060 B004                    STE    6,   4( 0,11)
```

Figure 9.4 - The "LIST" Listing of Example 4 (Extract)

```
003A 1881                    LR    8, 1
003C 9502 C004               CLI     4(12),X'02'
0040 4770 D188               BC    7, 392( 0,13)
0044 6060 C040               STD   6,  64( 0,12)
0048 6060 C048               STD   6,  72( 0,12)
004C 7060 8004               STE   6,   4( 0, 8)
                  *   ROUTINE HARBOR.MASTER GIVEN ACTION YIELDING STATUS
                  *   DEFINE ACTION AND STATUS AS INTEGER VARIABLES
                  *   DEFINE NEW.SHIP AND OTHER.SHIP AS INTEGER VARIABLES
                  *   IF ACTION = 1
0050 5820 8000               L      2,   0( 0, 8)
0054 5920 9008               C      2,   8( 0, 9) ;
0058 48F0 9050               LH    15,  80( 0, 9) ; $LABELS
005C 477A F000               BC     7,   0(10,15)
                  *   IF N.DOCK < 2,
0060 5820 901C               L      2,  28( 0, 9) ; $EXTRNS
0064 5820 2000               L      2,   0( 0, 2)
0068 5920 900C               C      2,  12( 0, 9) ;
006C 48F0 9052               LH    15,  82( 0, 9) ; $LABELS
0070 47BA F000               BC    11,   0(10,15)
                  *   IF DOCK IS NOT EMPTY,
                  **  THEN IF F.DOCK NE 0
0074 5820 9020               L      2,  32( 0, 9) ; $EXTRNS
0078 5820 2000               L      2,   0( 0, 2)
007C 1222                    LTR    2, 2
007E 48F0 9054               LH    15,  84( 0, 9) ; $LABELS
0082 478A F000               BC     8,   0(10,15)
                  *   FOR EACH OTHER.SHIP AT DOCK,
                  **  LET OTHER.SHIP = F.DOCK
0086 5820 9020               L      2,  32( 0, 9) ; $EXTRNS
008A 5820 2000               L      2,   0( 0, 2)
008E 5020 C044               ST     2,  68( 0,12)
                  **  GO L.3
0092 48F0 9056               LH    15,  86( 0, 9) ; $LABELS
0096 47FA F000               BC    15,   0(10,15)
                  **  ' L.1 '
                  **  DEFINE L.4 AS RECURSIVE 0 - DIM INTEGER VARIABLE
                  **  LET OTHER.SHIP = L.4
009A 5820 C048               L      2,  72( 0,12)
```

Figure 9.4 - The "LIST" Listing of Example 4 (Continued)

The other problem which is detectable at load time is that of duplicate routines. There are many well-known causes for duplicate routines, such as file collection problems, careless handling of source files, and making a temporary copy of a routine and forgetting to delete the original. The more subtle problem in SIMSCRIPT is the automatic generation of duplicate names through truncation to meet loader name restrictions. SIMSCRIPT allows very long names of routines, variables, attributes, etc. In fact, the only restriction on name length is the requirement that a name, keyword or constant be contained within a single record in the source program. This usually then restricts names to 80 characters!

However, these names are automatically truncated during compilation to satisfy the loader restrictions. To further complicate matters, SIMSCRIPT generates a number of names of attributes, global variables, and routines by prefixing from 1 to 5 characters to a user-supplied name.

A compiler enhancement is available on some implementations and is under development on others, which eliminates this problem. The names which conflict are translated into new names internally, but will be preserved for proper identification in error handling (next section). Where this enhancement is not available, the following procedure is suggested.

When it is determined that a duplicate name problem is caused by system truncation of names, insert a DEFINE TO MEAN in the preamble for one of each pair of duplicate names. The new name must differ from the old name in the first few (implementation dependent) characters.

For example, the following preamble fragment will produce duplicates on systems for which the loader names are eight characters (or less).

```
PREAMBLE
   PROCESSES
      EVERY TRACKING.MODULE
         HAS A TM.TRACK
         AND A TM.TRACKER
      EVERY TRACKER
         HAS A TK.TRACKING.MODULE
         AND A TK.TRACK
```

Three DEFINE TO MEAN statements will resolve the name conflicts. For example,

```
DEFINE TM.TRACK TO MEAN 1TM.TRACK
DEFINE TK.TRACK TO MEAN 1TK.TRACK
DEFINE TRACKER TO MEAN 1TRACKER
```

when inserted prior to any use of these names in the preamble will completely solve the problem.

Actually, many more duplicates would have been reported by the loader for all the names of routines or attributes generated from a process name (see Appendix D for the generated names and the specific user manual for the specific name restrictions, if any).

Another solution to the name conflict problem for attributes, is to assign specific word numbers to them (see Section 5.7). For example,

```
PREAMBLE
   DEFINE TRACKER TO MEAN 1TRACKER
   PROCESSES
      EVERY TRACKING.MODULE
         HAS A TM.TRACK IN WORD 7
         AND A TM.TRACKER IN WORD 8
      EVERY TRACKER
         HAS A TK.TRACK IN WORD 7
         AND A TK.TRACKING.MODULE IN WORD 8
```

The actual allowable placement is implementation-dependent (and diagnosed accordingly). In particular, the first several words of a process notice are reserved for system-defined attributes.

One note of caution with the use of DEFINE TO MEAN to resolve name conflicts: SIMSCRIPT derives many names from a PREAMBLE name. For example, a resource or permanent entity has an associated global variable N.entity. If the name of the entity is changed, this variable is also changed. This poses no difficulty unless the derived variable is referenced explicitly in the program.

For example, if a resource TELLER is for some reason renamed 1TELLER through a DEFINE TO MEAN, then the global variable associated with it becomes N.1TELLER and references to N.TELLER will be meaningless.

9.3 Run-Time Debugging Aids

When all compiler and loader detected errors have been corrected, there remains one last (and major) step; i.e., running the program. Many errors cannot be detected until the program is run because of the complex interrelationships of computations and data dependencies.

When a run-time error is detected in SIMSCRIPT, several actions are taken automatically. First, an error message is printed stating what error condition was found. Second, a program traceback is printed. Third, the values of several important system variables are printed. Finally, a call is made to a user-supplied routine to enable more information to be printed. (If this routine is not present, the program simply terminates.)

Error Message

There are over 100 separate messages describing error conditions that may arise during a SIMSCRIPT run. A dictionary of all the error messages is printed in each user manual. However, when an error is detected, the text of the relevant error is printed.

Traceback

A traceback is printed to pinpoint precisely where and under what circumstances the error occurred. This traceback starts from the routine where the error was detected. (Sometimes this will be a library or system routine and the traceback information about it will be of no value to the user.) Each traceback block will display the routine name and the precise line number on which the error occurred. The arguments to the routine and local variables are printed next. Some implementations provide the names of those variables. In others, the local variable values may be correlated with their source program name by referring to the cross-reference map for the routine. Then the same information is printed concerning the routine which called that routine, and so on, until the MAIN routine is reached in this "ascendancy tree."

System Conditions

Much useful information is available from SIMSCRIPT system-maintained variables. This includes simulation-related information such as the current simulated time (TIME.V), the contents of the "pending list" (EV.S). In addition, there is useful information on the current state of the dynamic storage and the input/output units. One implementation even produces a printout of all PREAMBLE-defined variables.

The entire debugging mechanism will now be illustrated by returning to Example 4.

9.4 Example 9: The Harbor Model Revisited

In the development of Example 4, a subtle error was introduced, which will serve to illustrate all the features of debugging presented thus far. The model (with errors) is shown in Figure 9.5. The error message and standard system output are shown in Figure 9.6.

The error is a rather typical one for the novice SIMSCRIPT user. The message indicates that an attempt has been made to file an entity in a set of which it is already a member.

```
                              CACI SIMSCRIPT II.5 IBM S/370 R9.1        PAGE     1
OPTIONS   TERM                                              03-NOV-1982 20:20 (   1)

      ''  EXAMPLE 9  --  A HARBOR MODEL (EXAMPLE 4 REVISITED)

   1  PREAMBLE
   2     PROCESSES INCLUDE SCHEDULER AND STOP.SIM
   3        EVERY SHIP HAS AN UNLOADING.TIME
   4           AND MAY BELONG TO THE QUEUE
   5           AND MAY BELONG TO THE DOCK
   6        DEFINE UNLOADING.TIME AS A REAL VARIABLE
   7     THE SYSTEM OWNS THE QUEUE AND THE DOCK
   8     ACCUMULATE MAXQ AS THE MAXIMUM,
   9        MEANQ AS THE MEAN OF N.QUEUE
  10     TALLY NUMBER.OF.SHIPS AS THE NUMBER,
  11        MINCT AS THE MINIMUM,
  12        MAXCT AS THE MAXIMUM
  13        AND MEANCT AS THE MEAN OF CYCLE.TIME
  14     DEFINE CYCLE.TIME AS A REAL VARIABLE
  15
  16     DEFINE .DOCK.IS.NOT.FULL TO MEAN N.DOCK < 2
  17     DEFINE .ARRIVING TO MEAN 1
  18     DEFINE .LEAVING TO MEAN 2
  19     DEFINE .OK TO MEAN 1
  20     DEFINE .NOT.OK TO MEAN 0
  21  END
```

C R O S S - R E F E R E N C E

NAME	TYPE		MODE	LINE NUMBERS OF REFERENCES	
.ARRIVING	DEFINE TO MEAN			17	
.DOCK.IS.NOT.FULL	DEFINE TO MEAN			16	
.LEAVING	DEFINE TO MEAN			18	
.NOT.OK	DEFINE TO MEAN			20	
.OK	DEFINE TO MEAN			19	
CYCLE.TIME	GLOBAL VARIABLE		REAL	13	14
DOCK	SET			5	7
MAXCT	GLOBAL VARIABLE		DOUBLE	12	
MAXQ	GLOBAL VARIABLE		DOUBLE	8	
MEANCT	ROUTINE		DOUBLE	13	
MEANQ	ROUTINE		DOUBLE	9	
MINCT	GLOBAL VARIABLE		DOUBLE	11	
N.QUEUE	PERMANENT ATTRIBUTE		INTEGER	9	
NUMBER.OF.SHIPS	GLOBAL VARIABLE		DOUBLE	10	
QUEUE	SET			4	7
SCHEDULER	PROCESS NOTICE			2	
SHIP	PROCESS NOTICE			3	
STOP.SIM	PROCESS NOTICE			2	
UNLOADING.TIME	TEMPORARY ATTRIBUTE	AUTO	REAL	3	6

Figure 9.5 - Example 9: The Harbor Model With Errors

```
                                   CACI SIMSCRIPT II.5 IBM S/370 R9.1        PAGE    2
OPTIONS   TERM                                         03-NOV-1982 20:20 (   1)

     1   MAIN
     2      ACTIVATE A SCHEDULER NOW
     3      ACTIVATE A STOP.SIM IN 80 DAYS
     4      START SIMULATION
     5   END
```

C R O S S - R E F E R E N C E

NAME	TYPE	MODE	LINE NUMBERS OF REFERENCES
SCHEDULER	PROCESS NOTICE		2
	+ GLOBAL VARIABLE	INTEGER	2*
STOP.SIM	PROCESS NOTICE		3
	+ GLOBAL VARIABLE	INTEGER	3*

```
                                   CACI SIMSCRIPT II.5 IBM S/370 R9.1        PAGE    3
OPTIONS   TERM                                         03-NOV-1982 20:20 (   1)

     1   PROCESS SCHEDULER
     2      UNTIL TIME.V > 80,
     3         DO
     4         ACTIVATE A SHIP NOW
     5         WAIT EXPONENTIAL.F(4/3,1) DAYS
     6         LOOP
     7   END
```

C R O S S - R E F E R E N C E

NAME	TYPE			MODE	LINE NUMBERS OF REFERENCES	
EXPONENTIAL.F	ROUTINE			DOUBLE	5	
PROCESS.V	PERMANENT ATTRIBUTE	SYS	73	INTEGER	7*	
SCHEDULER	PROCESS NOTICE				1	7
	+ GLOBAL VARIABLE			INTEGER	1	
SHIP	PROCESS NOTICE				4	
	+ GLOBAL VARIABLE			INTEGER	4*	
TIME.V	PERMANENT ATTRIBUTE	SYS	41	DOUBLE	2	

Figure 9.5 - Example 9 (Continued)

```
OPTIONS   TERM                 CACI SIMSCRIPT II.5 IBM S/370 R9.1        PAGE    4
                                                  03-NOV-1982 20:20 (    1)

    1  PROCESS SHIP
    2     DEFINE STATUS AS AN INTEGER VARIABLE
    3     DEFINE ARRIVE.TIME AS A REAL VARIABLE
    4     LET ARRIVE.TIME = TIME.V
    5     LET UNLOADING.TIME(SHIP) = UNIFORM.F(0.5,1.5,2)
    6     CALL HARBOR.MASTER GIVING .ARRIVING YIELDING STATUS
    7     IF STATUS = .NOT.OK,
    8        FILE SHIP IN QUEUE
    9        SUSPEND
   10     ALWAYS
   11     WORK UNLOADING.TIME(SHIP) DAYS
   12     REMOVE THIS SHIP FROM THE DOCK
   13     LET CYCLE.TIME = TIME.V - ARRIVE.TIME
   14     CALL HARBOR.MASTER GIVING .LEAVING YIELDING STATUS
   15  END
```

C R O S S - R E F E R E N C E

NAME	TYPE			MODE	LINE NUMBERS OF REFERENCES			
.ARRIVING	DEFINE TO MEAN				6			
.LEAVING	DEFINE TO MEAN				14			
.NOT.OK	DEFINE TO MEAN				7			
ARRIVE.TIME	RECURSIVE VARIABLE	WORD	2	REAL	3	4	13	
CYCLE.TIME	GLOBAL VARIABLE			REAL	13			
DOCK	SET				12			
HARBOR.MASTER	ROUTINE			INTEGER	6	14		
PROCESS.V	PERMANENT ATTRIBUTE	SYS	73	INTEGER	15			
QUEUE	SET				8			
SHIP	PROCESS NOTICE				1	15		
	+ GLOBAL VARIABLE			INTEGER	1	5	8	11
STATUS	RECURSIVE VARIABLE	WORD	1	INTEGER	2	6	7	14
TIME.V	PERMANENT ATTRIBUTE	SYS	41	DOUBLE	4	13		
UNIFORM.F	ROUTINE			DOUBLE	5			
UNLOADING.TIME	TEMPORARY ATTRIBUTE	AUTO		REAL	5	11		

Figure 9.5 - Example 9 (Continued)

OPTIONS TERM

```
  1  ROUTINE HARBOR.MASTER GIVEN ACTION YIELDING STATUS
  2     DEFINE ACTION AND STATUS AS INTEGER VARIABLES
  3     IF ACTION = .ARRIVING
  4        IF .DOCK.IS.NOT.FULL,
  5           IF DOCK IS NOT EMPTY,
  6              LET SHIP = F.DOCK
  7              INTERRUPT SHIP
  8              LET TIME.A(SHIP) = TIME.A(SHIP) * 2.0
  9              RESUME SHIP
 10           ELSE
 11              LET UNLOADING.TIME(SHIP) = UNLOADING.TIME(SHIP) / 2.0
 12           ALWAYS
 13           FILE THIS SHIP IN DOCK
 14           LET STATUS = .OK
 15        ELSE
 16           LET STATUS = .NOT.OK
 17        ALWAYS
 18     ELSE  ''ACTION IS .LEAVING
 19        IF QUEUE IS NOT EMPTY,
 20           REMOVE THE FIRST SHIP FROM QUEUE
 21           FILE THIS SHIP IN DOCK
 22           REACTIVATE THE SHIP NOW
 23        ELSE
 24           IF DOCK IS NOT EMPTY,
 25                 LET SHIP = F.DOCK
 26                 INTERRUPT SHIP
 27                 LET TIME.A(SHIP) = TIME.A(SHIP) / 2.0
 28                 RESUME SHIP
 29           ALWAYS
 30        ALWAYS
 31     ALWAYS
 32     RETURN
 33   END
```

C R O S S - R E F E R E N C E

NAME	TYPE			MODE	LINE NUMBERS OF REFERENCES			
.ARRIVING	DEFINE TO MEAN				3			
.DOCK.IS.NOT.FULL	DEFINE TO MEAN				4			
.NOT.OK	DEFINE TO MEAN				16			
.OK	DEFINE TO MEAN				14			
ACTION	ARGUMENT	NO.	1	INTEGER	1	2	3	
DOCK	SET				5	13	21	24
F.DOCK	PERMANENT ATTRIBUTE			INTEGER	6	25		
HARBOR.MASTER	ROUTINE			INTEGER	1			
N.DOCK	PERMANENT ATTRIBUTE			INTEGER	4			
QUEUE	SET				19	20		
SHIP	PROCESS NOTICE				7	9	22	26
	+ GLOBAL VARIABLE			INTEGER	6	7*	8*	9*
					21	22*	25	26*
STATUS	ARGUMENT	NO.	2	INTEGER	1	2	14	16
TIME.A	TEMPORARY ATTRIBUTE	WORD	3	DOUBLE	8*	9	27*	28
TIME.V	PERMANENT ATTRIBUTE	SYS	41	DOUBLE	9	28		
UNLOADING.TIME	TEMPORARY ATTRIBUTE	AUTO		REAL	11*			

Figure 9.5 - Example 9 (Continued)

```
                                    CACI SIMSCRIPT II.5 IBM S/370 R9.1       PAGE    6
OPTIONS  TERM                                            03-NOV-1982 20:20 (   1)

   1  PROCESS STOP.SIM
   2     PRINT 5 LINES WITH NUMBER.OF.SHIPS,TIME.V,MINCT,MAXCT AND MEANCT
   3        AS FOLLOWS
                SHIP AND CRANE MODEL
       * SHIPS WERE UNLOADED IN   *.** DAYS
     THE MINIMUM TIME TO UNLOAD A SHIP WAS    *.***
      "  MAXIMUM   "  "     "    "  "   "     *.***
      "  MEAN     "  "     "    "  "   "      *.***
   4     SKIP 3 LINES
   5     PRINT 2 LINES WITH MEANQ AND MAXQ THUS
     THE AVERAGE QUEUE OF SHIPS WAITING TO BE UNLOADED WAS    *.***
     THE MAXIMUM QUEUE WAS    *
   6     STOP
   7  END
```

```
                                C R O S S - R E F E R E N C E

  NAME                    TYPE                             MODE     LINE NUMBERS OF REFERENCES

MAXCT                GLOBAL VARIABLE                     DOUBLE     2
MAXQ                 GLOBAL VARIABLE                     DOUBLE     5
MEANCT               ROUTINE                             DOUBLE     2
MEANQ                ROUTINE                             DOUBLE     5
MINCT                GLOBAL VARIABLE                     DOUBLE     2
NUMBER.OF.SHIPS      GLOBAL VARIABLE                     DOUBLE     2
PROCESS.V            PERMANENT ATTRIBUTE     SYS 73      INTEGER    7*
STOP.SIM             PROCESS NOTICE                                 1        7
                   + GLOBAL VARIABLE                     INTEGER    1
TIME.V               PERMANENT ATTRIBUTE     SYS 41      DOUBLE     2
UIB.W                IMPLIED SUBSCRIPT       SYS 52      INTEGER    4
```

Figure 9.5 - Example 9 (Continued)

25e output in Figure 9.6 was generated from the implementation for the IBM computers. The output from other implementations will be formatted differently. Each User Manual has an example of the traceback information produced for that system.

From Figure 9.6, we can determine where the error occurred (or at least where it was first detected). In the traceback, the first routine mentioned is U.DOCK. U.DOCK is a routine generated from the PREAMBLE to support the DOCK set. Although more information is displayed about this routine, we can ignore it for now. We see that this routine was called from a routine "HARBOR.MASTER." (The rules for name prefixing and truncation are system-dependent and are contained in each User Manual.) In particular, the call to U.DOCK occurred on line 13 of HARBOR.MASTER Examination of the source program listing reveals this to be a FILE statement. From the location in HARBOR.MASTER, we deduce that we are processing an arriving ship. How can an arriving ship already be in the DOCK? (It can't!) Closer inspection of the HARBOR.MASTER routine reveals some confusion about the use of the SHIP variable. The argument to the routine contained a reference to the arriving ship. However, at line 6, this same variable was changed to now refer to another ship (the one already in the dock). In the corrected version in Example 4, another local variable, OTHER.SHIP, was introduced to reference the ship in the dock. The remainder of the traceback is not needed in this example.

The Simulation Summary in Figure 9.6 displays some interesting information. It shows the current simulation time, TIME.V = .1046... In addition, EVENT.V contains the priority class of the current event (process). From the PREAMBLE (and a review of Section 6.2, if necessary),

```
****** SIMSCRIPT II.5 ERROR 2006

****ATTEMPT TO FILE AN ENTITY IN A SET IT IS ALREADY IN

                    * * * S T A R T   O F   T R A C E B A C K * * *

        ERROR IN:
U.DOCK
        LOCATION 00013B78  OFFSET 0078 FROM LOAD POINT 00013B00
        REGISTER SAVE AREA AT: 0001F198

 F0-F6    40947CB1D6C11CD2  40947CB1D6C11CD2  4110000000000000  0000000000000000
 R2-R7                      00000001 0000003C 00000000 00714600 00000000 000143A0
 R8-R15  0001F148 00013C40 00013B00 0001F198 0001F150 0001B9F8 60013B78 00015648

         1 GIVEN AND  0 YIELD ARGUMENTS:
        E.1                                140436      INTEGER     00022494

        LOCAL RECURSIVE VARIABLES:
        E.2                                     0      INTEGER     00000000

        CALLED FROM:
 HARBOR.MASTER
        LOCATION 00014D4E  OFFSET 01DE FROM LOAD POINT 00014B70    IN LINE    13
        REGISTER SAVE AREA AT: 0001F150
         1 GIVEN AND  1 YIELD ARGUMENTS:
        ACTION                                  1      INTEGER     00000001
        STATUS                                  0      INTEGER     00000000

        CALLED FROM:
SHIP
        LOCATION 00014920  OFFSET 00E0 FROM LOAD POINT 00014840    IN LINE     7
        REGISTER SAVE AREA AT: 0001F108

        LOCAL RECURSIVE VARIABLES:
        STATUS                                  0      INTEGER     00000000
        ARRIVE.TIME                5.14755759E-85      REAL        00000001

        CALLED FROM:
TIME.R
        LOCATION 0001289E  OFFSET 00FE FROM LOAD POINT 000127A0
        REGISTER SAVE AREA AT: 0001F0A8

        LOCAL RECURSIVE VARIABLES:
        E.2                                     0      INTEGER     00000000
        N.3                                     0      INTEGER     00000000
        T.V                        NULL                TEXT        00000000
        E.1                                140500      INTEGER     000224D4

        CALLED FROM:
MAIN
        LOCATION 000144EA  OFFSET 014A FROM LOAD POINT 000143A0    IN LINE     4
```

Figure 9.6 - Example of Standard SIMSCRIPT Error Information

REGISTER SAVE AREA AT: 0001F050

* * * E N D   O F   T R A C E B A C K * * *

* * * S I M U L A T I O N   S U M M A R Y * * *

TIME.V = 1.04625950E-01   EVENT.V = 3   EVENTS.V = 3

EVENT CHAINS

CLASS	NUMBER	TIME.A(FIRST)	TIME.A(LAST)
1	1	2.40371489E+00	2.40371489E+00
2	1	8.00000000E+01	8.00000000E+01
3	1	SCHEDULED NOW	SCHEDULED NOW

* * * I / O   S U M M A R Y * * *

READ.V = 5   WRITE.V = 6

UNIT	STATUS	MODE	RECORD.V	COLUMN.V	EOF.V
5	INPUT		0	0	0
6	OUTPUT		0	0	0
98	OUTPUT	CHARACTER	80	56	0

* * * M E M O R Y   U S A G E   S T A T I S T I C S * * *

ENTITY SIZE	ACTIVE NUMBER	DISTRIBUTED OVER SUBPAGES/PAGES
8	1	1
16	4	1
40	2	1
48	1	1
56	1	1
64	5	1
104	3	1
184	1	1
200	1	1

0 NON-ACTIVE PAGE(S) AVAILABLE

Figure 9.6 - Example of Standard SIMSCRIPT Error Information (Continued)

we determine that SHIP processes are of priority 3. The listing of event chains reveals one pending process of class 1 (SCHEDULER) at time = 2.403 . . . , one STOP.SIMULATION at time = 80, and one SHIP at time NOW.

The next section (I/O Summary) does not add any information in our example. However, it can be very valuable in situations where data errors are found; the I/O Summary identifies the current input unit (READ.V) and the exact record and column number location of the erroneous data. EOF.V indicates whether an end-of-file has been encountered (EOF.V = 2).

The Dynamic Storage Summary is useful in debugging errors in which the program is overflowing storage. If an entity is being created in a loop, many copies of a particular size entity will stand out in this summary as the "ACTIVE NUMBER."

9.5 User-Written Debugging Routines

Two more features of SIMSCRIPT facilitate the debugging of simulation models.

SNAP.R -- User-Supplied Post Mortem Routine

Additional model specific information (which could not be anticipated by the system) can be printed when an error has been detected by the system.

To accomplish this, the user must provide a routine, called SNAP.R. This routine will automatically be called whenever any error is detected. If the user omits this routine, a default library version is included. This version produces no output. It merely satisfies the loader requirements.

One of the important purposes of SNAP.R is to print some (or all) of the attributes of processes, resources or entities which are in existence at the time an error was detected. These may exist in various sets or may be addressed through various global variables or attributes of other entities. As elaborate or simple a printout as desired may be produced. SNAP.R may also be called explicitly during the execution of a program; for instance, to test SNAP.R.

It is sometimes the case that the user has programmed detection of certain error conditions and may wish to force the same output that the system would produce. To produce the same output as described in this chapter, the user may specify use of the TRACE statement. For example, in a search of a set for some entity with a particular combination of attributes, if it is "impossible" not to find one, the following segment might be helpful:

```
FOR EACH...
   WITH...
FIND THE FIRST CASE
IF NONE,
   PRINT 1 LINE THUS
   ERROR IN SEARCHING...
   TRACE
   CALL SNAP.R
   STOP
OTHERWISE
```

BETWEEN.V - Tracing the Flow of Simulation

A very important aspect of simulation verification is the sequence in which events actually occur. To trace the sequence easily, SIMSCRIPT provides a mechanism for giving the user the option of printing a message just before each process or event is (re)executed. This feature is completely under user control. To activate it, a subprogram variable, BETWEEN.V, must contain the name of the routine to call. For example,

```
LET BETWEEN.V = 'DETAIL'
```

will activate the mechanism and call a user-supplied routine named DETAIL each time the timing routine (TIME.R) is ready to pass control to a process or event routine.

At the moment when the BETWEEN.V routine is called, the following conditions exist:

1. The next process/event to be executed has been selected. Let us refer to it as P.

2. The system clock, TIME.V, has been updated to TIME.A(P), the (re)activation time of process P.

3. EVENT.V has been set to the priority class of P, I.P.

4. The global variable named P has been set to the reference value of P, thus making it easy to reference attributes of P for output.

5. Control has <u>not</u> passed to the process.

It should be noted that this routine cannot be used to prevent the selected event or process from occurring (other than by stopping execution through a STOP statement).

The mechanism can be disabled at any time by setting BETWEEN.V to zero.

We shall illustrate the snapshot and trace mechanisms by adding them to Example 9.

The only change to the existing program is the addition of one line in the MAIN program,

```
LET BETWEEN.V = 'DETAIL'
```

Then the two additional routines are coded as shown in Figure 9.7.

Routine DETAIL uses EVENT.V to select a different PRINT statement for two of the three processes in the model. (No message is printed for STOP.SIMULATION.) Both routines DETAIL and SNAP.R use a library function, LINE.F, which returns an INTEGER value of the current line number of the process execution.

The additional output from the execution of this program is shown as Figure 9.8. The traceback is omitted since it is identical with Figure 9.6.

The SHIP.ID attribute has been added to the process SHIP. A counter in process GENERATOR is incremented each time a new ship is activated. The value is then assigned to the new ship's SHIP.ID. This attribute is used in the DETAIL printout (Figure 9.6) to uniquely identify the individual ships.

One might be tempted to use the value of the variable SHIP to identify the different ships which arrive. However, these numbers are really the actual storage address of the ship process notices. When a ship "leaves" the system, the process notice for it is destroyed. When a new ship is activated, this destroyed process notice is the first candidate for the new ship's process notice since dynamic storage is organized as a LIFO set, sorted by size. This can be very confusing, whereas the ID attribute presents a much clearer picture.

```
                                   CACI SIMSCRIPT II.5 IBM S/370 R9.1        PAGE     1
                                                     09-NOV-1982 17:13 (    1)
OPTIONS   TERM

         ''  EXAMPLE  9A  --  A HARBOR MODEL (EXAMPLE 9 WITH DEBUGGING FEATURES ADDED)
    1   PREAMBLE
    2      PROCESSES INCLUDE SCHEDULER AND STOP.SIM
    3         EVERY SHIP HAS AN UNLOADING.TIME
    4            AND A SHIP.ID
    5            AND MAY BELONG TO THE QUEUE
    6            AND MAY BELONG TO THE DOCK
    7         DEFINE SHIP.ID AS AN INTEGER VARIABLE
    8         DEFINE UNLOADING.TIME AS A REAL VARIABLE
    9      THE SYSTEM OWNS THE QUEUE AND THE DOCK
   10      ACCUMULATE MAXQ AS THE MAXIMUM,
   11         MEANQ AS THE MEAN OF N.QUEUE
   12      TALLY NUMBER.OF.SHIPS AS THE NUMBER,
   13         MINCT AS THE MINIMUM,
   14         MAXCT AS THE MAXIMUM
   15         AND MEANCT AS THE MEAN OF CYCLE.TIME
   16      DEFINE CYCLE.TIME AS A REAL VARIABLE
   17
   18      DEFINE .DOCK.IS.NOT.FULL TO MEAN N.DOCK < 2
   19      DEFINE .ARRIVING TO MEAN 1
   20      DEFINE .LEAVING TO MEAN 2
   21      DEFINE .OK TO MEAN 1
   22      DEFINE .NOT.OK TO MEAN 0
   23   END
```

C R O S S - R E F E R E N C E

NAME	TYPE		MODE	LINE NUMBERS OF REFERENCES	
.ARRIVING	DEFINE TO MEAN			19	
.DOCK.IS.NOT.FULL	DEFINE TO MEAN			18	
.LEAVING	DEFINE TO MEAN			20	
.NOT.OK	DEFINE TO MEAN			22	
.OK	DEFINE TO MEAN			21	
CYCLE.TIME	GLOBAL VARIABLE		REAL	15	16
DOCK	SET			6	9
MAXCT	GLOBAL VARIABLE		DOUBLE	14	
MAXQ	GLOBAL VARIABLE		DOUBLE	10	
MEANCT	ROUTINE		DOUBLE	15	
MEANQ	ROUTINE		DOUBLE	11	
MINCT	GLOBAL VARIABLE		DOUBLE	13	
N.QUEUE	PERMANENT ATTRIBUTE		INTEGER	11	
NUMBER.OF.SHIPS	GLOBAL VARIABLE		DOUBLE	12	
QUEUE	SET			5	9
SCHEDULER	PROCESS NOTICE			2	
SHIP	PROCESS NOTICE			3	
SHIP.ID	TEMPORARY ATTRIBUTE	AUTO	INTEGER	4	7
STOP.SIM	PROCESS NOTICE			2	
UNLOADING.TIME	TEMPORARY ATTRIBUTE	AUTO	REAL	3	8

Figure 9.7 - Example 9 With Diagnostic Programming Added

```
                                         CACI SIMSCRIPT II.5 IBM S/370 R9.1          PAGE    2
OPTIONS   TERM                                          09-NOV-1982 17:13 (    1)

    1  MAIN
    2
    3     LET BETWEEN.V = 'DETAIL'
    4
    5     ACTIVATE A SCHEDULER NOW
    6     ACTIVATE A STOP.SIM IN 80 DAYS
    7     START SIMULATION
    8  END
```

C R O S S - R E F E R E N C E

NAME	TYPE			MODE	LINE NUMBERS OF REFERENCES
BETWEEN.V	PERMANENT ATTRIBUTE	SYS	43	SUBPROG	3
DETAIL	ROUTINE			INTEGER	3
SCHEDULER	PROCESS NOTICE				5
	+ GLOBAL VARIABLE			INTEGER	5*
STOP.SIM	PROCESS NOTICE				6
	+ GLOBAL VARIABLE			INTEGER	6*

Figure 9.7 - Example 9 With Diagnostic Programming Added (Continued)

```
                                  CACI SIMSCRIPT II.5 IBM S/370 R9.1        PAGE    3
OPTIONS   TERM                                           09-NOV-1982 17:13 (   1)

    1  PROCESS SCHEDULER
    2     DEFINE SHIP.COUNTER AS AN INTEGER VARIABLE
    3     UNTIL TIME.V > 80,
    4     DO
    5        ACTIVATE A SHIP NOW
    6        ADD 1 TO SHIP.COUNTER
    7        LET SHIP.ID(SHIP) = SHIP.COUNTER
    8        WAIT EXPONENTIAL.F(4/3,1) DAYS
    9     LOOP
   10  END
```

C R O S S - R E F E R E N C E

NAME	TYPE			MODE	LINE NUMBERS OF REFERENCES		
EXPONENTIAL.F	ROUTINE			DOUBLE	8		
PROCESS.V	PERMANENT ATTRIBUTE	SYS	73	INTEGER	10*		
SCHEDULER	PROCESS NOTICE				1	10	
	+ GLOBAL VARIABLE			INTEGER	1		
SHIP	PROCESS NOTICE				5		
	+ GLOBAL VARIABLE			INTEGER	5*	7	
SHIP.COUNTER	RECURSIVE VARIABLE	WORD	1	INTEGER	2	6*	7
SHIP.ID	TEMPORARY ATTRIBUTE	AUTO		INTEGER	7		
TIME.V	PERMANENT ATTRIBUTE	SYS	41	DOUBLE	3		

Figure 9.7 - Example 9 With Diagnostic Programming Added (Continued)

```
                                   CACI SIMSCRIPT II.5 IBM S/370 R9.1        PAGE    4
OPTIONS   TERM                                             09-NOV-1982 17:13 (   1)

     1  PROCESS SHIP
     2     DEFINE STATUS AS AN INTEGER VARIABLE
     3     DEFINE ARRIVE.TIME AS A REAL VARIABLE
     4     LET ARRIVE.TIME = TIME.V
     5     LET UNLOADING.TIME(SHIP) = UNIFORM.F(0.5,1.5,2)
     6     CALL HARBOR.MASTER GIVING .ARRIVING YIELDING STATUS
     7     IF STATUS = .NOT.OK,
     8        FILE SHIP IN QUEUE
     9        SUSPEND
    10     ALWAYS
    11     WORK UNLOADING.TIME(SHIP) DAYS
    12     REMOVE THIS SHIP FROM THE DOCK
    13     LET CYCLE.TIME = TIME.V - ARRIVE.TIME
    14     CALL HARBOR.MASTER GIVING .LEAVING YIELDING STATUS
    15  END
```

C R O S S - R E F E R E N C E

NAME	TYPE			MODE	LINE NUMBERS OF REFERENCES				
.ARRIVING	DEFINE TO MEAN				6				
.LEAVING	DEFINE TO MEAN				14				
.NOT.OK	DEFINE TO MEAN				7				
ARRIVE.TIME	RECURSIVE VARIABLE	WORD	2	REAL	3	4	13		
CYCLE.TIME	GLOBAL VARIABLE			REAL	13				
DOCK	SET				12				
HARBOR.MASTER	ROUTINE			INTEGER	6	14			
PROCESS.V	PERMANENT ATTRIBUTE	SYS	73	INTEGER	15				
QUEUE	SET				8				
SHIP	PROCESS NOTICE				1	15			
	+ GLOBAL VARIABLE			INTEGER	1	5	8	11	12
STATUS	RECURSIVE VARIABLE	WORD	1	INTEGER	2	6	7	14	
TIME.V	PERMANENT ATTRIBUTE	SYS	41	DOUBLE	4	13			
UNIFORM.F	ROUTINE			DOUBLE	5				
UNLOADING.TIME	TEMPORARY ATTRIBUTE	AUTO		REAL	5	11			

Figure 9.7 - Example 9 With Diagnostic Programming Added (Continued)

```
 1  ROUTINE HARBOR.MASTER GIVEN ACTION YIELDING STATUS
 2     DEFINE ACTION AND STATUS AS INTEGER VARIABLES
 3     IF ACTION = .ARRIVING
 4        IF .DOCK.IS.NOT.FULL,
 5           IF DOCK IS NOT EMPTY,
 6              LET SHIP = F.DOCK
 7              INTERRUPT SHIP
 8              LET TIME.A(SHIP) = TIME.A(SHIP) * 2.0
 9              RESUME SHIP
10           ELSE
11              LET UNLOADING.TIME(SHIP) = UNLOADING.TIME(SHIP) / 2.0
12           ALWAYS
13           FILE THIS SHIP IN DOCK
14           LET STATUS = .OK
15        ELSE
16           LET STATUS = .NOT.OK
17        ALWAYS
18     ELSE  ''ACTION IS .LEAVING
19        IF QUEUE IS NOT EMPTY,
20           REMOVE THE FIRST SHIP FROM QUEUE
21           FILE THIS SHIP IN DOCK
22           REACTIVATE THE SHIP NOW
23        ELSE
24           IF DOCK IS NOT EMPTY,
25                 LET SHIP = F.DOCK
26                 INTERRUPT SHIP
27                 LET TIME.A(SHIP) = TIME.A(SHIP) / 2.0
28                 RESUME SHIP
29           ALWAYS
30        ALWAYS
31     ALWAYS
32     RETURN
33  END
```

C R O S S - R E F E R E N C E

NAME	TYPE			MODE	LINE NUMBERS OF REFERENCES
.ARRIVING	DEFINE TO MEAN				3
.DOCK.IS.NOT.FULL	DEFINE TO MEAN				4
.NOT.OK	DEFINE TO MEAN				16
.OK	DEFINE TO MEAN				14
ACTION	ARGUMENT	NO.	1	INTEGER	1 2 3
DOCK	SET				5 13 21 24
F.DOCK	PERMANENT ATTRIBUTE			INTEGER	6 25
HARBOR.MASTER	ROUTINE			INTEGER	1
N.DOCK	PERMANENT ATTRIBUTE			INTEGER	4
QUEUE	SET				19 20
SHIP	PROCESS NOTICE				7 9 22 26 28
	+ GLOBAL VARIABLE			INTEGER	6 7* 8* 9* 11* 13 21 22* 25 26* 27* 28*
STATUS	ARGUMENT	NO.	2	INTEGER	1 2 14 16
TIME.A	TEMPORARY ATTRIBUTE	WORD	3	DOUBLE	8* 9 27* 28
TIME.V	PERMANENT ATTRIBUTE	SYS	41	DOUBLE	9 28
UNLOADING.TIME	TEMPORARY ATTRIBUTE	AUTO		REAL	11*

Figure 9.7 - Example 9 With Diagnostic Programming Added (Continued)

```
  1  PROCESS STOP.SIM
  2     PRINT 5 LINES WITH NUMBER.OF.SHIPS,TIME.V,MINCT,MAXCT AND MEANCT
  3        AS FOLLOWS
                SHIP AND CRANE MODEL
       * SHIPS WERE UNLOADED IN  *.** DAYS
    THE MINIMUM TIME TO UNLOAD A SHIP WAS    *.***
     "  MAXIMUM   "  "    "    "  "   "      *.***
     "  MEAN      "  "    "    "  "   "      *.***
  4     SKIP 3 LINES
  5     PRINT 2 LINES WITH MEANQ AND MAXQ THUS
    THE AVERAGE QUEUE OF SHIPS WAITING TO BE UNLOADED WAS    *.***
    THE MAXIMUM QUEUE WAS    *
  6     STOP
  7  END
```

C R O S S - R E F E R E N C E

NAME	TYPE			MODE	LINE NUMBERS OF REFERENCES	
MAXCT	GLOBAL VARIABLE			DOUBLE	2	
MAXQ	GLOBAL VARIABLE			DOUBLE	5	
MEANCT	ROUTINE			DOUBLE	2	
MEANQ	ROUTINE			DOUBLE	5	
MINCT	GLOBAL VARIABLE			DOUBLE	2	
NUMBER.OF.SHIPS	GLOBAL VARIABLE			DOUBLE	2	
PROCESS.V	PERMANENT ATTRIBUTE	SYS	73	INTEGER	7*	
STOP.SIM	PROCESS NOTICE				1	7
	+ GLOBAL VARIABLE			INTEGER	1	
TIME.V	PERMANENT ATTRIBUTE	SYS	41	DOUBLE	2	
UIB.W	IMPLIED SUBSCRIPT	SYS	52	INTEGER	4	

Figure 9.7 - Example 9 With Diagnostic Programming Added (Continued)

```
                                    CACI SIMSCRIPT II.5 IBM S/370 R9.1        PAGE     7
OPTIONS   TERM                                           09-NOV-1982 17:13 (    1)

   1  ROUTINE SNAP.R
   2     START NEW PAGE
   3     PRINT 5 LINES WITH NUMBER.OF.SHIPS, TIME.V, MINCT, MAXCT AND MEANCT
   4        AS FOLLOWS
       SHIP AND CRANE MODEL OUTPUT AT ERROR CONDITION
     * SHIPS WERE UNLOADED IN   *.** DAYS
  THE MINIMUM TIME TO UNLOAD A SHIP WAS     *.***
   "  MAXIMUM   "  "    "    "  "   "       *.***
   "  MEAN      "  "    "    "  "   "       *.***
   5     SKIP 3 LINES
   6     PRINT 2 LINES WITH MEANQ AND MAXQ THUS
  THE AVERAGE QUEUE OF SHIPS WAITING TO BE UNLOADED WAS    *.***
  THE MAXIMUM QUEUE WAS    *
   7     PRINT 2 LINES WITH N.QUEUE AND N.DOCK THUS
THE NUMBER OF SHIPS IN QUEUE IS    *
THE NUMBER OF SHIPS IN THE DOCK IS    *
   8     SKIP 2 LINES
   9     FOR EACH SHIP IN QUEUE,
  10        PRINT 1 LINE WITH SHIP.ID(SHIP) THUS
     SHIP NO.  *** IS IN QUEUE
  11     FOR EACH SHIP IN DOCK,
  12        PRINT 1 LINE WITH SHIP.ID(SHIP), TIME.A(SHIP)
  13           AND UNLOADING.TIME(SHIP) THUS
     SHIP NO.  *** IS AT DOCK. LEAVE TIME=**.*** UNLOAD TIME=**.***
  14     STOP
  15  END  ''SNAP.R
```

C R O S S - R E F E R E N C E

NAME	TYPE			MODE	LINE NUMBERS OF REFERENCES			
DOCK	SET				11			
MAXCT	GLOBAL VARIABLE			DOUBLE	3			
MAXQ	GLOBAL VARIABLE			DOUBLE	6			
MEANCT	ROUTINE			DOUBLE	3			
MEANQ	ROUTINE			DOUBLE	6			
MINCT	GLOBAL VARIABLE			DOUBLE	3			
N.DOCK	PERMANENT ATTRIBUTE			INTEGER	7			
N.QUEUE	PERMANENT ATTRIBUTE			INTEGER	7			
NUMBER.OF.SHIPS	GLOBAL VARIABLE			DOUBLE	3			
QUEUE	SET				9			
SHIP	GLOBAL VARIABLE			INTEGER	9*	10	11*	12*
SHIP.ID	TEMPORARY ATTRIBUTE	AUTO		INTEGER	10	12		
SNAP.R	ROUTINE			INTEGER	1			
TIME.A	TEMPORARY ATTRIBUTE	WORD	3	DOUBLE	12			
TIME.V	PERMANENT ATTRIBUTE	SYS	41	DOUBLE	3			
UIB.W	IMPLIED SUBSCRIPT	SYS	52	INTEGER	5	8		
UNLOADING.TIME	TEMPORARY ATTRIBUTE	AUTO		REAL	12			

Figure 9.7 - Example 9 With Diagnostic Programming Added (Continued)

```
                                CACI SIMSCRIPT II.5 IBM S/370 R9.1        PAGE     8
OPTIONS   TERM                                    09-NOV-1982 17:13 (   1)

      1  ROUTINE DETAIL
      2     IF EVENT.V = I.SCHEDULER
      3        PRINT 1 LINE WITH TIME.V AND LINE.F(SCHEDULER) THUS
AT TIME    *.*** THE SCHEDULER IS (RE) ACTIVATED AT LINE NO.  *
      4        RETURN
      5     OTHERWISE
      6     IF EVENT.V = I.SHIP,
      7        PRINT 1 LINE WITH TIME.V, SHIP.ID(SHIP), LINE.F(SHIP), N.QUEUE
      8           AND N.DOCK THUS
AT TIME    *.*** SHIP *** EXECUTES LINE  * . N.QUEUE= *, N.DOCK= * .
      9        RETURN
     10     OTHERWISE
     11  END  ''DETAIL
```

C R O S S - R E F E R E N C E

NAME	TYPE			MODE	LINE NUMBERS OF REFERENCES	
DETAIL	ROUTINE			INTEGER	1	
EVENT.V	PERMANENT ATTRIBUTE	SYS	44	INTEGER	2	6
I.SCHEDULER	GLOBAL VARIABLE			INTEGER	2	
I.SHIP	GLOBAL VARIABLE			INTEGER	6	
LINE.F	ROUTINE			INTEGER	3	7
N.DOCK	PERMANENT ATTRIBUTE			INTEGER	7	
N.QUEUE	PERMANENT ATTRIBUTE			INTEGER	7	
SCHEDULER	GLOBAL VARIABLE			INTEGER	3	
SHIP	GLOBAL VARIABLE			INTEGER	7*	
SHIP.ID	TEMPORARY ATTRIBUTE	AUTO		INTEGER	7	
TIME.V	PERMANENT ATTRIBUTE	SYS	41	DOUBLE	3	7

Figure 9.7 - Example 9 With Diagnostic Programming Added (Continued)

```
AT TIME   0.0   THE SCHEDULER IS (RE) ACTIVATED AT LINE NO.  1
AT TIME   0.0   SHIP    1 EXECUTES LINE  1 . N.QUEUE= 0, N.DOCK= 0 .
AT TIME    .105 THE SCHEDULER IS (RE) ACTIVATED AT LINE NO.  8
AT TIME    .105 SHIP    2 EXECUTES LINE  1 . N.QUEUE= 0, N.DOCK= 1 .




          SHIP AND CRANE MODEL OUTPUT AT ERROR CONDITION
        0 SHIPS WERE UNLOADED IN    .10 DAYS
     THE MINIMUM TIME TO UNLOAD A SHIP WAS    0.0
      "  MAXIMUM    "  "    "    "  "   "     0.0
      "  MEAN      "  "    "    "  "   "      0.0



     THE AVERAGE QUEUE OF SHIPS WAITING TO BE UNLOADED WAS    0.0
     THE MAXIMUM QUEUE WAS    0
   THE NUMBER OF SHIPS IN QUEUE IS    0
   THE NUMBER OF SHIPS IN THE DOCK IS     1


          SHIP NO.     1 IS AT DOCK. LEAVE TIME=  .580 UNLOAD TIME=  .342
```

Figure 9.8 - User-Generated Diagnostic Output

Chapter 10
A COMPREHENSIVE EXAMPLE

10.0 Introduction

To summarize the principles of modelling and simulation in SIMSCRIPT, let us consider the design and implementation of a rather larger model than those previously considered. We first present the problem, which has to do with a waterway network, but is clearly analogous to many other situations. We then briefly introduce to one of the many design languages that have been developed recently. We use this language to design our model. Finally, we implement the design in SIMSCRIPT and discuss the execution of the model.

10.1 The Problem: A Waterways Network

As a part of a multimodal commodity-flow analysis done for the U.S. Army Corps of Engineers, it was necessary to construct a model of the traffic on the inland navigation system. The model in this chapter is a simplification of the model done in that study.

The aim is to study traffic on a portion (or all) of the waterway system to determine the capacities of its various components.

The traffic consists of freight barges that enter and leave the network at ports. Each port has parameters describing the amount of traffic it generates. The routes between origin and destination are deterministic and will be described as data to the model. Between origin and destination, both of which must be ports, the tows pass through other ports, forks in the rivers, and locks that delay shipping. A tow comprises a random number of barges. The locks can only accommodate a certain number of barges at a time and double lockages are required for oversize tows. The time for a lockage is specified with each lock. Some of the locks may contain more than one parallel chamber, permitting multiple tows to be served simultaneously. Each lock has an operating policy, such as "Serve m tows in one direction, then n in the other direction" or "Dedicate one chamber to each direction" or "Serve upbound tows for x hours, then serve downbound tows for y hours."

The network of ports, locks, and forks is connected by river segments, which are described by their length and current.

Our goal in the study is to determine the amount of traffic between ports, transit times for the traffic, and bottlenecks that occur, such as congestion at the locks.

10.2 An Introduction to the Software Design Documentation Language (SDDL)

The Software Design and Documentation Language (SDDL) is one of several tools developed to aid in the specification and design process for software development prior to the start of programming. SDDL was developed at the Jet Propulsion Laboratory by Henry Kleine.

Quoting from the introduction to SDDL [10]:

> The objective of SDDL is to satisfy the communications requirements of the software design and documentation process. This objective is met by providing:
>
> (1) A processor which can translate design specifications, expressed in SDDL syntax, into an intelligible, informative, machine-reproducible Software Design Document (SDD).
>
> (2) A design and documentation language with forms and syntax that are simple, unrestrictive, and communicative.
>
> (3) A methodology for effective use of the language and the processor.

The purpose of the SDDL processor is to translate the designer's creative thinking into an effective communications document. The processor must perform as many automatic functions as possible, thereby freeing the designer's energy for the creative design effort.

Some of the automatic functions which the processor performs are listed below:

1. Document Formatting

(1) Indentation by structure logic.
(2) Flow lines for accentuating structure escapes.
(3) Flow lines for accentuating module invocations.
(4) Line numbering for input editing.
(5) Logic error detection.
(6) Special handling for title pages and text segments.
(7) Input and output line continuation.
(8) Line splitting (i.e., printing part of the line so that the last character lines up at the right-hand margin).

2. Software Design Summary Information

(1) Table of contents showing all titles and modules, and the location of the summary tables provided by the processor.
(2) Module invocation hierarchy.
(3) Module cross-reference (where each module is invoked.
(4) Cross-reference tables for selected words or phrases appearing in the document. Selection is controlled by the user.
(5) Page reference numbers on module invocation statements.

3. Processor Control Capabilities

(1) Page width, length, numbering, heading, and ejection.
(2) Structure indentation amount.
(3) Deletion of preceding blank characters on input lines.
(4) Input line numbering sequence.

(5) Keyword specification.

(6) Selection of words for inclusion in the cross-reference tables.

(7) Number of right-hand columns for sequence numbers.

(8) Execution time options for suppressing selected processor features.

SDDL is implemented as a SIMSCRIPT II.5 program and is available from the U.S. Government Technical Information Service (COSMIC) or from CACI.

By default, SDDL recognizes a rather general set of keywords for determining the scope of design structures. These keywords are only recognized when they are the first word of a line and include:

PROGRAM - ENDPROGRAM
PROCEDURE - ENDPROCEDURE
IF - ENDIF
SELECT - ENDSELECT
etc.

It is possible to define additional (or replacement) keywords for SDDL. We have chosen to define a set of keywords close to those of SIMSCRIPT. The directives for this purpose are shown in Table 10.1. Note that some compromises must be made to accommodate SDDL in that a unique pairing of module delimiters is required. SIMSCRIPT normally uses END in many contexts, but SDDL requires a change to, for example, ENDMAIN, ENDPROCESS, etc. It is not our intention to write SIMSCRIPT at the design stage, but merely to ease the later transition to program implementation by using common keywords.

TABLE 10.1

SIMSCRIPT KEYWORD DEFINITIONS FOR SDDL

```
#WIDTH 100
#MARK .
#STRING '
#STRING "
#DEFINE MODULE SECTION,ENDSECTION
#DEFINE MODULE PROGRAM,ENDPROGRAM
#DEFINE MODULE PREAMBLE,ENDPREAMBLE
#DEFINE MODULE MAIN,ENDMAIN,STOP
#DEFINE MODULE ROUTINE,ENDROUTINE,RETURN
#DEFINE MODULE FUNCTION,ENDFUNCTION,RETURNWITH
#DEFINE MODULE ROUTINE,ENDROUTINE,EXITROUTINE
#DEFINE MODULE EVENT,ENDEVENT,STOPSIMULATION
#DEFINE MODULE EVENT,,EXITEVENT
#DEFINE MODULE PROCESS,ENDPROCESS,SUSPEND
#DEFINE MOUDLE PROCESS,,REQUEST
#DEFINE PROCESS,,WORK
#DEFINE PROCESS,,WAIT
#DEFINE BLOCK IF,ALWAYS,,ELSE
#DEFINE BLOCK IF,OTHERWISE
#DEFINE BLOCK IF,REGARDLESS
#DEFINE BLOCK DO,LOOP,CYCLE
#DEFINE BLOCK DO,LOOP,LEAVE
#DEFINE BLOCK BEGINHEADING,ENDHEADING
#DEFINE BLOCK BEGINREPORT,ENDREPORT
#DEFINE CALL NOW PERFORM  SCHEDULE  ACTIVATE REACTIVATE
```

10.3 The Model Design

This section presents the design of the waterways network model in the form of a completed SDDL output (SDD). (See Figure 10-1.)

The overall structure was definitely influenced by the fact that the intended implementation language is SIMSCRIPT. SDDL can, however, be used with a variety of target implementation languages. The power and generality of the high-level SIMSCRIPT world-view can be clearly exposed in SDDL without worrying about all the implementation details.

The level of detail presented in the SDD is a compromise. In actual design, there would be several such documents showing successively more detail.

```
*****************************
*  WATERWAYS NETWORK MODEL  *
*   SDDL DESIGN DOCUMENT    *
*         VERSION 1         *
*****************************
```

Figure 10.1 - Example 10: Waterways Network Model

TABLE OF CONTENTS PAGE I

Figure 10.1 (Continued)

```
PROGRAM OBJECTIVES
    ****************************************************
    *     THE OBJECTIVE OF THIS STUDY IS TO MODEL      *
    * A WATERWAYS NETWORK IN SUFFICIENT DETAIL         *
    * TO STUDY CONGESTION IN THE SYSTEM DUE TO         *
    * DELAYS EXPERIENCED BY TOWS AT LOCKS.  AS A       *
    * MEASURE OF CONFIDENCE, SIMULATED TRAFFIC         *
    * BETWEEN PORTS WILL BE MEASURED FOR COMPARISON *
    * TO ACTUAL DATA.  THE MODEL IS TO BE OPERATED  *
    * INTERACTIVELY, ALLOWING THE USER TO QUICKLY      *
    * MODIFY THE NETWORK, ADDING OR DELETING PORTS, *
    * OR RECONFIGURING LOCKS, AND CHANGING THE         *
    * TRAFFIC LOAD PARAMETERS BETWEEN SIMULATIONS.  *
    ****************************************************
ENDPROGRAM OBJECTIVES
```

Figure 10.1 (Continued)

```
PROGRAM PREAMBLE
      PROCESSES
         'TOW.GENERATOR'
         'TOW'
         'SIMULATION.REPORT'
      EVENTS
         'DEBUG.START'
      ENTITIES
         'NODE'
         'LINK'
         'CHANNEL'
         'CHAMBER'
      ROUTINES
         'PORT_OPERATION'
         'LOCK_OPERATION'
         'FORK_OPERATION'
         'NETWORK_INITIALIZATION'
      SETS
         'ROUTE'
            OWNER : NODE BY NODE
            MEMBER : LINK
         'LOCK_QUEUE'
            OWNER : NODE BY 'DIRECTION'
            MEMBER : TOW
         'LOCK.CHAMBER.SET'
            OWNER : LOCK
            MEMBER : CHAMBER
      STATISTICS:
         UTILIZATION OF CHAMBERS
         TOWS
            NO. TRANSITING PAIRS OF PORTS
            AVG. TIME TRANSITING PAIRS OF PORTS
         PORTS
            NO. TOWS RECEIVED
            NO. GENERATED
ENDPROGRAM
```

Figure 10.1 (Continued)

```
PROGRAM MAIN
      PERFORM NETWORK.INITIALIZATION---------------------------------->(  3)
      FOR EACH PORT
         ACTIVATE TOW.GENERATOR NOW----------------------------------->(  3)
      ACTIVATE SIMULATION.REPORT NOW---------------------------------->(  6)
      SCHEDULE DEBUG.START NOW---------------------------------------->(  7)
      START SIMULATION
ENDPROGRAM MAIN


PROGRAM NETWORK.INITIALIZATION
   ****************************************
   * THE INITIALIZATION OF THE MODEL IS    *
   * ACCOMPLISHED IN THE FOLLOWING MANNER: *
   * 1) AN OLD INPUT FILE IS ASSUMED TO    *
   *    EXIST REGARDLESS OF HOW OUT OF     *
   *    DATE ITS CONTENTS MAY BE.          *
   * 2) AFTER THE OLD INPUT FILE IS READ   *
   *    IN ITS ENTIRETY, AN INTERACTIVE    *
   *    ROUTINE GUIDES THE USER THROUGH    *
   *    THE DATABASE, ALLOWING CHANGES     *
   *    TO BE MODE.                        *
   * 3) AFTER ALL UPDATES HAVE BEEN        *
   *    COMPLETED, A NEW FILE IS           *
   *    OPTIONALLY WRITTEN.                *
   ****************************************
ENDPROGRAM


PROCESS TOW.GENERATOR
   ESTABLISH PARAMETERS FOR THIS PORT
   UNTIL  .END.OF.SIMULATION
   DO
      ACTIVATE TOW NOW------------------------------------------------>(  4)
      ESTABLISH TOW PARAMETERS
<-----WAIT PORT.INTER.TOW.GENERATION.TIME
   LOOP
ENDPROCESS
```

Figure 10.1 (Continued)

```
PROCESS TOW
    DETERMINE ROUTE FOR THIS TOW
    FOR EACH LINK IN ROUTE
    DO
        DETERMINE TRAVEL TIME TO NEXT NODE
<-----WORK TRAVEL TIME HOURS
        PERFORM NODE.ROUTINE YIELDING STATUS---------------------------->(    )
        IF STATUS = "DELAYED"
<--------SUSPEND
        ALWAYS
        IF PROCESSING TIME IS NOT ZERO
<--------WORK PROCESSING TIME
        ALWAYS
    LOOP
ENDPROCESS
```

```
ROUTINE PORT.OPERATION
    IF TOW IS DESTINED FOR THIS PORT
        UPDATE STATISTICS ON INCOMING TOWS
    ALWAYS
    REPORT STATUS "OK" AND PROCESSING TIME = 0
    TO TOW
ENDROUTINE
```

```
ROUTINE FORK.OPERATION
    REPORT STATUS "OK" AND PROCESSING TIME = 0
    TO TOW
ENDROUTINE
```

Figure 10.1 (Continued)

```
LINE                                                                          PAGE    5

ROUTINE LOCK.OPERATION
   IF STATUS = "ARRIVING"
      FOR EACH CHAMBER IN LOCK,
      WITH STATUS = IDLE
      FIND THE FIRST CASE
      IF NONE
         FILE TOW IN QUEUE (DIRECTION)
         REPORT STATUS "DELAYED" TO TOW
      ELSE
         ASSIGN TOW TO CHAMBER
         DETERMINE PROCESSING TIME
         REPORT STATUS "OK" AND PROCESSING TIME TO TOW
      ALWAYS
   ELSE ''STATUS IS LEAVING
      IF QUEUE(NODE,DIRECTION) IS EMPTY
         AND QUEUE(NODE,OPPOSITE) IS EMPTY
         SET CHAMBER STATUS TO IDLE
<--------RETURN
      OTHERWISE
      IF QUEUE(NODE,DIRECTION) IS EMPTY
         OR POLICY DICTATES CHANGE OF DIRECTION
         OF SERVICE
         CHANGE DIRECTION OF SERVICE
      ALWAYS
      REMOVE NEXT TOW FROM QUEUE
      ASSIGN TOW TO CHAMBER
      DETERMINE PROCESSING TIME
      REACTIVATE TOW NOW-------------------------------------------------->(   4)
   ALWAYS
ENDROUTINE
```

Figure 10.1 (Continued)

```
                                                                    PAGE    6

PROCESS SIMULATION.REPORT
    UNTIL .END.OF.SIMULATION
    DO
<-----WAIT REPORTING.PERIOD
        PERFORM PERIODIC.REPORT----------------------------------------->(  6)
    LOOP
    PERFORM FINAL.REPORT------------------------------------------------>(  6)
ENDPROCESS


ROUTINE PERIODIC.REPORT
    ****************************************
    * THE PERIODIC REPORT CONSISTS OF THE *
    * QUEUEING AND TRAFFIC SINCE THE LAST *
    * PERIODIC REPORT.  ALL "QUALIFIED"   *
    * STATISTICS ARE RESET AFTER REPORT.  *
    ****************************************
ENDROUTINE


ROUTINE FINAL.REPORT
    ******************************************
    * THE FINAL REPORT PRODUCES THE SAME     *
    * RESULTS AS THE PERIODIC.REPORT BUT     *
    * AGGREGATED OVER THE ENTIRE SIMULATION *
    * PERIOD.                                *
    ******************************************
ENDROUTINE
```

Figure 10.1 (Continued)

```
EVENT DEBUG.START
    ************************************************
    * THIS ROUTINE INFORMS THE USER THAT DETAILED *
    * TRACE IS BEGINNING AND QUERIES USER          *
    * FOR DESIRED SNAP SHOT OUTPUT                 *
    ************************************************
    IF SNAPSHOT IS DESIRED
       CALL SNAP.R----------------------------------------------------------->(  7)
    ALWAYS
    LET BETWEEN.V = "DEBUG"
ENDEVENT
```

```
ROUTINE DEBUG
    ***********************************************
    * AFTER A PRESCRIBED NO. OF LINES OF OUTPUT, *
    * THIS ROUTINE QUERIES THE USER AS TO         *
    * WHETHER TO CONTINUE DEBUG OUTPUT,           *
    * RESUME IT LATER OR TERMINATE RUN.           *
    ***********************************************
    IF CONTINUING TRACE
       SELECT CASE PER PROCESS_TYPE
       CASE(TOW)
          PRINT TOW INFORMATION
       CASE(TOW.GENERATOR)
          PRINT PORT INFORMATION
       ENDSELECT
    ALWAYS
ENDROUTINE
```

```
ROUTINE SNAP.R
    ******************************************************
    * PRINT ALL RELEVANT SYSTEM INFORMATION AND THE      *
    * STATUS OF EACH TOW ON DEMAND (FROM DEBUG ROUTINE) *
    * OR WHEN AN ERROR IS DETECTED (AUTOMATICALLY).      *
    ******************************************************
ENDROUTINE
```

Figure 10.1 (Continued)

```
    **************  MODULE REFERENCE TREE  ******                        PAGE     8
LN   PAGE


 1      1  OBJECTIVES

 2      2  PREAMBLE

 3      3  MAIN
 4      3  .  NETWORK.INITIALIZATION
 5      3  .  TOW.GENERATOR
 6      4  .  .  TOW
 7      *  .  .  .  NODE.ROUTINE
 8      6  .  SIMULATION.REPORT
 9      6  .  .  PERIODIC.REPORT
10      6  .  .  FINAL.REPORT
11      7  .  DEBUG.START
12      7  .  .  SNAP.R

13      4  PORT.OPERATION

14      4  FORK.OPERATION

15      5  LOCK.OPERATION
16      4  .  TOW
17            ** EXPANDED ON LINE   6

18      7  DEBUG
```

Figure 10.1 (Continued)

```
++++++++++++++++++++++++++++++++++++++++++++++++++++++++++++++++++++++++++++++++
IDENTIFIER    MODULE NAME                               LINE NUMBERS



CHAMBER
      PAGE   2  PROGRAM PREAMBLE                          56   71
      PAGE   5  ROUTINE LOCK.OPERATION                   147  154  161  170
CHANNEL
      PAGE   2  PROGRAM PREAMBLE                          55
DIRECTION
      PAGE   2  PROGRAM PREAMBLE                          67
      PAGE   5  ROUTINE LOCK.OPERATION                   151  159  164  165  167
FORK_OPERATION
      PAGE   2  PROGRAM PREAMBLE                          60
LINK
      PAGE   2  PROGRAM PREAMBLE                          54   65
      PAGE   4  PROCESS TOW                              119
LOCK_OPERATION
      PAGE   2  PROGRAM PREAMBLE                          59
LOCK_QUEUE
      PAGE   2  PROGRAM PREAMBLE                          66
NETWORK_INITIALIZATION
      PAGE   2  PROGRAM PREAMBLE                          61
NODE
      PAGE   2  PROGRAM PREAMBLE                          53   64   64   67
      PAGE   4  PROCESS TOW                              121
      PAGE   5  ROUTINE LOCK.OPERATION                   159  160  164
PORT_OPERATION
      PAGE   2  PROGRAM PREAMBLE                          58
ROUTE
      PAGE   2  PROGRAM PREAMBLE                          63
      PAGE   4  PROCESS TOW                              118  119
```

Figure 10.1 (Continued)

```
++++++++++++++++++++++++++++++++++++++++++++++++++++++++++++++++++++++++++++++++++++
IDENTIFIER     MODULE NAME                                    LINE NUMBERS



AVG.
    PAGE   2  PROGRAM PREAMBLE                                  76
BETWEEN.V
    PAGE   7  EVENT DEBUG.START                                210
.END.OF.SIMULATION
    PAGE   3  PROCESS TOW.GENERATOR                            110
    PAGE   6  PROCESS SIMULATION.REPORT                        176
LOCK.CHAMBER.SET
    PAGE   2  PROGRAM PREAMBLE                                  69
NO.
    PAGE   2  PROGRAM PREAMBLE                                  75    78    79
PORT.INTER.TOW.GENERATION.TIME
    PAGE   3  PROCESS TOW.GENERATOR                            114
REPORTING.PERIOD
    PAGE   6  PROCESS SIMULATION.REPORT                        178
```

Figure 10.1 (Continued)

REFERENCES

[1] Breiman, Leo., Statistics: With a View Toward Application, Houghton Mifflin Company, Boston, Massachusetts, 1973.

[2] Brooks, Fredrick P., Jr., The Mythical Man-Month, Essays on Software Engineering, Addison-Wesley Publishing Co., Reading, Massachusetts, 1975.

[3] CACI, Inc., SIMSCRIPT II.5 Reference Handbook, CACI, Inc., Los Angeles, California, 1976, 1983.

[4] Fishman, G. S., Concepts and Methods in Discrete Event Digital Simulation, John Wiley & Sons, New York, 1973.

[5] Fishman, G. S., Principles of Discrete Event Simulation, John Wiley & Sons, New York, 1979.

[6] Golden, D. G. and J. D. Schoeffler, "GSL -- A Combined Continuous and Discrete Simulation Language," SIMULATION, Vol. 20, pp. 1-8, Simulation Councils, Inc., La Jolla, California, January 1977.

[7] Gordon, Geoffrey, System Simulation, 2nd ed., Prentice-Hall, Englewood Cliffs, New Jersey, 1978.

[8] Kiviat, P. J., H. M. Markowitz, and R. Villaneva, SIMSCRIPT II.5 Programming Language, (edited by E. C. Russell), CACI, Inc., Los Angeles, California, 1973, 1983.

[9] Kiviat, P. J., R. Villanueva, and H. M. Markowitz, The SIMSCRIPT II Programming Language, Prentice-Hall, Englewood Cliffs, New Jersey, 1968.

[10] Kleine, Henry, Software Design and Documentation Lanaguage, Document 77-24, Jet Propulsion Laboratories, Pasadena, California, 1977.

[11] Law, Averill M., and W. David Kelton, Simulation Modeling and Analysis, McGraw-Hill, New York, 1981.

[12] Markowitz, Harry M., Bernard Hausner, and Herbert W. Karr, SIMSCRIPT, A Simulation Programming Language, Prentice-Hall, Englewood Cliffs, New Jersey, 1963.

[13] Payne, W. H., J. R. Rabung, and T. P. Bogyo, "Coding the Lehmer Pseudorandom Number Generator," Communications of the ACM, Vol. 12, No. 2, ACM, New York, February 1969.

[14] Pritsker, A.A.B., The GASP IV Simulation Language, John Wiley & Sons, New York, 1973.

[15] Schriber, Thomas J., Simulation Using GPSS, John Wiley & Sons, New York, 1974.

[16] Shannon, Robert E., Systems Simulation -- The Art and the Science, Prentice-Hall, Englewood Cliffs, New Jersey, 1975.

[17] Solomon, Susan L., "Simulation as an Alternative to Linear Programming," Simuletter (a quarterly publication on Modelling and Simulation) by SIGSIM (ACM), Vol. 8, No. 2, pp. 13-15, ACM, New York, January 1977.

APPENDIX A
SIMSCRIPT REFERENCE SYNTAX

A.1 Basic Constructs

The notation employed in describing SIMSCRIPT II.5 is an improved version of conventions used in several computer programming language descriptions. In the following pages:

1. Words in capital letters denote required statement keywords, as well as optional words or phrases used either for clarity or to use an optional feature.

2. Primitives are shown in lowercase and denote words for which values must be supplied, unless denoted as optional.

3. Metavariables, such as expressions, selection clauses, etc. (defined below), are shown in lowercase also. Again, actual expressions must be supplied.

4. A statement is a combination of keywords, primitives, and metavariables that follow a certain pattern called the syntax of the statement.

5. Brackets [ ] and braces { } denote choices. When brackets appear, a choice *may* be made from the options indicated. When braces appear, a choice *must* be made. The items available for selection appear within the brackets or braces separated from one another by a vertical bar |. When the choice can be repeated, a symbol (or symbols) that must separate the items in that list of choices is written immediately after the right-hand brace or bracket enclosed in angles. For example,

   { A | B } < , > represents a sequence of any number of A's and B's separated by commas. For example,

      A, A, B, A, B

   whereas,

      { A } < , >

   is equivalent to,

      A [,A] [,A] ... [,A]

6. The null separator < > is used to indicate that no symbol need separate the items in a list. An example of { A | B } < > might be AABAB...A. The choice represented by { A } < > is equivalent to A[A][A]...[A].

7. A list separator symbol can itself be complex, involving choices and repetitions, as in { A | B } < AND | OR >. An instance might be,

    A AND B OR B OR A

8. Plural keywords ending in S such as VARIABLES or LINES, can be written in singular form as VARIABLE or LINE when called for by the grammar of a statement.

A.2 Primitives

integer: Sequence of digits delimited by blanks, special characters, or an end of record.

name: Any sequence of letters and digits containing at least one letter and delimited by blanks, special characters, or an end of record.

special_names:

The syntax of special names is the same as name; however, each special_name is required in the context specified.

Each of the following names must be defined in the program preamble before use in other contexts:

attribute_name
event_name
permanent_entity_name
process_name
qualifier_name
resource_name
set_name
temporary_entity_name

routine_name, while not necessary to be defined in the preamble, must correspond to a user-defined routine.

word:

```
{ integer
| name
| number
| special_character
| string
}
```

Words must be separated from each other by one or more blanks unless one of them is a special character.

Periods (.) are ignored between words and at the end of statements.

Comments can be inserted between any two words in a program by enclosing them in quotation marks ('') formed by two consecutive apostrophes. The right-hand set of quotes is not necessary if the comment is the last item on the line.

A.3 Metavariables

In order to compress the syntax description of the statements, several commonly repeated expressions, or metavariables, are defined here rather than at each permissible usage.

```
arithmetic_expression: = [ + | - ]  { ( expression )
                                      | number
                                      | subprogram_constant
                                      | string_constant
                                      | [ -$ ] variable
                                    } < + | - | * | / | ** >
```

```
array_reference: = ( [ expression ] < , > { * } < , > )
```

```
comma: = { , | AND |, AND }
```

for phrase:

```
FOR { name {  BACK FROM | = } expression TO expression [ BY expression ]
      | { EACH | ALL | EVERY }
        { permanent_entity_name | resource_name [ CALLED variable ]
        | name [ { FROM | AFTER } expression ]
         { OF | IN | ON | AT } set_name [ subscript ]
          [ IN REVERSE ORDER ]
         }
        }
      } [ , ] [ selection clause | termination clause ] < >
```

format:

format_1 = { B expression | S expression | / }

format_2 = { format_1, | integer A expression
| integer C expression
| integer I expression
| integer D (expression, expression)
| integer E (expression, expression)
| integer T expression | integer T *
}

```
logical_expression:

    { { ( logical_expression )
      | expression { [ IS ] relational_operator expression } < >
      | expression [ IS ][ NOT ] { POSITIVE | NEGATIVE | ZERO }
      | MODE [ IS ][ NOT ] { REAL | INTEGER | ALPHA | TEXT }
      | DATA [ IS ][ NOT ] ENDED
      | CARD [ IS ][ NOT ] NEW
      | PAGE [ IS ][ NOT ] FIRST
      | [ THE | THIS ] set_name [ subscript ] IS[ NOT ] EMPTY
      | [ THE | THIS ] expression IS [ NOT ]
        IN [ A | AN | THE | SOME ] set_name
      | { EVENT | PROCESS } IS [ NOT ]
        { INTERNAL | ENDOGENOUS
        | EXTERNAL | EXOGENOUS
        }
      } [ IS ] { TRUE | FALSE }
    } { AND | OR }
```

```
number: = { integer | .integer | integer [ .integer ] }
```

```
program_label: = ' { name | number } '
```

```
relational_operator:

        { { = | EQ | EQUALS | EQUAL TO }
        | { - = | NE | NOT EQUAL TO }
        | { < | LS | LT | LESS THAN }
        | { > | GR | GT | GREATER THAN }
        | { < = | LE | NOT GREATER THAN | NO GREATER THAN }
        | { > = | GE | NOT LESS THAN | NO LESS THAN }
        }



selection_clause:

        { WITH
        | [ EXCEPT ] WHEN
        | UNLESS
        } logical_expression [ , ]



string_constant:  =   " { name | number | blank } <> "



special_character:  =  { ( | ) | + | - | # | / | ** | $ }
```

subscript: = ({ expression } < , >)

subprogram constant: = { ' routine_name ' }

termination_clause: = { WHILE | UNTIL } logical_expression [,]

variable: = name [subscript | array_reference]

A.4 The Statement Syntax

```
{ ACCUMULATE | TALLY }
  { name { = | AS } [ THE ] [ qualifier_name ]
   { AVERAGE | AVG | MEAN
   | SUM
   | NUMBER | NUM
   | VARIANCE | VAR
   | STD.DEV | STD
   | SUM.OF.SQUARES | SSQ
   | MEAN.SQUARE | MSQ
   | MINIMUM | MIN
   | MAXIMUM | MAX
   }
  | name ( [ + | - ] { name | number } TO [ + | - ] { name | number }
           BY { name | number } )
    { AS | = } [ THE ] [ qualifier_name ] HISTOGRAM
  } < comma > OF name
```

Specifies automatic data collection and analysis.

```
{ ACTIVATE | CAUSE | REACTIVATE | SCHEDULE | RESCHEDULE }
  { A | AN | THE [ ABOVE ] | THIS }
  { process_name | event_name } [ CALLED variable ]
   [ { GIVEN | GIVING } { expression } < comma >
    | ( expression } < comma > )
   ]
   { AT expression
     | NOW | NEXT
     | { IN | AFTER } expression { UNITS | DAYS | HOURS | MINUTES }
   }
```

Creates (for A or AN) and places an event or process notice in the pending list in proper chronological order.

ADD expression TO variable

Adds the value of expression to the value of the variable.

AFTER - see BEFORE

```
[ ALSO ] { for | termination clause }
       [ for | termination clause | selection clause ] < >
       DO [ THIS | THE FOLLOWING ]
```

Logical phrases control the execution of statements that follow them. When more than one statement is to be controlled, the words DO and LOOP must bracket the statements. Multiple control phrases terminating control on the same LOOP statement are preceded by the word ALSO.

ALWAYS - see IF

```
{ BEFORE | AFTER }
{ { CREATING | DESTROYING } < comma >
      [ A | AN | THE | ANY ] temporary_entity_name
| { FILING | REMOVING } < comma >
      [ IN | FROM ] { A | AN | THE | ANY } set_name
| { ACTIVATING | CAUSING | CANCELLING | INTERRUPTING | SCHEDULING } < comma >
  [ A | AN | THE | ANY ] { process_name | event_name }
} CALL routine_name
```

Specifies a call to the named routine whenever the indicated statement is executed. Inputs to the routine (automatically supplied) are:

	BEFORE	AFTER
CREATE	not allowed	entity identifier
DESTROY	entity identifier	not allowed
FILE	entity identifier, subscripts	entity identifier, subscripts
REMOVE	entity identifier, subscripts	entity identifier, subscripts
ACTIVATE	entity identifier, time	entity identifier, time
CAUSE	entity identifier, time	entity identifier, time
SCHEDULE	entity identifier, time	entity identifier, time
CANCEL	entity identifier	entity identifier
INTERRUPT	entity identifier	entity identifier

BEGIN HEADING

Marks the beginning of a heading section within a report section.

BEGIN REPORT [ON A NEW PAGE] [PRINTING for ,IN GROUPS OF integer
[PER PAGE]]

Marks the beginning of a report section with optional new page and column repetition features.

BREAK { event_name | process_name } TIES{{ BY | ON } [HIGH | LOW]
attribute_name } < comma THEN >

Establishes the priority order within a process or event class in case of time-tie.

{ CALL | PERFORM | NOW } routine_name

[{ GIVEN | GIVING | THE | THIS } { expression } < comma >
| ({ expression} < comma >)] [YIELDING { variable } < comma >]

Invokes a routine used as a procedure.

```
CANCEL [ THE [ ABOVE ] | THIS ] event_name [ CALLED variable ]
```

Removes a scheduled event notice from the pending list.

CAUSE - see ACTIVATE

```
COMPUTE

  { variable { = | AS } [ THE ]
    { AVERAGE | AVG | MEAN
     | SUM
     | NUMBER | NUM
     | VARIANCE | VAR
     | STD.DEV | STD
     | SUM.OF.SQUARES | SSQ
     | MEAN.SQUARE | MSQ
     | MINIMUM | MIN
     | MAXIMUM | MAX
     | { MINIMUM | MIN } ( variable )
     | { MAXIMUM | MAX } ( variable )
    }
  } < comma > OF expression
```

Must be controlled by a logical control phrase. Computes the indicated statistics of the expression after the LOOP statement if the control is over a DO...LOOP block.

```
CREATE { [ A | AN ] { temporary_entity_name | process_name | event_name }
            [ CALLED variable ]
       | { EACH | ALL | EVERY } { { permanent_entity_name | resource_name }
          [ ( expression ) ] } < comma >
       }
```

Obtains a block of words of the appropriate size for the named entity.

```
CYCLE | NEXT
```

Returns control immediately to the top of a loop for testing and next iteration. Must be contained within a DO...LOOP block.

```
DEFINE { set_name } < comma > AS [ A | AN ] [ LIFO | FIFO ] SET

  [ RANKED {{BY | ON } [ HIGH | LOW ] attribute_name }
       < comma THEN > ]

  [ WITHOUT { F | L | N | P | S | M } ATTRIBUTES ]
  [ [ , ] WITHOUT { FF | FL | FB | FA | F | RF | RL | RS | R } < comma >
  ROUTINES ]
```

Defines set ranking and optional deletion of owner and member attributes and processing routines.

```
DEFINE { routine_name } < comma > AS [ A | AN ]

  [ INTEGER | ALPHA | REAL | DOUBLE | TEXT ]
  [ RELEASABLE | FORTRAN | NONSIMSCRIPT ] { ROUTINE | FUNCTION }
  [ { GIVEN | GIVING | WITH } integer [ VALUES | ARGUMENTS ] ]
  [ [ comma ] YIELDING integer [ VALUES | ARGUMENTS ] ]
```

Defines routines, their mode and the number of given/yielding arguments for consistency checking.

```
DEFINE { name } < comma > AS [ A | AN ]

  [ [ INTEGER | REAL | DOUBLE | ALPHA | TEXT | SIGNED INTEGER ]
    [ integer - { DIM | DIMENSIONAL } ]
    [ DUMMY | SUBPROGRAM | STREAM { name | integer } ]
  ] < [ comma ] >
    { VARIABLE | ARRAY }
    [ MONITORED ON { [ THE ] { LEFT | RIGHT } } < comma > ]
```

Defines the properties of global variables.

```
DEFINE { name } < comma > AS [ A | AN ]

  [ [ INTEGER | REAL | DOUBLE | ALPHA | TEXT ]
    [ integer - { DIM | DIMENSIONAL } ]
    [ SUBPROGRAM ]
    [ SAVED | RECURSIVE ]
  ] < [ comma ] >
    { VARIABLE | ARRAY }
```

Defines the properties of local variables.

DEFINE word TO MEAN { word } < >

Instructs the compiler to substitute the words following the keyword MEAN for the indicated word in all subsequent statements, before they are compiled. The sequence of words to be substituted is terminated by the first end of record following MEAN.

```
DESTROY { [ THE | THIS ] { temporary_entity_name | process_name
        | event_name } [ CALLED variable ]
        | EACH { permanent_entity_name | resource_name } }
```

Releases the block of storage for the specified entity "name."

DO [THIS | THE FOLLOWING]

Used with LOOP to delimit a group of statements controlled by one or more logical control phrases.

ELSE - see IF

END

Marks the physical end of a program preamble, routine, report section, or heading section within a report section.

ENTER WITH variable

Used to transfer a right-hand expression to a local variable within a left-handed function.

ERASE { name }

Used to release storage used for TEXT variables.

{ EVENT | UPON } [TO | FOR] event_name

[{ GIVEN | GIVING | THE | THIS } { name } < comma >
| ({ name } < comma >)]
[SAVING THE EVENT NOTICE]

Event routine heading. Unless SAVED, the associated event notice is automatically destroyed when the event routine is executed.

{ EVENT NOTICES | EVENTS } [{ INCLUDE | ARE } { event_name } < comma >]

Preamble statement marking the start of event declarations.

```
EVERY { entity_name } < comma > [ MAY | CAN ]
  { HAS { A | AN | THE | SOME } attribute_name
    [ ( { integer/integer | */integer | integer-integer } ) ]
    [ IN {ARRAY | WORD } integer | FUNCTION ]
  | OWNS { { A | AN | THE | SOME } set_name } < comma >
  | BELONGS TO { { A | AN | THE | SOME } set_name } < comma >
  | HAS { A | AN | THE | SOME } attribute_name
    RANDOM [ STEP | LINEAR ] VARIABLE
    [ IN { WORD | ARRAY } integer ]
  } < comma >
```

Entity-attribute-set structure declaration. Specifies optional attribute packing, equivalences, word assignments, and functions.

```
{ EXTERNAL | EXOGENOUS }

  { EVENT | PROCESS } UNITS ARE
  { name | integer } < comma >
```

Logical input devices from which external event/process data will be read.

```
{ EXTERNAL | EXOGENOUS }

  { EVENTS | PROCESSES } ARE { event_name | process_name } < comma >
```

Declares the names of the events and processes which can be triggered externally.

```
FILE [ THE | THIS ] expression

     [ FIRST | LAST | { BEFORE | AFTER } expression ]
       IN [ THE | THIS ] set_name [ subscript ]
```

Places an entity in a set.

```
FIND { THE FIRST CASE
     | { variable = [ THE ] [ FIRST ] expression } < comma >
     } [ , ]
     [ IF { FOUND | NONE } [ , ] ]
```

Must be controlled by a FOR phrase with a selection clause, but cannot be within a DO...LOOP block. The option IF statement directs control after the control phrase has been completed, depending upon the outcome of the FIND.

```
GO [ TO ] { 'program_label [ ( expression ) ] '
          | program_label [ ( expression ) ]
          | { 'program_label' | program_label } < OR > PER expression
         }
```

Transfers control to a labelled statement or one of several labelled statements in a list according to the integer value of the transfer expression expression.

IF logical_expression [,]
   [statement] < >
[ELSE | OTHERWISE]
   [statement] < >
{ ALWAYS | REGARDLESS }

The IF statement directs control to one of two possible groups of statements, depending on the outcome of logical expression. IF statements may be nested to any complexity. (For more explanation see Section 3.5.)

INTERRUPT [THE | THIS | THE ABOVE] process_name [CALLED variable]

Removes a processess from the pending list, computes the "time to go" (TIME.A - TIME.V) and stores it in TIME.A (process_name)
[or TIME.A (variable)]

LAST COLUMN { IS | = } integer

Directs compiler to ignore columns beyond integer on subsequent input records.

LEAVE

Transfers control to the statement immediately following the next LOOP statement.

```
LET variable = expression
```

Assigns the value of expression to the variable. If variable is integer and expression is real, the result is rounded before storing.

```
LIST { expression
     | ATTRIBUTES OF { entity [ CALLED expression ]
                     | EACH entity
                       [ { FROM | AFTER } expression ]
                       [ { IN | OF | AT | ON } set_name [subscript ] ]
                       [ IN REVERSE ORDER ]
                       [ , { selection_clause | termination_clause } < > ]
                     }
     } < comma >
```

A free-form output statement that labels and displays values of expressions, and one- or two-dimensional attributes or arrays.

```
{ LOOP | REPEAT }
```

Used with DO to delimit a group of statements controlled by one or more logical control phrases.

```
MAIN
```

Marks the beginning of the main routine in a program. Execution commences at the first executable statement after MAIN.

```
MOVE { FROM expression
     | TO variable
     }
```

Used only within a routine defined for a monitored variable to access or set the value of that variable.

```
NOTE:  MOVE TO right-monitored variable
       MOVE FROM left-monitored variable
```

NEXT - see CYCLE

```
NORMALLY [ , ]

  { MODE { IS | = } { INTEGER | REAL | DOUBLE | ALPHA | TEXT | UNDEFINED }
  | TYPE { IS | = } { SAVED | RECURSIVE | UNDEFINED }
  | { DIMENSION | DIM } { IS | =} integer
  } < comma >
```

Establishes background conditions for properties of variables and functions that are effective unless overridden by subsequent DEFINE declarations or, in the case of local arrays, first use.

NOW - see CALL

OTHERWISE - see IF

PERFORM - see CALL

PERMANENT ENTITIES [INCLUDE { permanent_entity_name } < comma >]

Preamble statement marking the start of permanent entity declarations.

[NEW | OLD | VERY OLD] PREAMBLE

Marks the beginning of the program preamble.

PRINT integer [DOUBLE] LINES
  [WITH { expression | A GROUP OF { expression }
    < comma > FIELDS }   < comma >]
  [SUPPRESSING FROM COLUMN integer]
  { THUS | LIKE THIS | AS FOLLOWS }

The "integer LINES" following the PRINT statement are format lines containing text and pictorial formats for the display of indicated expression values.

The phrases, A GROUP OF { expression }< comma > FIELDS and SUPPRESSING FROM COLUMN integer, can only be used within report sections that have column repetition.

PRIORITY ORDER IS { event_name | process_name } < comma >

This preamble statement assigns a priority order to different classes of processes and events to be used to resolve time-ties in scheduling.

PROCESS [TO | FOR] process_name
  [{ GIVEN | GIVING | THE | THIS } { name } < comma >
    | ({ name } < comma >)]

Process routine heading declaration. The process name process must be declared in the preamble.

PROCESSES [{ INCLUDE | ARE } { process_name } < comma >]

Preamble statement marking the start of process entity declarations.

READ { { variable } < comma > [AS { [DOUBLE] BINARY
    | [(expression)] { format$_2$ } < comma > }]
    | AS { format$_1$ } < comma >
  }
  [USING { THE BUFFER | [TAPE | UNIT] expression }]

Reads data, either formatted or free-form, from a specified device or the previously established input device.

REGARDLESS - see IF.

RELEASE { variable } < comma >

Frees storage occupied by variables (either arrays or attributes of permanent entities or resources).

RELINQUISH expression [UNITS OF] resource_name [(subscript)]

Makes the specified number of units of the resource available for automatic reallocation.

```
REMOVE [ THE ]
  { { FIRST | LAST } variable
  | [ THIS | ABOVE ] expression
  } FROM [ THE | THIS ] set_name [subscript ]
```

Removes an entity from a set.

REPEAT - see LOOP.

REQUEST expression [UNITS OF] resource [(subscript)]
[[,] WITH PRIORITY expression]

Makes a request for the specified number of units of the resource. If not available, the requesting process is enqueued in PRIORITY order and suspended awaiting availability of the resource.

RESCHEDULE - see ACTIVATE

RESERVE { { variable } < comma > AS { expression }
< BY > [BY *] } < comma >

Allocates blocks of storage of the specified size to the variables. If BY * is specified, only pointer space (for multi-dimensioned arrays) is allocated. Otherwise, the data storage is also allocated.

RESET [THE] [qualifier_name] < comma >
TOTALS OF { variable } < comma >

Initializes ACCUMULATE or TALLY counters associated with variable. If TOTALS is not preceded by qualifier_name(s), all counters of variable are (re)initialized. Otherwise, only those counters with the matching qualifiers are reset.

RESOURCES [{ INCLUDE | ARE } { resource_name } < comma >]

Preamble statement marking the start of resource entity declarations.

RESUME [THE | THIS | THE ABOVE] process_name [CALLED variable]

Used to restore a previously interrupted process to the pending list with the remaining "time-to-go" taken from TIME.A (process_name).

RESUME SUBSTITUTION

Used to reinstate the substitutions previously nullified by a SUPPRESS SUBSTITUTION statement.

RETURN [(expression) | WITH expression]

Used in a procedure, this statement returns control to its calling program. Used in a function, this statement returns control and a value to its calling program.

REWIND [TAPE | UNIT] expression

Rewinds an input/output device.

```
[ LEFT | RIGHT ] { ROUTINE | FUNCTION | SUBROUTINE }
  [ TO | FOR ] routine_name

  [ { GIVEN | GIVING | THE | THIS } { name } < comma >
    | ( { name } < comma > ) ]
  [ YIELDING { name } < comma > ]
```

Routine heading declaration. The prefix LEFT or RIGHT is for declaring monitoring routines. A routine used as a function has only GIVEN arguments.

SCHEDULE - see ACTIVATE

```
SKIP expression { FIELDS
                | [ INPUT | OUTPUT ] { CARDS | LINES | RECORDS }
                }
```

Applies to the current input or current output unit. SKIP expression FIELDS applies only to the current input unit. If neither INPUT nor OUTPUT is specified, CARDS and RECORDS imply INPUT and LINES implies OUTPUT.

```
START NEW { PAGE
          | [ INPUT | OUTPUT ] { CARD | LINE | RECORD }
          }
```

Applied to the current input or output unit. If neither INPUT nor OUTPUT is specified, CARD and RECORD imply INPUT, and LINE implies OUTPUT.

START SIMULATION

Causes the timing routine (TIME.R) to begin selecting and executing events and/or processes.

STOP

Halts program execution and returns control to the operating system.

STORE expression IN variable

Assigns the value of expression to variable without regard to mode.

SUBSTITUTE { THIS | THESE } integer LINES FOR word

Instructs the compiler to substitute the next integer lines following "word" for each occurrence of "word" in all subsequent statements before they are compiled.

SUBTRACT expression FROM variable

Subtracts the value of expression from the value of variable and stores the difference in variable.

SUPPRESS SUBSTITUTION

Used to nullify current substitutions (possibly in order to modify the substitutions).

SUSPEND [PROCESS]

Used to place the current process in the passive state and return control immediately to the timing routine without destroying the current process.

TALLY - see ACCUMULATE

TEMPORARY ENTITIES

Preamble statement marking the start of temporary entity declarations.

```
THE SYSTEM [ MAY | CAN ]
  { HAS { { A | AN | THE | SOME } attribute_name
        [ ( { integer/integer | */integer | integer-integer } ) ]
        [ IN { ARRAY | WORD } integer | FUNCTION ]
        } < comma >
  | OWNS { { A | AN | THE | SOME } set } < comma >
  | HAS { A | AN | THE | SOME } attribute_name
    RANDOM [ STEP | LINEAR ] VARIABLE
    [ IN { WORD | ARRAY } integer ]
  } < comma >
```

Specifies attributes of the system and sets owned by the system. Also specifies optional attribute packing, equivalences, word assignments, and functions.

[THEN] IF - see IF

```
TRACE [ USING [ TAPE | UNIT ] expression ]
```

Produces a backtrack of the current function and subroutine calls. TRACE is executed automatically when SIMSCRIPT detects an error during execution. In this case, the standard listing device is used.

UPON - see EVENT

```
USE { THE BUFFER | [ TAPE | UNIT ] expression } FOR { INPUT | OUTPUT }
```

Establishes the indicated input or output device as the current input or output unit. All subsequent input/output statements that do not specify their own devices in USING phrases use these current units. Specifying THE BUFFER causes reading or writing to an internal file.

```
{ WAIT | WORK } expression { UNITS | DAYS | HOURS | MINUTES }
```

Introduces a delay of expression time-units into a process.

WORK - see WAIT

```
WRITE { expression } < comma > { AS { [ DOUBLE ] BINARY
                   | [ ( expression ) ] { format2 } < comma >
                   }
      | AS { format1 | * }
      }
      [ USING { THE BUFFER | [ TAPE | UNIT ] expression }
      ]
```

Writes data to the specified device or the previously established output device according to the specified format.

A.5 Preamble Statement Precedence Rules

The following statements may only appear in the program preamble (except where otherwise noted). No other statements may appear in the preamble.

Statement Type	Statement	Rules
1a	NORMALLY	Can appear anywhere in preamble.
1b	DEFINE TO MEAN	
1c	SUBSTITUTE	
1d	SUPPRESS SUBSTITUTION	
1e	RESUME SUBSTITUTION	
1f	LAST COLUMN	
2a	TEMPORARY ENTITIES	A preamble may contain many types of 2a, 2b, 2c, 2d, and 2e statements.
2b	PERMANENT ENTITIES	
2c	EVENT NOTICES	
2d	PROCESSES	
2e	RESOURCES	
3a	EVERY	Many can follow a type 2 statement. An entity can appear in more than one EVERY statement.
3b	THE SYSTEM	
4	DEFINE variable	No precedence relation if it defines a global variable. Must follow all Type 3a statements if it defines an attribute named in them. A variable, attribute, or function can appear in only one DEFINE statement.

Statement Type	Statement	Rules
5	DEFINE set	Must follow Type 3 statements which declare the MEMBER or OWNER entity.

No type 6-9 statement can precede any Type 2-3 statements.

Statement Type	Statement	Rules
6a 6b 6c 6d	BREAK TIES EXTERNAL EVENTS EXTERNAL PROCESSES EXTERNAL UNITS	One statement allowed for each process or event notice.
7	PRIORITY	Must follow all Type 2c, 2d, and Type 6b and 6c statements (and their EVERY statements).
8a	BEFORE AFTER	One of each per entity/set action.
9a 9b	ACCUMULATE TALLY	One statement allowed for each attribute or unsubscripted global variable.

Appendix B

SIMSCRIPT II.5 CODING CONVENTIONS

The following conventions are not formally a part of SIMSCRIPT. They are, in fact, in addition to the requirements of the language as specified in the "SIMSCRIPT II.5 Reference Handbook" and related materials (i.e., "Simulating with Processes and Resources in SIMSCRIPT II.5" and the various user manuals). The purpose of these conventions is two-fold: (1) to minimize the chance for errors in coding large, complex models, and (2) to standardize the form of programs so as to simplify the reading of programs prepared by others.

The SIMSCRIPT concepts of processes, events, functions and subroutines lend themselves to the construction of very modular programs. Each module should be written to perform one major function. The interfaces between modules must be clearly defined. If data are passed from one module to another either explicitly or implicitly, this must be specified. (One of the major sources of confusion and error in attempts to modify existing, unstructured programs, is the lack of clarity of expression of module interrelationship).

Within modules, the conventions of structured programming should be adhered to, to the extent that they aid the clarity of expression and do not obscure it! An occasional "GO TO" may actually improve the readability of a program even though "pure" structured programming might preclude its use.

Top-down-structured programming is accomplished in SIMSCRIPT II.5 very naturally. The PREAMBLE is actually a top-level specification of the model. All of the modelling elements are defined in the preamble. Each passive element (ENTITY) and each dynamic element (PROCESS or EVENT) is listed together with its attributes and set relationships.

PREAMBLE-related coding standards:

1. All processes and entities should have single-word names which can easily be abbreviated to two characters (uniquely).

2. Each attribute name should be of the form "XX.name" where "XX" is the two-character abbreviation of the process or entity having the attribute and name is the descriptive attribute name.

3. All sets should be named so as to include a word such as "set" or "list" in the title.

4. All entity names should be defined locally in every routine by means of a "SUBSTITUTE" statement such as:

   ```
   SUBSTITUTE THESE 2 LINES FOR DEFINE.LOCAL.ENTITIES
   DEFINE LINK, MESSAGE, NODE, BLIP and TRACK AS INTEGER
   VARIABLES
   ```

   (This is to avoid the "side-effect" errors of inadvertently changing entity references in subroutines or co-routines (parallel processes).)

5. Process attributes should be restricted to the information required external to the process. All remaining data should be defined locally to the process (explicitly).

6. No default definitions should be used. Attributes and system variables should be defined explicitly.

7. Sets should be explicitly defined even though they could be satisfied by default.

Code Indentation Conventions

1. The basic intent of indentation is to improve the appearance and readability of the code. A basic increment for indentation should be adopted. If a statement overflows a line, it should be indented further. The amount of additional indentation is left to the user.

2. Only one statement should be coded per line.

3. Conditional statements should be are indented as follows:

```
a)  IF __________
          __________
          __________
          (no explicit transfer statement)
    ELSE
          __________
          __________
    ALWAYS
    ======
```

```
b)  IF __________
          __________
          __________
          (explicit transfer statement)
    OTHERWISE
    __________
    __________

c)  IF __________
       __________
          __________
    ALWAYS
```

4. Loops are indented as follows:

```
a)  FOR
       WITH
       UNTIL
    DO
       __________
       __________
       __________
    LOOP

b)  FOR
       WITH
    LET
```

(Any single statement under the control of a FOR is not indented further).

5. The "CASE" statement can be implemented as follows:

```
GO TO L(case)
L(1)
    __________
    __________
    GO TO END CASE
L(2)
    __________
    __________
    GO TO END CASE
    .
    .
    .
__________
__________
__________
'ENDCASE'
```

6. Nested situations imply further indentation.

7. The "THEN IF" construct of SIMSCRIPT should not be used.

Structured Programming

While "pure" structured programming would enforce the rule of single-entry-single-exit to any program module, it is sometimes less confusing to use a RETURN, CYCLE, LEAVE or STOP at the end of one path rather than to collect several ALWAYS at the end of the structure. GO TO statements should be avoided wherever possible.

Implied Subscripts

Considerable use is made of the implied subscripting feature of SIMSCRIPT II.5. Generally, the value of the implied subscript should be set in the same routine in which it is used. The only exception to this is a process or event routine wherein references to the attributes of that process or event notice are made via the global pointer which was set by the timing routine. To identify implicitly subscripted attributes in program statements, two periods are suffixed to the attribute name. The following statement illustrates this convention:

```
LET TK.BETA..=(TK.G..*DELTA.T+TK.BETA..)
              /(TK.F..+1
```

where, in this case, all implicit subscripts are references to the entity abbreviated TK.

For example, this entity may have been defined thus:

```
EVERY TRACK HAS
   A TK.ALPHA IN WORD 1,
   A TK.BETA IN WORD 2,
   A TK.F IN WORD 3,
   A TK.G IN WORD 4
etc.
```

APPENDIX C

SIMSCRIPT II.5 RANDOM DEVIATE GENERATOR

Routine Listings

The algorithms used for generating random deviates are shown in this appendix as they are actually coded in SIMSCRIPT II.5. The one exception is RANDOM.F; it is actually implemented in computer-dependent assembly language. The result of all RANDOM.F routines is identical with the exception of the Control Data SIMSCRIPT implementation.

If it is desired to replace a system function, such as RANDOM.F or GAMMA.F, the routine name must not be declared in the PREAMBLE. The routine is automatically declared by the system and an additional DEFINE statement would be taken as an error.

Initial Random Number Stream Seeds

(SEED.V)

SEED.V(1) = 2,116,429,302
SEED.V(2) = 683,743,814
SEED.V(3) = 964,393,174
SEED.V(4) = 1,217,426,631
SEED.V(5) = 618,433,579
SEED.V(6) = 1,157,240,309
SEED.V(7) = 15,726,055
SEED.V(8) = 48,108,509
SEED.V(9) = 1,797,920,909
SEED.V(10) = 477,424,540

For the CDC implementation, the following initial seeds are supplied:

SEED.V(1) = 88,251,033,025,441
SEED.V(2) = 183,503,209,621,313
SEED.V(3) = 41,716,398,375,649
SEED.V(4) = 98,700,237,180,545
SEED.V(5) = 45,258,732,784,161
SEED.V(6) = 180,800,743,732,673
SEED.V(7) = 56,654,300,844,385
SEED.V(8) = 179,321,787,784,449

```
ROUTINE BETA.F(K1, K2, STREAM)
   DEFINE K1, K2 AND X AS DOUBLE VARIABLES
   DEFINE STREAM AS AN INTEGER VARIABLE
   IF K1 <=  0
      LET ERR.F = 147
      RETURN
   OTHERWISE
   IF K2 <=  0
      LET ERR.F = 148
      RETURN
   OTHERWISE
   LET X = GAMMA.F(K1, K1, STREAM)
   RETURN WITH X/(X + GAMMA.F(K2, K2, STREAM))
END
```

```
ROUTINE BINOMIAL.F(N, P, STREAM)
   '' IF N IS A LARGE INTEGER OR INCORRECTLY INITIALIZED TO A REAL VALUE
   '' COMPUTATION TIME FOR THIS FUNCTION MAY BE EXCESSIVE
   DEFINE N, I, SUM AND STREAM AS INTEGER VARIABLES
   DEFINE P AS A DOUBLE VARIABLE
   IF N <= 0
      LET ERR.F = 141
      RETURN
   OTHERWISE
   IF P <= 0
      LET ERR.F = 142
      RETURN
   OTHERWISE
   FOR I = 1 TO N
      WHEN RANDOM.F(STREAM) <= P
   ADD 1 TO SUM
   RETURN WITH SUM
END
```

Figure C.1 - SIMSCRIPT II.5 Random Deviate Generator Routine Listings

```
ROUTINE ERLANG.F(MU, K, STREAM)
   '' IF K IS A LARGE INTEGER OR INCORRECTLY INITIALIZED TO A REAL VALUE
   '' COMPUTATION TIME FOR THIS FUNCTION MAY BE EXCESSIVE
   DEFINE MU AND E AS DOUBLE VARIABLES
   DEFINE I, K AND STREAM AS INTEGER VARIABLES
   IF MU <= 0
      LET ERR.F = 133
      RETURN
   OTHERWISE
   IF K <= 0
      LET ERR.F = 134
      RETURN
   OTHERWISE
   LET E = 1
   FOR I = 1 TO K
      LET E = E * RANDOM.F(STREAM)
   RETURN WITH -LOG.E.F(E) * MU / K
END
```

```
ROUTINE EXPONENTIAL.F(MU, STREAM)
   DEFINE MU AS A DOUBLE VARIABLE
   DEFINE STREAM AS AN INTEGER VARIABLE
   IF MU <=  0
      LET ERR.F = 132
      RETURN
   OTHERWISE
   RETURN WITH -MU * LOG.E.F(RANDOM.F(STREAM))
END
```

Figure C.1 (Continued)

```
ROUTINE GAMMA.F(MEAN, K, STREAM)
   DEFINE MEAN, K, KK, I, Z, A, B, D, E, X, Y AND W AS DOUBLE VARIABLES
   DEFINE STREAM AS AN INTEGER VARIABLE
   IF MEAN <= 0
      LET ERR.F = 145
      RETURN
   OTHERWISE
   IF K <= 0
      LET ERR.F = 146
      RETURN
   OTHERWISE
   LET Z = 0
   LET KK = TRUNC.F(K)
   LET D = FRAC.F(K)
   IF KK NE 0
      LET E = 1
      FOR I = 1 TO KK
         LET E = E * RANDOM.F(STREAM)
      LET Z = -LOG.E.F(E)
      IF D = 0 AND K < 5
         RETURN WITH ( MEAN / K ) * Z
      OTHERWISE
   ALWAYS
   LET A = 1 / D
   LET B = 1. / ( 1. - D )
   LET Y = 2.0
   WHILE Y > 1.0
   DO
      LET X = RANDOM.F(STREAM)**A
      LET Y = RANDOM.F(STREAM)**B + X
   LOOP
   LET W = X/Y
   LET Y = -LOG.E.F(RANDOM.F(STREAM))
   RETURN WITH (Z + W * Y) * (MEAN / K)
END
```

Figure C.1 (Continued)

```
ROUTINE LOG.NORMAL.F(MU, SIGMA, STREAM)
   DEFINE MU AND SIGMA AS DOUBLE VARIABLES
   DEFINE S AND U AS DOUBLE VARIABLES
   DEFINE STREAM AS AN INTEGER VARIABLE
   IF MU <= 0
      LET ERR.F = 135
      RETURN
   OTHERWISE
   IF SIGMA <= 0
      LET ERR.F = 136
      RETURN
   OTHERWISE
   LET S = LOG.E.F((SIGMA*SIGMA)/(MU*MU) + 1)
   LET U = LOG.E.F(MU) - 0.5*S
   RETURN WITH EXP.F(NORMAL.F(U, SQRT.F(S), STREAM))
END
```

```
ROUTINE NORMAL.F(MU, SIGMA, STREAM)
   DEFINE MU AND SIGMA AS DOUBLE VARIABLES
   DEFINE STREAM AS AN INTEGER VARIABLE
   DEFINE R, S, X, XX, Y, YY AS DOUBLE VARIABLES
   IF SIGMA <= 0
      LET ERR.F = 137
      RETURN
   OTHERWISE
   LET S = 2.0
   WHILE S > 1.0
   DO
      LET X = RANDOM.F(STREAM)
      LET Y = 2*RANDOM.F(STREAM) - 1
      LET XX = X*X
      LET YY = Y*Y
      LET S = XX + YY
   LOOP
   LET R = SQRT.F(-2*LOG.E.F(RANDOM.F(STREAM)))/S
   RETURN WITH MU + (XX - YY)*R*SIGMA
END
```

Figure C.1 (Continued)

```
ROUTINE POISSON.F(MU, STREAM)
   DEFINE MU, X AND Y AS DOUBLE VARIABLES
   DEFINE N AND STREAM  AS INTEGER VARIABLES
   IF MU > 6
      RETURN WITH ABS.F(NORMAL.F(MU, SQRT.F(MU), STREAM))
   OTHERWISE
   IF MU <= 0
      LET ERR.F = 138
      RETURN
   OTHERWISE
   LET Y = EXP.F(-MU)
   LET X = RANDOM.F(STREAM)
   WHILE X >= Y
   DO
      ADD 1 TO N
      LET X = X * RANDOM.F(STREAM)
   LOOP
   RETURN WITH N
END
```

```
ROUTINE RANDI.F(I, J, STREAM)
   DEFINE I, J AND STREAM AS INTEGER VARIABLES
   IF J < I
      LET ERR.F = 139
      RETURN
   OTHERWISE
   RETURN WITH TRUNC.F(RANDOM.F(STREAM)*(J - I + 1)) + I
END
```

Figure C.1 (Continued)

```
ROUTINE UNIFORM.F(A, B, STREAM)
   DEFINE A AND B AS DOUBLE VARIABLES
   DEFINE STREAM AS AN INTEGER VARIABLE
   IF B < A
      LET ERR.F = 140
      RETURN
   OTHERWISE
   RETURN WITH A + RANDOM.F(STREAM)*(B - A)
END
```

```
ROUTINE WEIBULL.F(SHAPE, SCALE, STREAM)
   DEFINE SHAPE AND SCALE AS DOUBLE VARIABLES
   DEFINE STREAM AS AN INTEGER VARIABLE
   IF SHAPE <= 0
      LET ERR.F = 143
      RETURN
   OTHERWISE
   IF SCALE <= 0
      LET ERR.F = 144
      RETURN
   OTHERWISE
   RETURN WITH SCALE*((-LOG.E.F(RANDOM.F(STREAM)))**(1.0/SHAPE))
END
```

Figure C.1 (Continued)

APPENDIX D

SYSTEM-DEFINED NAMES

The names defined by the SIMSCRIPT language system are described below. Additional names are defined to support special features of particular hardware.

VARIABLE	MODE	DESCRIPTION	DEFAULT
BETWEEN.V	Subprogram	Subprogram variable called before each event is executed.	0
BUFFER.V	Integer	The length of the internal buffer.	132
EOF.V	Integer	End-of-file code; 0 denotes that an end-of-file marker is an error; 1 indicates return control with EOF.V set to 2 when end-of-file is encountered; one for each input unit.††	0
EVENT.V	Integer	Code representing the event/process class to occur next.	0
EVENTS.V	Integer	The number of event/process classes.	0
F.EV.S(*)	Integer	Array containing the first-in-set pointers for the event set, EV.S.	0
HEADING.V	Subprogram	A subprogram variable tested by the system for each new page. ††	0
HOURS.V	Real	Number of hours per simulated day.	24
L.EV.S(*)	Integer	Array containing the last-in-set pointers for the event set, EV.S.	0

†† A separate value is maintained for each unit; only the currently used value is accessible to the program.

VARIABLE	MODE	DESCRIPTION	DEFAULT
LINE.V	Integer	Number of the current output line. ††	1
LINES.V	Integer	Number of lines per page. ††	55
MARK.V	Alpha	Termination character required on external event cards and on the input for random variables.	*
MINUTES.V	Real	Number of minutes per simulated hour.	60
N.EV.S(i)	Integer	Function returning the number of events in class i.	n/a
PAGE.V	Integer	Number of the current output page. ††	1
PAGECOL.V	Integer	If ≠ 0, column number in which PAGE and the value of PAGE.V are to be printed on the output listing. ††	0
PARM.V(*,*)	Alpha	Array containing parameters passed to program from control card (see particular implementation manual)	no
RCOLUMN.V	Integer	Pointer to the last column read in the input buffer. ††	0
READ.V	Integer	Number of the current input unit.	5
RECORD.V(n)	Integer	The number of records read from or written on the indicated unit.	0

†† A separate value is maintained for each unit; only the currently used value is accessible to the program.

VARIABLE	MODE	DESCRIPTION	DEFAULT
RRECORD.V	Integer	The number of records read from current input unit, or the most recent line number read. ††	
SEED.V(*)	Integer	Array containing initial random numbers. Mode is REAL on the VAX.	yes
TIME.V	Real	Current simulated time.	0
WCOLUMN.V	Integer	Pointer to the column last written in the output buffer. ††	0
WRECORD.V	Integer	The number of records written to current output unit, or the most recent line number written. ††	0
WRITE.V	Integer	Number of the current output unit. ††	5

CONSTANTS

CONSTANT	MODE	DESCRIPTION
EXP.C	Real	2.7182818284590452
INF.C	Integer	Largest INTEGER value that can be stored.
PI.C	Real	3.1415926535897932
RADIAN.C	Real	57.295779513082321 degrees/radian.
RINF.C	Real	Largest REAL value that can be stored.

†† A separate value is maintained for each unit; only the currently used value is accessible to the program.

SYSTEM-DEFINED ATTRIBUTES

ATTRIBUTE	ENTITY	MODE	DESCRIPTION
TIME.A	Processes and Events	Real	Time at which event (process) is to occur.
EUNIT.A	Processes and Events	Integer	External event unit number (0 for internal).
P.EV.S	Processes and Events	Integer	Pointer to predecessor in event set (EV.S).
S.EV.S	Processes and Events	Integer	Pointer to successor in event set (EV.S).
M.EV.S	Processes and Events	Integer	Event set membership flag: 1 if in set 0 if not in set
IPC.A	Processes	Integer	Process class number (subscript for EV.S attributes).
RSA.A	Processes	Integer	Pointer to the recursive save area for this process.
STA.A	Processes	Integer	State of the Process: 1 if in WORK statement 2 if in SUSPEND statement 3 if INTERRUPTed 0 otherwise
F.RS.S	Processes	Integer	Pointer to QC.E for first resource held or requested by process.
WHO.A	QC.E	Integer	Pointer to process requesting the resource.
QTY.A	QC.E	Integer	Number of units of resource requested.
PTY.A	QC.E	Integer	Priority of the request.
P.RS.S	QC.E	Integer	Pointer to predecessor QC.E in resource list for a process.

ATTRIBUTE	ENTITY	MODE	DESCRIPTION
S.RS.S	QC.E	Integer	Pointer to successor QC.E in resource list for a process.
PROB.A	RANDOM.E	Real	Cumulative probability value.
IVALUE.A	RANDOM.E	Integer	Integer name for sample use.
RVALUE.A	RANDOM.E	Real	Real name for sample value.

SYSTEM-GENERATED NAMES

The following variables are generated by the SIMSCRIPT system in conjunction with user-defined entities:

VARIABLE	ENTITY	MODE	DESCRIPTION
N.pe	Permanent Entity	Integer	Number of entities of type "pe."
N.resource	Resource	Integer	Number of "kinds" of resource.
K.entity	Temporary Entity, Event, and Process	Integer	Size of entity in computer words.
I.event	Event and Process	Integer	Event/Process class number (subscript for EV.S attributes).

The following attributes are generated by the SIMSCRIPT system in conjunction with user-defined entities:

ATTRIBUTE	ENTITY	MODE	DESCRIPTION
F.Q.resource	Resource	Integer	Pointer to QC.E for first process currently waiting for the resource.
F.X.resource	Resource	Integer	Pointer to QC.e for first process currently using the resource.
N.Q.resource	Resource	Integer	The number of requests for the resource currently waiting.
N.X.resource	Resource	Integer	The number of requests for the resource currently being satisfied.
P.Q.resource	QC.E	Integer	Pointer to predecessor QC.E waiting for resource.
P.X.resource	QC.E	Integer	Pointer to predecessor QC.E using resource.
S.Q.resource	QC.E	Integer	Pointer to successor QC.E waiting for resource.
S.X.resource	QC.E	Integer	Pointer to successor QC.E using resource.
U.resource	Resource	Integer	Number of units of resource currently available.
F.set	Set Owner	Integer	Pointer to first member of set.
L.set	Set Owner	Integer	Pointer to last member of set.

ATTRIBUTE	ENTITY	MODE	DESCRIPTION
M.set	Set Member	Integer	Set membership flag: 1 if in set 0 if not in set
N.set	Set Owner	Integer	Number of entities in the set
P.set	Set Member	Integer	Pointer to predecessor entity in set
S.set	Set Member	Integer	Pointer to successor in set
F.variable	Entity Having RANDOM VARIABLE Attribute	Integer	Pointer to first RANDOM.E in "variable" random distribution
S.variable	RANDOM.E	Integer	Pointer to successor RANDOM.E in "variable" random distribution

FUNCTIONS

FUNCTION MNEMONIC	ARGUMENTS †	FUNCTION MODE	DESCRIPTION
ABS.F	e	Mode of e	Returns the absolute value of the expression.
AND.F	a,b	Integer	Logical product of a and b.
ARCCOS.F	e	Real	Computes the arc cosine of a real expression; $-1 \geq e \geq 1$.
ARCSIN.F	e	Real	Computes the arc sine of a real expression; $-1 \geq e \geq 1$.

†e = expression that can be of any complexity, including functions
v = variable

FUNCTION MNEMONIC	ARGUMENTS	FUNCTION MODE	DESCRIPTION
ARCTAN.F	e_1, e_2	Real	Computes the arc tangent of e_1/e_2; $(e_1, e_2) \neq (0.0)$.
ATOT.F	e	Text	Converts an alpha expression to a text value.
BETA.F	e_1, e_2, e_3	Real	Returns a random sample from a beta distribution. e_1 = power of x; real e_2 = power of (1-x); real; $e_1 > 0$ e_3 = random number stream; integer
BINOMIAL.F	e_1, e_2, e_3	Integer	Returns a random sample from a binomial distribution. e_1 = number of trials; integer e_2 = probability of success; real e_3 = random number stream; integer
CONCAT.F	a,b	Text	Concatenates two text values to produce a text value containing the characters of each.
COS.F	e	Real	Computes the cosine of a real expression given in radians.
DATE.F	e_1, e_2, e_3	Real	Converts a calendar date to cumulative simulation time, based on values given to ORIGIN.R. e_1 = month, integer e_2 = day, integer e_3 = year, integer

FUNCTION MNEMONIC	ARGUMENTS	FUNCTION MODE	DESCRIPTION
DAY.F	e	Integer	Converts simulation time to the day portion based on values given to ORIGIN.R. e = cumulative simulation time, real
DIM.F	v(*)	Integer	Returns the number of elements pointed to by the pointer variable v, in the dimension of the array v.
DIV.F	e_1, e_2	Integer	Returns the truncated value of (e_1/e_2). e_1 = dividend, integer e_2 = divisor, integer; $e \neq 0$
EFIELD.F	none	Integer	Returns the ending column of the next data field to be read by a READ Free Form Statement. May affect file position.
ERLANG.F	e_1, e_2, e_3	Real	Returns a sample value from an Erlang distribution. e_1 = mean, real e_2 = k, integer e_3 = random number stream, integer
EXP.F	e	Real	Computes EXP.C to the eth power; e must be real.
EXPONENTIAL.F	e_1, e_2	Real	Returns a random sample from an exponential distribution. e_1 = mean, real e_2 = random number stream, integer
FRAC.F	e	Real	Returns the fractional portion of a real expression.

FUNCTION MNEMONIC	ARGUMENTS	FUNCTION MODE	DESCRIPTION
GAMMA.F	e_1, e_2, e_3	Real	Returns a random sample from a gamma distribution. e_1 = mean, real e_2 = k, real e_3 = random number stream, integer
HOUR.F	e	Integer	Converts event time to the hour portion. e = cumulative event time, real
INT.F	e	Integer	Returns the rounded integer portion of a real expression.
ISTEP.F	v,e	Integer	Returns a random sample from a look-up table without interpolation. v = variable that points to the look-up table e = random number stream, integer
ITOA.F	e	Alpha	Converts an integer expression to an alphanumeric value, (one digit only).
LENGTH.F	a,b	Integer	Returns the length of a TEXT variable in characters.
LIN.F	v,e	Real	Returns a random sample from a look-up table, using linear interpolation. v = variable that points to the look-up table e = random number stream, integer
LINE.F	p	Integer	Returns the source program line number of the last statement executed in process p.

FUNCTION MNEMONIC	ARGUMENTS	FUNCTION MODE	DESCRIPTION
LOG.E.F	e	Real	Computes the natural logarithm of a real expression; $e > 0$.
LOG.NORMAL.F	e_1,e_2,e_3	Real	Returns a random sample from a lognormal distribution. e_1 = mean, real e_2 = standard deviation e_3 = random number stream, integer
LOG.10.F	e	Real	Computes log of a real expression.
LOR.F	a,b	Integer	Logical sum of a and b.
LOWER.F	e	Text	Converts letters in a Text string to lower case.
MATCH.F	e_1,e_2,e_3	Integer	Returns the location of a text substring with a text string or 0 if not found. e_1 = source, text e_2 = pattern to be matched, text e_3 = number of characters of source to be skipped, intege
MAX.F	$e_1,e_2,\ldots e_n$	Real if any e_i real; if none, integer	Returns the value of the largest e_i
MIN.F	$e_1,e_2,\ldots,e_n$	Real if any e_i real; if none, integer	Returns the value of the smallest e_i..
MINUTE.F	e	Integer	Converts event time to the minute portion. e = cumulative event time, real
MOD.F	e_1,e_2	Real if either e_i real; if not, integer	Computes a remainder as e, - TRUNC.F $(e_1/e_2)*e_2$; $e_2 \neq 0$

FUNCTION MNEMONIC	ARGUMENTS	FUNCTION MODE	DESCRIPTION
MONTH.F	e	Integer	Converts simulation time to month portion based on values given to ORIGIN.R. e = cumulative simulation time, real
NDAY.F	e	Integer	Converts event time to the day portion. e = cumulative event time, real
NORMAL.F	e_1, e_2, e_3	Real	Returns a random sample from a normal distribution. e_1 = mean, real e_2 = standard deviation, real e_3 = random number stream, integer
OUT.F	e	Alpha	Sets or returns the eth alphabetic character in the current output buffer; e must yield an integer value; e > 0; both right- and left-handed function.
POISSON.F	e_1, e_2	Integer	Returns a random sample from a Poisson distribution. e_1 = mean, real e_2 = random number stream, integer
RANDI.F	e_1, e_2, e_3	Integer	Returns a random sample uniformly distributed between a range of values. e_1 = beginning value, integer e_2 = ending value, integer e_3 = random number stream integer

FUNCTION MNEMONIC	ARGUMENTS	FUNCTION MODE	DESCRIPTION
RANDOM.F	e	Real	Returns a pseudorandom number between zero and one e = random number stream, integer
REAL.F	e	Real	Converts an integer expression to a real value.
RSTEP.F	v,e	Real	Returns a random sample from a look-up table. v = variable that points to the look-up table e = random number stream, integer
SFIELD.F	none	Integer	Returns the starting column of the next data field to be ready by a READ Free Form statement. May affect file position.
SHL.F	w,n	Integer	Shift w left n positions.
SHR.F	w,n	Integer	Shift w right n positions.
SIGN.F	e	Integer	Indicates the sign of a real expression. 1 of e > 0 0 if e = 0 -1 if e < 0
SIN.F	e	Real	Computes the sine of a real expression given in radians.
SQRT.F	e	Real	Computes the square root of a real expression; e > 0.

FUNCTION MNEMONIC	ARGUMENTS	FUNCTION MODE	DESCRIPTION
SUBSTR.F	e_1, e_2, e_3	Text	Sets or returns in substring of a text value; both left- and right-handed function. In the left-handed usage, e_1 must be an unmonitored variable. e_1 = string, text e_2 = position, integer e_3 = length, integer
TAN.F	e	Real	Computes the tangent of a real expression given in radians.
TRUNC.F	e	Integer	Returns the truncated integer value of a real expression.
TTOA.F	e	Alpha	Converts first character of text expression to alpha.
UNIFORM.F	e_1, e_2, e_3	Real	Returns a uniformly distributed random sample between a range of values. e_1 = beginning value, real e_2 = ending value, real e_3 = random number stream, integer
UPPER.F	e	Text	Converts letters in a text string to uppercase.
WEEKDAY.F	e	Integer	Converts event time to the weekday portion. e = cumulative event time, real
WEIBULL.F	e_1, e_2, e_3	Real	Returns a sample value from a Weibull distribution. e_1 = scale parameter, real e_2 = shape parameter, real e_3 = random number stream, integer

FUNCTION MNEMONIC	ARGUMENTS	FUNCTION MODE	DESCRIPTION
XOR.F	a,b	Integer	Logical difference of a and b.
YEAR.F	e	Integer	Converts simulation time to the year portion based on values given to ORIGIN.R. e = cumulative simulation time, real

ROUTINES

ROUTINE	ARGUMENTS	DESCRIPTION
EXIT.R	e	Terminate execution, passing status code to command level. e = status, integer
ORIGIN.R	e_1,e_2,e_3	Establishes an origin time when the calendar format is used. e_1 = month, integer e_2 = day, integer e_3 = year, integer
SNAP.R	none	User supplied routine called by SIMSCRIPT II.5 when an execution error is detected.
TIME.R	none	Compiler-generated custom-made routine that controls simulation timing and selects events.

INDEX

Reader Comment Form

☐ Building Simulation Models with SIMSCRIPT II.5®

Your comments and suggestions are appreciated.

Errors (Show Page Number) __________

Omitted Material __________

Suggestions for Improvement __________

Tear Out

CACI publishes a quarterly newsletter directed to the simulation community. It contains abstracts of models, publications and upcoming conferences. If you would like to receive the newsletter, simply return the coupon.

send simsnips!

☐ Send SIMSNIPS directly to the individuals listed. They are actively involved with simulation projects.

☐ Information about my simulation projects is enclosed.

Name

Organization

Address

City State Zip

Telephone ( )

Name

Organization

Address

City State Zip

Telephone ( )

Name

Organization

Address

City State Zip

Telephone ( )

Fold Here

No
Postage Stamp
Necessary
If Mailed in the
United States

BUSINESS REPLY MAIL

First Class Permit No. 53844 Los Angeles, California

POSTAGE WILL BE PAID BY

C.A.C.I.
12011 San Vicente Boulevard
Los Angeles, California 90049

Attention: Dr. E. C. Russell

Staple Here

SIMSCRIPT II.5 Publications Available from CACI

Building Simulation Models with SIMSCRIPT II.5
SIMSCRIPT II.5 modelling taught by using case studies.

The SIMSCRIPT II.5 Programming Language
The SIMSCRIPT II.5 language teaching text.

SIMSCRIPT II.5 Reference Handbook
An accurate, convenient reference source for the SIMSCRIPT II.5 language.

A Quick Look at SIMSCRIPT II.5
An introduction to the SIMSCRIPT II.5 language and concepts.

CDC/6000-7000 SIMSCRIPT II.5 User Manual
Reference guide to the CDC/6000-7000 implementation of SIMSCRIPT II.5.

Honeywell H/600-6000 SIMSCRIPT II.5 User Manual
Reference guide to the H/600-6000 implementation of SIMSCRIPT II.5.

IBM SIMSCRIPT II.5 User Manual
Reference guide to the IBM implementation of SIMSCRIPT II.5.

VAX SIMSCRIPT II.5 User Manual
Reference guide to the VAX implementation of SIMSCRIPT II.5.

UNIVAC/1100 SIMSCRIPT II.5 User Manual
Reference guide to UNIVAC/1100 implementation of SIMSCRIPT II.5.

PR1ME SIMSCRIPT II.5 User Manual
Reference guide to the PR1ME implementation of SIMSCRIPT II.5.

SIMSCRIPT II.5 Course Book
Paper copies of the transparencies comprising the SIMSCRIPT II.5 course.

Quarterly SIMSNIPS
A newsletter directed to the Simulation Community.

A publication price list as well as SIMSCRIPT training and modelling services information are available from:

C.A.C.I.

12011 San Vicente Boulevard, Los Angeles, California 90049 (213) 476-6511